Diary of a Wartime Affair

Diary of a Wartime Affair

THE TRUE STORY OF A SURPRISINGLY MODERN ROMANCE

DOREEN BATES

VIKING

an imprint of

PENGUIN BOOKS

VIKING

UK | USA | Canada | Ireland | Australia
India | New Zealand | South Africa

Viking is part of the Penguin Random House group of companies
whose addresses can be found at global.penguinrandomhouse.com.

First published 2016
001

Copyright © Margaret Esiri and Andrew Evans, 2016

The moral right of the copyright holders has been asserted

Typeset in 10.75/12pt Bembo Book MT Std by Palimpsest Book Production Limited, Falkirk, Stirlingshire
Printed in Great Britain by Clays Ltd, St Ives plc

A CIP catalogue record for this book is available from the British Library

ISBN: 978–0–241–25006–8

Contents

List of Illustrations

List of Illustrations

All photographs not acknowledged belong to Doreen Bates' estate.

Acknowledgements

We should first like to acknowledge the work of Doreen's late sister, Margot, who began the long process of transcribing Doreen's diary after her death. She was assisted in learning how to use a computer for this purpose by a friend, Hywel Davies.

Between September 1940 and November 1944 Doreen submitted an abridged version of her diary to Mass Observation, whose archive is now at Sussex University. The current archivist, Fiona Courage, has been most helpful to us and to enquirers interested in exploring the Mass Observation entries of 'Diarist 5245'.

We are grateful to social historian Tanya Evans for her encouragement and help in getting the diary published. She originally discovered Doreen as a diarist through the Mass Observation Archive.

Eleo Gordon, our editor at Penguin, has been an invaluable source of encouragement and knowledge as we have proceeded with the publication process. She has made the whole enterprise a great pleasure.

Finally, we'd like to thank Serena Esiri-Bloom (one of Doreen's great-granddaughters) for her help with organizing and digitally scanning the family photos.

Introduction

Doreen Mary Bates, the author of this diary, was born on 25 April 1906, the first child of Rosa and (George) Wyndham Bates. Her parents had been born and brought up near Plymouth and it was there that they met and married. Rosa was the youngest daughter of a gunner in the Royal Navy and went to the village school at Kingsand, just across Mount Edgcumbe Bay from Plymouth. She taught in the same school for several years after she finished as a pupil in the top class, and then obtained a post as a cashier at a large Plymouth store. Wyndham was the fifth eldest child in a family of fourteen. After leaving school he went to Birmingham to learn retailing. After their marriage in 1904 they moved to the outskirts of London, renting a small house in Tooting. It was there that Doreen was born. Both Rosa and Wyndham had strong religious convictions and Wyndham eventually became a church warden in an Anglican church for many years. Wyndham worked at Crittalls, a department store in Victoria, and later at Waring & Gillow, before going into partnership with a friend to form a company that imported furnishing fabrics from continental Europe. The company flourished modestly for several years.

Rosa found Doreen an active, restless and challenging toddler who was intelligent, determined and hard to distract, but also loving and rewarding to care for. When Doreen was four she was joined by a sister, Margaret (known as Margot). Doreen was disappointed in the new arrival at first; she had expected a playmate, not a helpless baby. However, they were soon on good terms and remained close for the rest of their lives. The family moved to a house they bought in Thornton Heath, where they lived until 1928. In that year they moved to a newly built house in Riddlesdown, near Purley in Surrey.

Rosa was a firm believer in the importance of education, and Doreen and Margot were first sent to a school near their home. Rosa taught them both to read before they went to school. Doreen learnt quickly and developed a love of reading from an early age. Melbourne College was strict and ladylike and not very inspiring, but it taught the basics well enough. Much later in life Doreen wrote a short memoir of her time at Melbourne College:

> I went to my first school on May 6th 1912 when I was six. It was conducted by the survivor of two Victorian sisters, Miss Blanch, as she was always called. She wore long skirts and high necks to her blouses, and mousy hair plaited and arranged in a kind of bird's nest on top of her head. She was pale and dry with a severe expression. The worst punishment was to be 'sent to Miss Blanch'. I was sent to her only once, for pulling the long plaits of a girl who was very tall and delicate and liable to faint.
>
> It was a small school and its fees in the top form were about £2/15 shillings a term.
>
> One of the objects must have been to produce 'young ladies'. We always had to wear gloves out of doors; we were supposed to walk, not run; never shout, always be polite. We did not wear uniform except our large flat straw hats with the red school hat band. I never remember any discussion about the future or careers although we took Oxford Preliminary Junior and Senior School examinations. The great virtue of the school for me is that it taught me to work. There was no possibility of shirking. If you did not learn your lesson it was returned. You were given a 'detention'. It was returned till you could demonstrate that you had learned it. Having observed this arrangement I decided that I might just as well learn my lesson the first time and avoid detentions. I kept this resolve except for one awful occasion when the whole form was given a detention because we had failed to master Henry II's legal reforms.
>
> I had one term in the Kindergarten. I remember learning to subtract with buttons (there was one much coveted button with a Dutch boy on it). I had a year in the first form but I remember little of what I learned except some of Blake's *Poems of Innocence*. In the second form I remember some 'natural history' all out of a book about dragonflies and their development; about shepherd's purse, and about hedgehogs. In the third form we read *Hiawatha* and learned fractions and I remember a detailed lesson on the Panama Canal. In the fourth form when I was nine we did decimals, Tennyson's 'Ode on the Death of the Duke of Wellington' and 'Morte d'Arthur' and *The Princess*, and began geometry. I was interrupted in this form by

going to Plymouth for a spell during the First World War. In May 1918 I resumed after we had returned home following my father being invalided out of the Royal Flying Squad. Perhaps this was why my first Shakespeare in the fifth was *Twelfth Night* which I found difficult, although we had read Lamb's *Tales* in the second form at seven. We went on to *Julius Caesar* and I was thrilled. We did some Roman history to go with it and I developed a passion for it. I shall never forget the experience of seeing the play at St James Theatre with my father. I could have prompted any of the cast from the gallery and I could hardly bear the play to go on and reach its end. We also 'learned' *As You Like It* and *Henry Vth*, reciting passages at elocution and working hard at the notes and glossary. These lessons gave me a life-long interest in Shakespeare and apart from anything else would have justified the school for me.

At the end of each term we had a function called 'Poetry Saying' in the hall before the whole school. One or two girls from each form were chosen to recite a selection of what they had learned during the term. I loved this. I remember speaking the part of Cassius in the quarrel scene from *Julius Caesar*. Once five of us recited the whole of Macaulay's 'Armada'. I had what I still regard as the best bit from, 'With his white hair unbonneted the stout old sheriff comes' down to 'our glorious Semper Eadem'. 'The Lady of Shalott' was another – I loved the dramatic bits – 'She left the web, she left the loom, she made three paces through the room; she saw the waterlily bloom; she looked down to Camelot.'

Doreen, their mother Rosa and Margot, 1914

The school library was quite inadequate. We were allowed to change our books on Wednesday mornings and take one book at a time. Mine never lasted me the week. I never had enough to read before I was fourteen. I read my own books over and over again. Nevertheless, besides Shakespeare, we had also read and studied *Ivanhoe*, *Kenilworth*, *The Talisman* and another Scott which no one seems to know, *Anne of Geierstein*, as well as *Adam Bede*, *Silas Marner* and *Robinson Crusoe*.

Doreen was eight years old when the First World War broke out and Wyndham was called up to join the Royal Flying Corps, later the RAF. Before he left for the war he took Doreen aside and asked her to look after her mother and little sister. Doreen took this responsibility seriously. She became co-operative and helpful. The family was short of money and had to budget carefully to make ends meet. This period of frugality made a strong impression on Doreen, who husbanded her resources carefully throughout her life. Although she was reluctant to spend money on herself, however, she took much pleasure in being generous to others and enjoyed spending money in this way when it was available. In 1917 Wyndham was invalided out of the Royal Flying Corps after being wounded in a shoulder. The family rented rooms to be near him in hospital while he was recovering at Dungeness. They were then able to be re-united as a close and loving family.

When the war ended Wyndham resumed his fabric importation and Rosa and Wyndham started to think about sending Doreen to a school with higher standards and greater intellectual ambition than Melbourne College. They decided on Croydon High School, one of the schools run by the Girls' Public Day School Trust. It was only a bus ride away from Thornton Heath and it opened up new horizons for Doreen, as she records in this memoir:

> When I reached the top form at Melbourne College my mother looked further afield and her choice lighted on Croydon High School which had been founded in 1875. I did an entrance exam but was told I should have to wait a year for a vacancy. Hence I did not go to the school until September 1921 when I was fifteen. I went into the Upper Fifth – a class of about thirty – which was working for the London General Schools Exam the following June. I found the transition difficult. The girls were noisier, more assured and I felt an outsider. The fees had increased to 10 guineas a term and I felt guilty at costing my parents so much. It was an effort to provide the school uniform and in fact the navy skirt and white blouse which the prospectus prescribed was hardly worn in my form. Nearly everyone wore a navy gym slip which I chose for my birthday present after two terms of feeling

wrongly dressed. I was very shy and hardly ever volunteered to answer questions in class. I was inevitably behindhand in some subjects. I began Euclid in the middle; I had missed the first year's botany; I had done less Latin than the rest of the form. The teaching was good. I had extra informal botany; the English and history thrilled me. We read European history, a new slant for me. The history mistress was a magnificent teacher as I was to discover in my two years in the Sixth but I was afraid of her sarcastic tongue in the Fifth and hardly uttered a word. The freer discipline and noise scared me but I did reasonably well in the end of term exams and managed (in company with only one other girl) to get Matric exemption in the General School exam in which I took 8 subjects. So, elated, yet abashed, I entered the Sixth at 16 in September 1922.

My two years in the Sixth form were a revelation and I loved every minute. The girls were more congenial. The rougher, tougher ones had left or gone to 'Home Studies' – a course of domestic arts which, of course, we more academic girls despised. We had the run of the school library and a common room of our own where we enjoyed our picnic lunch. There were school societies and expeditions, play-readings and music and art. I need play nothing but tennis – I was still afraid of the games mistress, and with luck need never see her. I began to make friends and, best of all, in my second year had history lessons either to myself or with one other girl. I remember those lessons best in the summer term sitting under a tree in the school garden – Roman history, nineteenth-century English and European. I learned to work independently – to read and make notes – to write rudimentary essays. At no time have I encountered better teaching – certainly not at the University – enthusiastic, yet disciplined. It ranged wide and yet kept to the point.

I cannot remember that we ever discussed careers but I was encouraged to try for a university education as the greatest prize. There seemed no question that it was to be desired. The whole atmosphere of the form was of enthusiasm for learning as the best way of spending the years from 16 to 21. We were very young emotionally. I remember no problems with boyfriends or make up. My activities were centred on school. I rarely went to the theatre, though I loved it – more rarely to a film. There was no radio or TV. We had no car. I went to school which was one and a quarter miles either by bus, or walked and kept my penny fare.

We rarely saw the headmistress who was a mild Victorian old lady who must have been 64–65. When I was not quite 18 I was going to Westfield College London with 2 other girls to take the Scholarship and Entrance exam and we saw her in her study to be patted on the head and we were told to 'keep together' and be very careful on the journey, especially if it was foggy. Of course, there must have been more to her than I experienced. The general spirit of the school, which was very good, must have been due in some measure to her guidance at the top if only because of her part in the selection of staff. Perhaps I see the school through rose-tinted glasses as two thirds of my time was in the Sixth where I felt privileged to be in touch with teachers whose intellectual and personal qualities seemed to be quite above any ambition of mine. What they gave me then was beyond price and with their help I managed to get an entrance scholarship to a residential college of London University and a State Scholarship to enable me to take advantage of it. This was the gift of the first Labour government, and on the result of the Higher School Certificate exam in June 1924 I was able to start at once on the London Honours Course in History. Those two years 1922–24 were marvellous years when I worked harder than I have ever done, enjoyed every minute of it and when circumstances conspired to give me, for once, just what I wanted and needed.

Her years at Royal Holloway College from 1924 to 1927 were decisive ones for Doreen. For the first time she was living away from home during the term. She encountered young women from many different backgrounds and made lifelong friends among her fellow students, some of them mentioned in her diary: Mary Roney, who read History and later joined her father's firm of solicitors; Elsie Fisher, reading English, who later worked indefatigably to promote literacy among the gypsy population; and Ella Hewson, who read English and later worked in publishing and was eventually to write fiction herself. These young women were among the first to take advantage of the new opportunities in women's education and saw themselves not first and foremost as wives and mothers-to-be but as budding professionals in their own right. They questioned accepted norms in society and tried out new and more independent ways of living. Doreen entered into the spirit of this different life with enthusiasm and pleasure. She played a particularly active part in dramatic productions and play readings. She perhaps neglected her academic work to some extent without quite the same inspiration from her University teachers as she obtained from her Sixth form school teachers, but she nevertheless achieved a respectable 2.1 degree at the end of her three years. There are brief diary entries from this period which refer to the active life she led at Royal Holloway College but it seems to have been some years after she left this place of intellectual ferment and returned to her home surroundings that she started writing the more comprehensive and revealing diary that is published here.

After graduating Doreen wanted a job that would give her a regular and secure salary, bringing with it the chance of more permanent independence and also a chance to contribute to the family finances. She was keenly aware that Rosa and Wyndham had made considerable financial sacrifices to enable her to go to college and she wanted to repay that debt. She became a civil servant working for the Inland Revenue and the diary commences in 1934 when she was twenty-seven and working in one of the London offices of the Inland Revenue to which she commuted by train from the family home in Riddlesdown.

Margot, Wyndham and Doreen

At this time one senses that she did not greatly enjoy her work but regarded it as a secure way of earning her bread and butter. Most of her satisfaction in life came from the activities she participated in outside work. She joined an amateur dramatic society, the Croydon Players, read books voraciously, went to plays, lectures and concerts, met her friends and went on stimulating holidays with her family or with friends. She bought a car and learnt to drive (there was no test to be passed in those days) and resumed piano lessons. In this way she laid down the lifelong habit of filling every day with as much activity and interest as she could cram in.

But it was her work as a civil servant that led to the most significant emotional encounter of her life. This was with an older colleague, William (Bill) Evans, referred to in the diary mainly as E. William Evans was born in 1894 in Stoke-on-Trent. He was the eldest of a family of seven, one of whom died of diphtheria at the age of five. His mother had been a teacher before her marriage and his father ran a bicycle shop and was also a fiery preacher in a local non-conformist church. The family was poor but Bill gained entrance to the local grammar school where he was able to stay until he was seventeen, when he had to leave school to obtain employment. However, that was not the end of his education, for he was able to take advantage of evening classes run by the Workers' Educational Association, eventually obtaining a degree in Economics while working as a civil servant in the Customs and Excise Department. He continued his education throughout his life, gaining a degree in Mathematics and, after his retirement, a Diploma in Archaeology from London University.

When Doreen joined the Inland Revenue E had been working there for several years and was married to Kathleen (referred to in the diary as K), a ballet teacher. They lived in Kingston-upon-Thames and had no children.

E's intellectual interests and temperament were very different from Doreen's. His main interests were in mathematics, science and philosophy while hers were in history, literature, drama and travel. They both enjoyed music and shared a strong sense of intellectual enquiry, a hatred of hypocrisy or dishonesty and an open-mindedness about politics and social progress. Their emotional attachment developed slowly and posed a great dilemma for them both, but particularly for Doreen, as becomes clear as her diary unfolds.

Her honesty in facing this dilemma, the joy but also the depression that at times engulfed her, and the eventual resolution of her situation are told with startling frankness.

E and K with her parents

1934

Doreen joined the Inland Revenue in 1927, when she was twenty-one years old. Initially she worked in an office in Croydon which was quite close to her home in Riddlesdown, but at the end of 1930 she was transferred to an office in Paddington, where she was to share a room with E. There she would find herself discussing *Jude the Obscure*, E's childhood and school days and the philosophy lectures by C. E. M. Joad that they went to together, as well as tax case dilemmas.

According to the diary, which she started writing intermittently in 1931, it was not until 1933 that a romantic element became insistent in their relationship, with E declaring to her that 'she had the most fascinating mind he had come across', and they started going for picnic lunches in Kensington Gardens, where they read plays and books together. In time this intellectual meeting of minds led to sexual encounters, probably starting in October 1933, but from the start both E and Doreen were smitten with guilt about E's wife, Kathleen. This was to continue as a backdrop to their developing deep love, giving it a bitter-sweet quality that is clearly apparent in the diary entries that follow.

The diary starts with a short account of one of the numerous walks Doreen took with E in countryside around London that was easily reached by train.

Easter Tuesday, 3 April

This is a quick note of a secret day. Met E at Victoria at 10.12. Hastily changed my stockings and put on walking socks and cloaked my case of library books there before tubing to Euston for King's Langley. I was hardly expecting to see him and he came panting from a hurried change at Clapham Junction. A slow puffing train and a carriage to ourselves to King's Langley, but we just talked.

The Grand Union Canal, King's Langley

Walked ten and a half miles along the canal without touching a road. Rather disappointing at first, though interesting in a sordid way – an Ovaltine factory and hundreds of chickens for eggs, 2 or 3 huge paper factories – but gradually growing hills – innumerable locks, barges with brightly painted points, shining brass, each with a bicycle. Sat by a lock for lunch and beheld the complete reward for any walk – a kingfisher, first reddish-orange front and long bill, then a flash of blue-green back in the sun – iridescent, startling – too lovely to be true, but 3 times we saw it.

Monday 30 April

I have reached the stage now of quite definitely getting pleasure out of physical contact with E. Apart from some satisfaction derived from the fact that it gives him pleasure I am still a little afraid and I still shudder now and then but I am much closer to him. If there was any prospect of having a child in the future I should be almost happy. He is marvellously patient considering the strength of his desire. It is this that still frightens me. I can see it in his eyes, growing as he looks at me. His hair is very fine and thick altho', owing to its fineness, it doesn't bush out much. He has queer hazel-grey eyes flecked with brown. At lunchtime we sat on the hearth rug after F E Shaw (FES)⋆ had gone till I nearly missed the 5.50 train.

Tuesday 1 May

To the Rep with E for *A Doll's House*. He said I was hard and cruel. In the 2nd Act I loosened my brassière. Heavens, but I have too much feeling, yet I dread it – a foreboding. But he is so sweet – 'I would rather die than give you up' – 'Is it not sweet to feel my hand on your cheek?' He loves the *shape* of my face – so queer! I love his dependence, his helplessness – a childish clinging.

Saturday 12 May

I slept badly last night after the AIT† dinner.

Tea, pie, orange and then changed quickly upstairs with E's assistance and hastened, very hot, to Victoria. Train to Merstham, walked up on to the hills, took off my vest in a copse and we sat on a tree trunk in a clump of beeches looking at bluebells growing up the shady side of a hollow. After 20 minutes we climbed higher and eventually sat in a field under an ash tree till 5.30. E was sweet, very gentle and patient. I was happy and yet sad.

E with his dog

⋆ The tax office boss.
† Association of Inspectors of Tax.

We go perfectly together – that makes it worse. I said, 'Everyone starts like this and yet look at most of them.' He said, 'No, it is generally just physical satisfaction that the man wants and economic independence and society position that a woman wants. We are different!' I told him, 'I do want a boy with your queer grey eyes and hair standing on end and my digestion,' and, E added, 'your laughing eyes'.

Monday 14 May

Sunny but a gusty cold wind. It clouded over this afternoon and at dinner a heavy shower fell, to be followed by a magnificent rainbow – high, complete and brilliant. As the rain stopped a blackbird whistled joyously (at the prospect of worms I suppose).

At lunch E produced a map and said it must be a real hike or K⋆ would want to come and I felt awful – we both do. To deceive her seems worse to me than the fact. He thought she would suffer more, tho' was gloomy all the afternoon. We talked and talked from 4.30 to 5.45. She is no worse off because he is happier – he is nicer to her than before – and it seems cruel not to give him what small happiness I can. He said, 'We'll cancel it, then?'

They didn't cancel and instead spent the Whitsun weekend, 19–21 May, from Saturday until Monday evening walking in the Cotswolds.

Wednesday 23 May

I am still bemused by the happiness of last weekend. A lovely afterglow, as it were, lingers and warms my eyes as I look at him in such different surroundings in the office. We have no regrets and not a moment's remorse.

⋆ E's wife, Kathleen.

Thursday 24 May

We are still much in love. I kept having warm rushes of love as I looked at his hair. I must be more sensible and do more work. Couldn't go to *Sixteen* with him as my aunts Alice and Gladys★ were coming. Mac† was severe but pleasant.

Sunday 27 May

The family are at lunch and I am sitting down in our bedroom to make a record of today. The sun is shining in on me and making my face burn and my mind feels stiff and cannot achieve any nimbleness with words. They keep slipping away just out of reach.

Last night my sister, Margot, and I went to see *The Voysey Inheritance*. I took my rucksack with a woolly coat and a thermos of tea. The play was well acted and interesting. At 10.35 Margot insisted on going, to give me time to have coffee and an egg before catching the 11.05 to Waterloo Junction. Felt rather guilty leaving her in the train to go home.

Charing Cross was buzzing with hikers off on a special train to Battle – very long with a Pullman restaurant car. I found a corner in the front coach opposite two middle-aged female ornithologists with shooting sticks. I despaired of seeing E at Surbiton as there were crowds at Clapham, Wimbledon and Surbiton. However, he got in. Trees looked beautiful against the sky as their branches swayed in the breeze, blotting out the stars. The moon was golden and almost full, but was not high.

The wind was fresh but not so cold as I expected. E said it would be much colder in the morning. I didn't feel at all nervous till I saw Clandon church standing up black and sinister against the moonlit sky. We heard no nightingales till we left the road and took the footpath to Newlands Corner. We sat down to listen but they were rather far off – we could hear the songs distinctly but rather faintly. We walked on down the road from Newlands Corner. The wind was less cold and the view looked eerie. The

★ Paternal aunts.
† Her piano teacher.

hills showed up dark in the moonlight with light mist between. It looked quite uninhabited and dead – like the north pole – completely remote and frozen. Down in the valley we heard an owl hoot, very near. The church clock in Albury struck 1.30 and we took a steep narrow road south to Black Heath. It had very high banks so that the moon could not shine into it. At times it was completely black dark, like a tunnel. I was frightened – couldn't see anything – could just feel E's hand, warm and friendly, but I kept drifting away. He grew remote and might have been a stranger. It was like a dream with an air of unreality. I was relieved to get out into the moonlight again and see his face.

On the top of Black Heath we rested and watched the moon sink, getting more orange and fatter. The wind had dropped and we gave up hope of hearing any more nightingales when suddenly two began to sing, while far away we heard a cock crow. We were rather cold but were close and finally we slept for half an hour. When I awoke the sky was light behind and the stars had faded. We were quaking and cramped with cold. We drank my tea (which had gone tepid and rather rank) and ate sandwiches. At 4.30 we started walking again. A white mist rose and fell, shrank and spread among the trees and the air was damp and chill. The sky was streaked with pale pink but there was a good deal of cloud. The path was beautiful – sandy, with gorse, broom and bluebells and pines. The bracken was about 6 inches high, pale green and very curly. At first we heard little but incessant cuckoos and cocks but gradually more and more birds woke up and sang till the air was full of their songs and the whirr of their wings. They flew slowly and happily and seemed confident that they were safe. Rabbits were frisking everywhere – would suddenly sit still, examine us and scamper away. Here and there we left dark green footprints on the silvery grey-green of the dewy grass. Everything was still and looked quite newly made in the grey-blue light.

We reached Shere about 7.35 and it was beginning to grow warm, altho' a fresh breeze had sprung up as the sun increased in strength. We climbed up through the beeches on the path to Horsley. At the top we lay down to rest in the sun and fell asleep. When we woke it was 8.45. A lovely path nearly all the way to Horsley, twisting through beeches with clear pale green leaves against the deep blue of the sky, or letting the sunshine through thin larches, a sober but fluffy green in the bright light; pools of

Shere Memorial Cross

bluebells standing in the new green grass, and everywhere birds.
We reached Horsley station at 10.05 and found a shop for coffee with a
notice Open. The proprietor and his wife were surprised to see us, tho',
and we interrupted their breakfast when we ordered coffee. Got home
about 11.50 so hungry I could hardly wait till dinner was ready. Apart from
two aching little toes and eyes slightly strained I wasn't very tired but I
slept for an hour and a half this afternoon. The sun has dropped out of
sight now and the family will be home in a few minutes. Another day is
done. May my memory remain fresh and unblurred.

Saturday 2 June

An unsatisfactory day. I worked quite hard. E irritated me slightly. He had
a day's leave yesterday – he took Elsie★ to Chelsea Flower Show. He

★ Elsie Evans, E's sister.

wouldn't have gone except for her. Then at 12.15 he said, 'Come upstairs.' I scarcely let him touch me. He said, 'You're lucky, aren't you – always to have to be stirred up. It's not sour grapes, it's just that you don't want any grapes.' I felt quite cool and level-headed and detached and remote. Partly pique, I suppose, but mainly the effect of *The Country Wife* on Thursday night. It takes very little even now to disgust me and make me feel that the physical side of sex is degrading. I felt sorry in the bus – he looked so miserable and yet the hot look in his eyes made me recoil. He said, 'I'm sorry you're dismal – I shan't see you till Monday – a weekend is a long time – you know how long it can be.'

Monday 4 June

Dismal, miserable day! I was snappy and cold to E all the morning – wouldn't lunch with him in the office – said I could buy a new hat but really had no intention of doing so. Felt quite forlorn. The magic had quite gone – Whitsun seemed incredible. Lunched at Lyons, still miserable, couldn't read, even. Decided to try and get over this. He was looking for the 'plumed troop' passage in *Othello* when I got back. I found it and said I was sorry I'd been bad-tempered in the morning. He said he was. We were better after that. He was gloomy – 'a sense of utter failure'. Before I went to the library he kissed me suddenly – passionately.

Thursday 7 June

After the Derby yesterday a day's work – rather restful, even assessing! At lunchtime we went to *A Man of Aran* – magnificent photography. I've never seen a film in which one lost oneself so. The shark hunt was revolting. The man was fine and the woman beautiful (reminded me of Epstein's *Madonna* but with some gaiety), the son attractive. The finest part was the storm – towering black cliffs, waves tossing to the top and a boat with 3 men. After seeing it who could say the universe is friendly? Yet after they had reached the land (tho' the boat was lost), serenity and calm victory over sea and sky.

E had to see a Colonel in the afternoon who wouldn't divulge his history to anyone else. He resented my presence till E told him I was an Inspector. He looked at me in horror and said, 'My God!' but later, rather softened, he said, 'You seem young for so responsible a position.'

During the interval since the last entry Doreen spent two weeks on holiday with her family in Greece.

Monday 25 June

Sultry, damp and thundery. First day in my own room at the office. Rather depressed. Picnic with E in Kensington Gardens interrupted by (1) a shower (2) a squirrel which was too tame. He said, 'I was more dismal on Sat than all through the fortnight you were away. It seemed so awful to lose you after three quarters of an hour.' What is different about you is that when you are away from a person you forget his irritations till you see him again, then you say, 'Oh, yes, of course' – but you are nicer than I thought each time I see you again.

Thursday 28 June

A day of sudden downpours, thunder claps, massed clouds with hot sunshine in the intervals making the ground steam. Wore my new coat and wide-brimmed hat but had to wear my mac to lunch in the Park. Halfway through we had to hurry to the new cafeteria where we had coffee. A wild and unexpected sweetness about the whole day: as we stood under the umbrella under a chestnut which was almost thick enough to keep out the heavy rain; as we sat drinking coffee and E said my diary this year was different – 'You seem to "ingest" things more, they affect you more deeply – it is impossible to get too near you'; as we squelched over the wet grass – 'All sorts of clothes suit you well' – he meant the hat.

Quite elated altogether. I have had marvellous flashes of joy today.

Saturday 30 June – Sunday 1 July

A midnight walk. I was doubtful about the weather when I arranged with E in the morning but it was perfect – bright moonlight, warm. We had coffee in Croydon and got to Merstham at 12.30. I called him Billy for the first time – he quoted Browning and adapted Coleridge to 'Your flashing eyes, your floating hair' – not a walk, but a 'flight to heaven's gate'. We walked to a hayfield facing north where we watched the dawn and listened to the first faint chorus of the larks. The morning star rose low in the east and looked too large and bright to be real. A heavy dew, but not cold – scent of wild roses and elder blossom. We walked from 4.30 – Upper Caterham, Lower Caterham, Tillingdown and Marden Park. I felt bad – shaky, and couldn't eat much breakfast. Slept for one and a half hours. The mist had cleared and the sun was very strong when I awoke at 7.45. Felt better. We stayed there by the beeches just above Godstone and loved. Then to Godstone for lunch. I was so happy I felt it could not possibly last – our joy was so precarious. Up White Hill we had a long discussion about Kathleen and the attitude of the office and the family. It was very hot and we had too many clothes so we lay down by the ash tree again to cool. We wanted to love but there were too many people out for Sunday afternoon walks.

Monday 9 July

I was rather dismal this morning. I think it was the effort of going to see Roy and Marjorie★ yesterday. It seems such plain sailing for them – a nice little house, furnished in quite good taste – complete with fish eaters and tea cloths. Yet look at Roy – the complete materialist – 'stew the gooseberries in the oven while the joint is cooking and so save gas!' Perhaps this isn't fair to them – sour grapes perhaps.

Reading T E Lawrence's letters – extraordinarily interesting – comforting too. There is something so akin about him. He had such misery and ecstasy; he didn't shrink from doing what he had to do in the face of everyone – strong, even in hurting people.

★ Roy was D's first cousin and Marjorie was his wife.

I had gusts of intense love for E today – when he kissed me this evening we both bruised our lips.

Tuesday 10 July

Read Lawrence's letters in the train. It struck me that there is a similarity between his views and mine. E read Huxley's *Introduction* at lunchtime and said this afternoon, 'Of course, in so many ways you are rather like Lawrence.'

Wednesday 11 July

We lunched (late) in Kens Gdns and talked about Lawrence's letters – a highbrow conversation following a remark of mine that our conversation had descended steadily in quality. A discussion, too, on the physical element in our relations. E said it made the permanent core all the stronger but I feel it makes it more precarious. He is so sure of the permanent core, yet the physical element for him is greater than for me.

Thursday 12 July

I have felt so dismal all day. It has rained, thank heaven – quite a heavy downpour this morning after growing so dark I nearly switched on the light. Then – swish! And it poured with rain as I was dictating. But I couldn't rejoice in it. All the zest had gone and I just felt empty – negative, dull, stranded. I made E unhappy too. He thought I doubted his love or disliked the physical side of it. But it was just gloom. At bottom, I think, I distrust myself – my faith had disappeared. I don't know why, tho' it is perhaps remotely related to Roy and Marjorie. It seems so tragic that they have the perfect opportunity without, I am certain, the spirit to make the most of it. I am a poor thing – I am lazy, lack originality and intelligence and application and feel dismal because I can so clearly see what not to be and do – I hate materialism and the 'let's get to the top and be jolly' spirit and I humbly, and from a distance, love beauty and sensitiveness of spirit. I cannot overcome an inhibition which prevents me from revealing just what I feel is important.

Saturday 14 July

I was still recovering my spirits in spite of working hard but getting nowhere except thro' the post for E and for FES. Too many people about for us to love so he kissed me about 3 times and we went to Victoria for coffee. He is fed up with work.

There is a possibility that he and K may be at Regent's Park Theatre on the same night as Margot and I are. I told him I couldn't talk to her. I should tell her everything if I saw her. He was rather disturbed about it but I feel I couldn't actively deceive her to her face. On the way up the hill I invented interviews with her in which I triumphantly vindicated my action and explained her shortcomings to her!

Monday 16 July

A heavy, woeful day. E has been worrying all the weekend over what I told him on Sat – that I couldn't go on deceiving K if I saw her. 'It would be the end – yet Doreen, you go down to my very depths.' I have such a headache and my eyes are smarting with tears.

Friday 27 July

Rather a depressed week. E has been working hard and late. First I felt very edgy – I don't know if I let the work get on my nerves (as he said, and I said at home) or whether I missed him. Wednesday was the worst. Yesterday and today I have been gradually recovering. I have begun to get more detached. I know if we have to stop I shall survive. I feel more confidence now because, in spite of our love, I am independent. He gives me much and I take it but I haven't shifted my whole weight on to him. I should suffer – be lost for a time – but I can get through by myself.

Monday 30 July

A brilliant sunny day, fresh this morning but unbearably hot in the 6.10. Lunched in Kens Gdns, happily – just a glimmering of love for each other. E said, 'I think I dream of you every night . . . Sex is a queer thing – you had no feeling for me on Saturday and I hadn't much more for you – I had a first touch then and you felt it too.' He doesn't really know me in the slightest emotionally, yet he tries to get close to me. Perhaps it's my fault. He is clearly more penetrating and sensitive than most men, yet he can be quite mistaken.

Thursday 2 August

At last I have lost the depression which has hung over me since last Sunday week. Quite suddenly I felt better. I woke up to hear the rain pelting down last night. A westerly wind has been roaring and leaping all day, but these things cannot have transformed my whole outlook. It is inexplicable. I can hardly believe I am the same person today as yesterday. E says: which is the minor personality and which the normal? It is only with intellectual, detached effort that I can apprehend my feelings of yesterday. If I could only control it. I am not only lighter in feeling but quicker (if not so clear and detached) in mind.

Friday 3 August

Two days ago I thought I could never have loved as I did this evening – so sweet yet so light, so passionate and so close. 'Your eyes are beautiful.' I used to feel afraid and uncomfortable when his eyes turned hot as he looked at me. Now I am not afraid and I suppose I like to feel my power.

Tuesday 14 August

I went to Lyons at lunchtime and read some of Rees' book *The Health of the Mind*. It is simple and didn't say anything I didn't know but it is practical and sane. There are times when I long for a child, but it's probably better for the child as it is.

Thursday 13 September

An eventful gap since I last wrote here – including a week in Shropshire with E. I must try to make a record of this gossamer happiness – soon, before its memory fades into golden and indistinguishable distance. Already it seems like a dream passed not in the darkness of the night but in the sunshine of heaven. I say to myself – only a fortnight ago today we walked Wenlock Edge and slept at the Plough. I look at him and remember how I lay in his arms, and slept and awoke to look into his eyes and we set out in the mornings with nothing to consider but the beauty of the earth and sky and the happiness of our love.

Taking a break

Monday 17 September

An unsatisfactory yet inspiring day with E. I felt a pressing sense of uncertainty, as tho' every time he kisses me may be the last. I live in the spirit of de la Mare's 'Look thy last on all things lovely every hour . . .' I don't know how far this is due to the uncertainty of the concrete position – the possibility of external interference and how far it is due to my own fear of becoming too dependent on him or of his dependence on me; and the fear that we are suffering from the delusion that we are one and can transcend ourselves through sex. This is not true – it must remain experience to stimulate the self and not a basic support for life or a screen against reality. I must make something concrete from the experience – give back something in return or it will corrupt both our lives. Moreover the bridge between us is intellectual. If we had not attained some unity of mind we could never feel the deep passion as we do. 'It is the play of your mind in your face that is so attractive.' I must write a big novel some time. Meantime, some short stories for practice in expression.

Friday 21 September

Laziness is my besetting sin. Whatever resolutions I make I seem to do no better. I do not even keep level with the day's post, let alone overtake the arrears; a snag or two, claims and post, and a caller, and the day has gone. So sweet, our secret love-making before we hurry for the train. I played for long tonight – tried the new Heller studies. I fancy at times I am making progress. I think it is simpler and I have more grasp of detail + whole, but I still have tremendous difficulty with laddering – a kind of physical conflict.

Tuesday 25 September

A joyful day! My heart soared high in happiness before, I suppose, crashing to dull despair tomorrow or the next day. It was due primarily to seeing *The Moon in the Yellow River* with E last night, a stimulating play of ideas – conflicts pinned down and adequately expressed by the characters – mainly the do-ers and the see-ers. Caught 11.46 and talked till quarter to two – not sleepy then. One would expect a bleary-eyed weariness all day with a gradually intensifying headache. But no!

So sweet to find anew that we have the same approach, view things sufficiently from the same angle to be able to comprehend. 'I should have hated you if it hadn't been good' – he pretended to quake and said he'd never take such a risk again.

I looked to see if there were interesting films to go to – only *Dr*

Maurice, a Study of Hypnotic Power. A little later he said, 'In this room is a study of hypnotic power. Every time I look at you, you stir me, fascinate me, hold me.' We were nearly caught by Scott at 1.15, but the sweetness of his kiss at 5.00 before I rushed off to have tea with Elsie.* She said I was looking extraordinarily well.

Sunday 7 October

A warm steamy day with no sunshine and intermittent drizzle. Went to church. Harvest Festival – the gorgeous 104 Psalm. Its only weakness is the last verse and that has a savage triumphant shout, but its beauty – the whole plan and spirit – its unspoilt ecstasy and unclouded joy in the harmony of nature. In detail and style so direct, simple and concrete. 'Thou coverest thyself with light as it were a garment' – magnificent simplicity, dazzlingly effective – 'the wings of the wind'. It would be a good thing to learn by heart. That was the best thing in the service. The prayer for all sorts and conditions of men is lovely. The cadences of the sentences are perfect. The sermon was awful, the man sounded quite drunk at times. What he said was rubbish. I felt terribly angry that he should have nothing better for that big congregation than a musty collection of old tags not even strung together with any consistency. It made me so sick I couldn't sing the last two hymns and nearly had to go home. Didn't recover until Mr Henderson sang something from Haydn's *Creation*. This was lovely, a jolly thing, and his voice is a heavenly boom.

Tuesday 9 October

A heavenly day – sunny, fresh and dry with a light blue sky. I have been dismal and cross all day due mainly to (1) general effect of Aunt Alice (Rosa† took her to Brighton and to a meeting about witchcraft this evening and was fed up because she was staying until tomorrow); (2) K's restrictions

---

* Elsie Fisher, a friend from college days.
† Doreen's mother.

on E's activities. I don't know how long it will be before the difficulties of our relations loom so large before me that I shall cut myself off and sacrifice the happiness which we do achieve. I am afraid I am growing to dislike her. Jealousy does not enter into this feeling – envy, perhaps – but it mainly is an obstacle, a barbed wire entanglement which has to be surmounted or threaded before we can do anything together.

Friday 12 October

A marvellous sunny day and yet I have been melancholy, so much so that I have had to make myself work hard to prevent myself from crying. All this week I have been unhappy and restless, probably because I love E too much and am so dissatisfied with our limitations. I could give him so much more, could make his home lovely, give him children to keep him young, and gaiety to make him laugh. (In fact I should probably be cross and discontented and edgy as I am now.) He has applied for a job in Statistics and Intelligence and I have done my best to persuade him to do so and typed his application. We had lunch in Queen's Rd and this evening we went to University College (experiment on images).*

Tuesday 16 October

To old Mac. He is superhumanly patient – how my stumbling through Beethoven must grind his sensibilities. He grows enormous chrysanthemums.

One of the difficulties with E is that I feel frustrated – can't do anything concrete for him. That's why it gave me such disproportionate pleasure to type his application. I don't know, I hope I don't just fizzle out about him. I wonder if now is the time for a clean break. I have quite recovered from my ecstasies.

* E and Doreen were doing a course in psychology.

Thursday 18 October

A crowded day; Brown (builder) in the morning and Wood and solicitor (for E, who was at an Appeal meeting with FES). She stayed nearly an hour telling me sickening stories of how hotels are run in Oxford and Cambridge Terrace and Eastbourne Terrace. It made me so sick that I felt horrified when E touched me. She had a small old dog with her. Mrs Beadle this afternoon, dress maker and linen draper – for the sake of her nerves she must keep going and likes the work. Met Doreen Hosier* at 6.0. She was very cordial.

Saturday 20 October

Very tired this morning after taking Rosa to the Gate to see *Miracle in America* after Practical Psychology at UC. E was tired too. After a long gap and not even seeing each other last Sat we both felt strongly moved. For me I recaptured some of the sweetness and felt some of the fear from our early love-making. E felt queer at the end. I think he over-exerted himself in his weary state. I was rather frightened – his lips were quite blue. I gave him some water but he looked shaky even at Victoria.

Monday 22 October

A joyful day of exhilaration. Cloudy and strong west wind this morning after heavy rain in the night. Took Asquith's letters to the office and bickered with E all day as to whether he should read them. Saw Wise re the Enquiry and a nice pale accountant re Carr-Glyn (actress but not 'exotic' or extravagant), otherwise little work. Played with E for a long time + a lengthy discussion on the profits from brothels in Eastbourne Terrace. When he kissed me tonight I wondered how I had doubted whether I still loved him. In the bus he said, 'Nicer tonight than on Sat because of the bickering today.'

* A former colleague, who had remained a friend.

Tuesday 23 October

Another glorious sunny day. Lunch in Kens Gdns. E had not slept well 'as I longed and longed for you'. It made me happy that he wanted me. I suppose that is mean. He said, 'I could pick you out in the dark from fifty women, you are so small and rubbery!'

Thursday 25 October

St Crispin's Day – I am 28 and a half today! I don't mind. This year has really been a year – more than a year – of happiness and sorrow, longing and fulfilment.

To a lecture at UC this evening to hear Pryns-Hopkins on 'Current Events Viewed Psychologically'. I quite liked him. We were late and the lecture room was full so we had to sit on an experiment table next to a brain on some blotting paper. Afterwards we went down the stairs at Goodge St and E kissed me twice so fiercely that it was almost agony.

Tuesday 30 October

A queer jumbled crowded day so that I am tired. It has been cold – the coldest night I think. Have been intensely in love today. He said, 'I should like to shout to all the world, "She belongs to me." I should be so proud of you – thousands of little things I love you for – so many that each seems fresh – the way your lips quiver, the tiny movements of your eyebrows – your face is never still. Yes, you are sometimes wearing – when you won't listen. I wish you wouldn't talk about babies. You have made me want them too.'

Wednesday 7 November

Had to see Mrs Lewis and her accountant Goldwyn for F. E. Shaw. At the end she said, 'I expected to see a tall thin person with grey hair and a beard, when the Inspector said, "Miss Bates".'

Glimmers of liking for E – I could just comprehend the possibility of really loving him. He came to Clapham Junction and just kissed me quietly for 2 mins.

Wednesday 14 November

Just a word or two. E kissed me quietly today. The first time since last Wed, so sweet after an interval. We had an hour and a half's inconclusive discussion on the value of religious institutions and the nature of religion.

Saturday 17 November

A good day to begin in this most excellent of notebooks, in which it seems profanation to write in pencil. I met Rosa and Margot and after coffee we went to *Eden End* – the best Priestley play yet and beautifully acted by Beatrix Lehmann, Ralph Richardson and Edward Irwin. It is odd how people apply plays to themselves. E says he must identify himself with the hero; M said, 'Lilian is like me'; Rosa said, 'Stella is like me.' The people are alive, the situation is real but the play is descriptive only, tho' it seems true. It is a little depressing, like an Arnold Bennett novel. You feel like saying, 'This is true, not sentimental; it is real and represents life, tho' it refrains from comment.' So different from *Lear* or even *Within the Gates*.

Sunday 18 November

The chalk path showed ghostly in the silver light on the way to church. A thin sun shone into the hall as I was playing 'Let the people praise thee, Lord' for the children. I wrote my budget letter* and consequently felt depressed after tea; so did Margot, so we talked while my bath got cold. I simplified and crystallized what I think in the course of our conversation. Contemplation and creation sum up the whole art of living so far as *I* am concerned – my ideas are quite clear that far, but I am sadly undecided

---

* An account for herself of the achievements and shortcomings of the year.

about other people – How far should one consider other people? Should one try to influence them? – interfere with them? – give them what they want of you? – withhold oneself? I don't know.

Wednesday 21 November

Fog – so gloomy that I had the light on all day. Went to *Sunday Times* book exhibition at lunchtime. We had tea before I caught the 5.40 for a music lesson. E had said, 'I can go to Burnham next week,' which means the weekend for us. I said at tea, 'The weather will be awful.' He said, 'The only thing to do is to go to bed early' – then 'expose yourself to the blind passion of man – you are divided about it, ambivalent'. I am not really, but he looks quite transformed.

Friday 30 November

More than a week since I last wrote here and a period of ups and downs, exhilaration and despair, joy and sorrow, excitement and boredom. Saturday, Sunday and Monday morning with E, Winchester cathedral on Sat afternoon in the gloom of white mist on a darkening winter's day. The choir in purple cassocks came to practise. We sat down in the dim nave to listen. E said, 'It's more than time you put on the ring,'★ and polished it on his cap. It was partly this and partly the piercing sweetness of the boys' voices, so fresh and young in that old, old place where so many thousands have chanted and died; I cried a little and said, 'We must have tea.' We went to Smith's café, pseudo-Tudor, and then I bought Margot a Poole mug and we found a hotel and had dinner. E rang K up to say his cold was better and we went to the Regal to see *The House of Rothschild* – not bad, but I felt dismal and went on feeling dismal all night till I fell asleep. I could think of nothing but K. He was sweet and just said, 'I am glad you told me why you couldn't bear me to come near you or touch you.' We both slept badly and in the morning I felt better. He came to me for a quarter of an hour. We took our lunch out on Sunday. We went first to

★ A wedding ring, purchased at Woolworths.

St Cross (avoiding the attention of a professional photographer). After dinner I insisted on walking and we explored the town, and so back and to bed and an hour of love 'three times in one day – even Elsie Fisher would think that good'.

I have missed E so this week. I have counted the days. I have also had occasional misgiving in spite of our precautions till tonight and am now relieved.

Saturday 1 December

Aunt Emily and Uncle Harry[*] came. Aunt May,[†] just the image of Grandma – in spite of their having had such different lives – Grandma with 14 babies, Aunt May dried up and wasted. It rather suggests experience may not make much difference, but she was eagerly interested in the royal wedding.

Friday 7 December

Rosa was depressed about poverty this morning and I missed the 9.11 talking to her. I felt rather mean that I gave only £1 to Gray[‡] for Christmas. Last night E said he'd rank me 5 (next to bottom) for Moral Worth, 1 for Intelligence and 2 or 3 for Good Looks. It was just a joke but it seems awful – 5! He also said, 'If you would only think before you act, i.e. bring your intelligence into play, you would be one of the most remarkable women the world has seen!'

Monday 10 December

E taught me about permutations and combinations (difficult) and said, 'It would be quite interesting to teach you mathematics – one has to get your mind working and then it's easy, but you won't let it unless one persuades

[*] Paternal uncle.
[†] Another paternal aunt.
[‡] A clerk at the office.

you it's easy!' Then for half an hour he held me in his arms and kissed me. I loved him so, I suppose because I had felt dismal at lunchtime and he had seen it and stayed till 2.15 and then said, 'Feeling better? No? Well, it was wasted? – yes, a little – you will probably be conscious you are brighter in half an hour.' When I went back to my room at 6.20 I found that Elsie had dropped in and gone away again without a word. 'What colossal tact,' said E. She must have seen his light and not him at his desk and gone away having drawn the correct conclusion that we did not want to be disturbed.

Friday 14 December

E said on Tues we must do something more practical on Friday and we could do a theatre after. With some wrangling I cancelled my evening with Margot, and also said I might be late. Just after lunch today he said, 'I haven't announced that I shall be late and I think it would do me good to get to bed early, I'm rather tired – we'll see, later on.' I wasn't cross – at all – but I felt idiotically hurt at his lack of thought, if only he'd said so yesterday. It is his sensitiveness and consideration, I think, that I love best about him and then to find him apparently falling so short. I made things worse, of course, by thinking of how eager he was a year ago to do anything with me. I didn't intend to convey anything to him, but he did sense it. Without a word he rang up and said he would be late and then when we were going to UC said, 'What about the Westminster Theatre?' I said I was going home and he said, 'I suppose you wouldn't enjoy going now anyway? I have made a mess of tonight.' Later on, over a rather dismal coffee, 'I am sorry I have made you unhappy.'

I wish I knew why he didn't want to go. Was it just weariness or distaste for arranging, or the game not worth the candle? Or merely nothing worth seeing? I don't know, but may I never persuade him to do anything or let him do anything merely out of consideration or pity. Heaven grant that I have the decency or pride or self-respect to feel what he wants and make him do it. He has no idea how I feel except that he vaguely felt that I was miserable and he was responsible. He said, 'I wish I knew why you were dismal – is it being at the mercy of chance, not being able to do what we'd like always?' I said, 'Probably.'

Saturday 15 December

A little better, perhaps, except that I am feeling a deeper unparticularized gloom which I suspect will last till after Christmas, probably, if I could analyse it, due to the essentially family feeling at Christmas and the contrast with E and me. Oh, I would give so much to have children, and the right to love him. He was quite sweet at lunch, taught me a little more permutations and combinations, and held me so gently and sweetly and humbly affectionately that it nearly made me cry.

Sunday 16 December

I have, I think, passed the deepest part of this bog of depression. This morning I played at the children's church and during the prayers and lessons and address (from old Biddell) I thought to myself and managed to achieve some slight detachment and – perhaps it was the effect (unconscious) of the thanksgiving – saw the advantages instead of, or as well as, the disadvantages of the situation. Whatever happens and however miserable I may be fated to be, there are some enormous benefits to be remembered – (1) I have lost the fear of sex that I must have had even 18 months ago and dug up at least some of the repressions I had, and that before I was too old to wake up and find that everything had passed; this is entirely due to E – his consideration and understanding and restraint and honesty; this is a priceless gift which he has given me, worth all the pain and misery I may have to suffer; (2) whether we ever achieve everything – by this I mean a home and children – I have even now had more than most women – love and complete happiness for a spell. Our unions have sometimes been all that Shaw describes in *A Village Wooing*. This is one of the twin peaks of a woman's life (the other being the creation of a baby) and I rejoice in the experience, however dismal I am. I shall try not to lose the sense of fulfilment which love gives; (3) I shall never regret what I have done because I truly believe E has become alive again through his love for me. I think that nobody else could have inspired him to rise again and that he spoke truly when he said once that to lose me would be like sinking back into the grave. So tho' the heavens fall I must not despair, i.e. if K finds out and we have to part, or the Board finds out and separates us by the length of the UK, or even the Irish Sea – or even, what would be far worse, he sinks into routine or even ceases to feel anything, or I do. I must rejoice in 1934 and its memories and not compare the past, present and future and repine and analyse and look out with fear and foreboding on the future and try to survive any catastrophe. Quite a confession and sermon!

Now for a stronger will and good resolution and a lively heart!

Saturday 22 December

So tired, and it is colder. Read almost all of *Mutiny* in the train and so a long discussion with E on martial law etc., out of which I came best (a noteworthy exception in most discussions of this sort). He has gone to Sheffield till Monday week – 9 days. After picnicking comfortably he said as I was going, 'I'd better not kiss you as we don't seem able to kiss sensibly,' and just touched my cheek. I think he loves me a lot still. Anyway, yesterday he got some pleasure from touching and feeling me. I wonder, does he think of me when I am not there as much as I think of him?

Monday 31 December

As 1934 draws to a close and 1935 dawns I am going to pause to look back and to look forward.

E came back to the office this morning full of Helen's sweetness and David's brightness.* He made me feel sad quite without intending it. He would revel in children of his own, if only we were free. To keep the gloom away I bickered desperately but now, all alone, I could cry dismally. This is a poor end to a year which has given me glorious moments so I will make an effort and just dwell on the bright things; the early sweetness of the walk from Seaford to Eastbourne on the gloomy chilly February day; lying on the cliff out of the wind after lunch, then sheltered by the gorse

* His niece and nephew.

bush on Crowlink; then as it grew dark on the seat by Beachy Head, and last in the train. I was still afraid but just awakening. The mixed ecstasy and pain of the walk from Amersham; I kept him at arm's length in the wood, while a blackbird sang, piercing sweet, just overhead; but later that evening at *The Merchant of Venice* I let myself go; so to the hot Saturday afternoon at Merstham a week before Whitsun when he made me cry by saying, 'Perhaps you'll think of me when you really love someone else.' I won't cry now; and so to Whitsun – a joyous honeymoon when we just lived in a dream from Saturday afternoon to Monday evening; strenuous walking over the Cotswolds, exploring churches, lying in the sun and under trees. A perfect sequel to the sickening fear and lonely cowardice of the afternoon when I went to Dr Malleson.★ The two dream-like midnight walks and finally the week in Shropshire.

Since then – for me – is the gradual decrease in happiness and increase in my consciousness of the gloomy side. I want children and can't have them. My nerves are perhaps a bit threadbare from the continual secrecy and the constant vigilance – the false position at the office – I don't know. If I thought I would get a district no worse than Paddington I think I would ask for a move and cut it off now, before I become continually unhappy and too low to react to new surroundings. In any case it may be the best thing to do. I don't want the happiness of February to September overshadowed. Perhaps I haven't enough work to do or don't find enough. It is clearly bad to have office and love mixed up.

★ She was probably afraid she was pregnant.

1935

Thursday 3 January

I have been quite jubilant on the whole. E has really been very sweet the
last 2 days; he would be so nice with his own children. What would I not
give to make them! – but that way depression lies.

Sunday 6 January

I warded off a threatened fit of gloom yesterday by going by myself to see
The Snow Maiden at the Vic. E was nice to me. He said, 'It is as sweet now
as it was a year ago – we can tell Joad that it lasts a long time, can't we?' He
had arranged to meet K to go to *Toad of Toad Hall*. I felt rather at a loose
end and not very keen on the Vic but I decided finally to go. Two minutes
after the music began I knew I had been right. It was lovely – suggestions
of *The Immortal Hour* and Chekhov, all minor and blue with bright relief,
red and yellow, sad and lovely and transient, strange and yet familiar.
I tipped my speech for Saturday's History Luncheon* and felt quite elated.
It is not particularly good but it is fine to have done it in good time, and
also to have made it. It has quite good patches and is subtle in places. I
think what is the matter with me is that I don't work hard enough.

Monday 7 January

Showed E my History speech (with great sinkings). Though he suggested
sundry improvements he thought it quite good, which led to some
pleasant argument on intelligence and finally to a kiss as sweet as any since

* She was to be the speaker at a reunion of history graduates from Royal Holloway
College.

the beginning. 'We fit in so beautifully,' he said, and before that, 'Because I know you are clever I am so proud that you love me, and that you feel the same about me makes it so sweet.'

Richmond Park

Tuesday 8 January

This is a day to remember. E said he had not slept last night. We went to UC and found nothing doing so, altho' it was very cold, we went to Richmond Park to love. After coffee we reached the Park – almost no wind, quite dark. We were able to see the trees with their bare branches against the sky. So sweet to feel his hands moving so quietly and gently over me. He was nice, immediately responsive. It seemed like a dream – the darkness, the sweetness, the bitter cold – yet a dream shared with him.

Sunday 13 January

I must write something about yesterday – it was too full and unique to leave out altogether and I was too weary to do any diary last night. It was the History Luncheon at Craig Court at 1.15. I wore my Vienna brown frock – more office-y and warmer than the velvet I originally intended to wear – my new brown felt hat and borrowed Rosa's brown coat.

I was too busy to think about the speech till 11.15, then had a bad attack of nervousness, a sick feeling at the bottom of my stomach, a clammy feeling of the hands and shivering whenever I thought about it. E was very sweet and sympathetic – told me how awful he felt before his first Appeal meeting. Rosa rang up and wished me luck. E gave me an orange and kissed me and for just a minute I thought, 'What a fool I am – as tho' anything matters except that we love each other.'

Tubes crowded and I didn't get to the Restaurant till 1.25. HJ* was quite cordial; gave me Burgundy and we had some discussion of cruises. Mary Roney† on the other side of me. I was relieved that Misery‡ was not there (tho' not at the reason, which was that her mother had just died). I decided that I didn't really care about anyone there. In spite of this fortunate decision the meal had a nightmarish quality of unreality. My first sentence kept creeping through my mind. When it came to the point I did not have to pause to think nor did I forget. I was conscious of feeling weak about the knees once, and once I was afraid my voice was going but I paused deliberately to cough. The first part was funnier and I was tremendously encouraged when people laughed. I was distinctly aware of HJ's fat 'Ha, ha!' at my elbow. I felt it must sound obviously learnt by heart and very pompous towards the end. When I had finished I seemed to hear with deafening distinctness the noise of people pushing their chairs back and whispering the toast – 'The History School and Prof Johnstone'. HJ was quite appreciative – whispered to me privately 'One of the best speeches we have ever had' – and made the expected joke

---

* Her university history professor.
† A friend from college days.
‡ Nickname for a history lecturer.

about giving thanks to an Inspector of Taxes. Many said, 'Marvellously fluent – you did not repeat a word once.' I felt it was not too bad, but – Oh – the joy of a weight of anxiety lifted from my heart. I shouldn't have cared what happened.

Mary and I taxi-ed to Victoria where E was waiting for me. We went to Richmond and walked three miles along the river. It was bitterly cold but beautiful and very few people about and the sun sinking red immediately ahead. I told him all about the lunch and we said very little. I just felt exhilarated. It was still only dusk at 5.0 when we bus-ed back to Richmond. In the train from Victoria he kissed me and said, 'I have never kissed anyone smelling of Burgundy before!'

Wednesday 16 January

Three full nice days since I wrote. We have loved each other almost too much. Psychology yesterday – work curves – I did the arithmetic and he did the cancellation. You have to mark the 5 second intervals and I forgot towards the end of the 10 minutes. 'You have spoilt the experiment,' he said. I said I was sorry. Then he did the same. 'You have spoilt the experiment,' I said, and we laughed. He said today that when he is bad-tempered I know just what to do and am never bitter. I must have a nice nature. Today he said, 'It must be very rare – such joy as ours – so continuous – your dancing eyes, that's what I shall remember longest.' There is a peculiar light-heartedness and gay quality in our love which I think must be uncommon – we laugh at ourselves and yet still enjoy it – a detachment which does not spoil the intimacy but makes it more healthy – disinfects our passion so-to-speak. I am so happy. I looked at myself in the bath tonight and thought, 'No, this is not wasted whatever happens – it has made him happy – a miracle – this peculiar, knobbly body has yet that power – for that is the basis for our love.'

Sunday 20 January

E and I have had a good week. Apart from the office we have lunched together on Monday, Tuesday, Friday and Saturday. We went to

Psychology on Tuesday and *The Little Plays*, dinner and the Choral Symphony on Thursday, the AIT dinner on Friday and half an hour of violent loving and *Figaro* at the Vic yesterday.

We walked through the Park to Mandes for dinner. E was sweet. 'No meditating,' he said. The concert was fine – Beethoven's No 1, Mozartish and gay, and the Ninth (Choral). The first and 4th movements are the most intoxicating. E said it had the same effect on me as a sex orgasm. The 2nd movement (Scherzo) and the 3rd (Adagio) were like interludes, the first lively and dancing, the second sweet and melancholy. It is as if Beethoven thought – this shall be the epitome of my life as I have felt it – gay and tragic, trivial and serious. Weingartner★ is 72 (according to E) but he is tall and very straight and gives German bows from the waist. The Ninth is the first thing E told me to hear, so appropriate to go with him.

In bed 11.20pm:

Went to church this evening; special service with Te Deum and during the sermon I clearly thought what I must do: I must reconcile myself to having no children and not being E's wife. To do this I must work hard at something, if possible with E, but if necessary on my own.

Monday 28 January

Hideous nightmare day! Got up this morning with a great effort to see frozen snow over the Downs and roads, and hard-frosted windows. Caught 9.31 (late) and got to the office feeling rather shaky and croaking with a lost voice. Started dictating and Mrs Shaw rang up to say that F E Shaw died suddenly yesterday morning. She sounded quite firm – a post mortem today, an inquest. Her brother had arrived; who should she write to at Somerset House? It seemed unbelievable. Miss Hale, who seems so superficial, did not know what to say; Greenfield and Rimmer turned pale. I felt weak and shaky and shivered violently with the cold – trembled for a long time. E rang me about 1.00, Rimmer was rather nice but I felt so alone and knocked over. I shouldn't have thought it would be such a shock because I always thought it would be sudden and at any time, but probably

---

★ The conductor.

my cold and happing* made it worse. After lunch I wondered if I had misunderstood on the phone and I kept seeing him and hearing his voice, and his slow heavy footsteps coming along the passage to my room, and in the lift with his bowler hat and tweed overcoat and his small tight smile and his podgy hands. Still bitter, bitter cold – it always affected him. Foreseeing his end I felt obscurely responsible for it – 'Death lays his icy hand on kings.'

Thursday 31 January

Met E at Surbiton station and we had a coffee and then to St Mark's church for F E Shaw's funeral. The flowers were beautiful but incongruous when you thought of the shell of F E Shaw inside the small coffin. His boys looked much older than we expected, and tall, all turning after Mrs Shaw, not FES. The service was cold and short. I felt that the parson tried to put some conviction into it but was incapable. I thought the Epistle had no application and I could hardly see its beauty. I was glad to get back to the station leaving E to go on to the cemetery. E was miserable this afternoon. We talked of him for ages. It is amazing how much we knew of him and how continually he fills our thoughts. I have felt his death more than Granny's or Uncle Arthur's.

Saturday 2 February

At last the interminable week has nearly ended! I don't know when I remember a longer week. We went to the Centre meeting which I loathed, crowds of revolting men drinking beer. The two things had stirred up E's feeling about the Higher Grade and he slept badly and was still depressed this morning. I feel so unsettled now at the office. Legge is pleasant but uninterested and hasn't enough to do. He has no repose – never is quite still – a contrast to F E Shaw, so genially placid. I should like a move but I don't know what to do about E. I feel that unless he does something definite that would be the end. We have less and less time together apart from the office

* Menstruation.

and I am not sure whether it is because he doesn't want more or can't get more. I wish K knew about us. I feel it would decide the whole thing and I should finish one way or the other with this unsettled precariousness.

Tuesday 5 February

A joyful day – brilliant sunshine and blue sky. I wore my Tudor jumper. I don't know why – perhaps the sunshine, perhaps I really had overcome my depression and reached some serenity but I felt happier this morning. The effect of this was to make me 'jaunty' and E said this had an immediate effect on him especially after I had been subdued for some days. I knew almost at once that he was actively interested in me. He said, 'You are wearing the "holey" vest – I can see right through the holes in your jumper and vest to your skin in the sunlight.'

In the afternoon a little bickering about dictation (I said 'Damn', which pleased him), then to Psychology. Fidelity of report, Nonsense syllables, Mazes. He kissed me and said, 'I should like to go to bed with you – queer how one suddenly wakes up.' With his hand half round my waist, 'You are so frail – so small and nice.' It is still sweet to love – there is a sweetness in recognizing it leaping in him.

Wednesday 6 February

We heard this morning that Goldstein is coming to Paddington from Sutton on 18th. It doesn't sound nice – a new Senior Inspector, younger than E and a worker. We both wish we could get a shift.

Thursday 7 February

The cold wind has dropped but it has been very cold again, with sunshine this morning. Very tiring interview with Miss Horlock at 3.0. She nursed King Edward VII in 1898 till 1910, then went to US. Lost her money and had arthritis there and retired to the UK in 1929. In 1931 she had a stroke which left her very deaf.

From 5.0 till 6.05 – on and off – we loved. It is heavenly to feel I can give him pleasure. Altho' it is mainly (I suppose) physical I feel it is somehow big and sacred. I am so glad that it is not the least bit sordid and material – that money and presents and outside considerations do not come into it.

Saturday 9 February

A happy day. I gave up having coffee with E so that we should love and it was so sweet and slow and conscious almost all the time till the passionate climax, hot and inexorable, complete as doom. I feel I can give him full satisfaction and happiness and this makes me so proud.

Saturday 16 February

Blowing a gale – the wind gets on my nerves. I am afraid of it, even out of doors. It seems so relentless and alive, roaring in the trees and driving the rain in clouds along the road. One feels so helpless. It must be an appalling experience to be at sea in a small boat in a gale. E came in late this morning. I was snappy at first to him as I felt edgy and he was still not too well. But gradually I loved him.

Tuesday 19 February

The great Goldstein has arrived. I know not what he looks like except that he is big and fat, wears rimless glasses, has a thick sensual mouth and fat podgy hands. He is clearly determined to make a stir at Paddington – wants to get a typist for himself for official and private correspondence, is going to revolutionize the files and is fond of sending chits and typed memos all over the office. He and Legge strolled into my room before lunch and he made a few preliminary remarks on the untidy files – 'Doesn't it offend your sense of feminine neatness?' I didn't dislike him seriously till this afternoon when he signed a letter of mine that I hadn't even seen. Also, Rimmer came in with a tale of woe and a heap of chits such as 'Am I not entitled to (1) a noticeboard, (2) a calendar?' He is clearly upsetting Rimmer. Well, we shall see.

Lunched with E at the Plane Tree and then went to the British Museum and looked at the Mexican and other Central American things. They were interesting and have surprising resemblances to Egyptian. The faces have surprising variety. E said there must be a mixture of races but I doubt it in America before the discovery.

Saturday 23 February

So ends one of the longest weeks of my life! I would never have believed that one man coming into the district could have had so much effect in such a short time. Goldstein has to my own knowledge upset Rimmer, Harrod, Creasey, Miss Hale, Miss Elliott, Hollingsworth, reduced Williams to a state of mirthless sarcasm and made E and me quite miserable. It is not that his ideas are bad – it is his method and his personality. He insists on being addressed 'To Inspector . . .', he likes typed 'Submissions', as if to Head Office, tho' he is ready for 'consultations' on anything. He must have first claim on the typist, everyone at his beck and call. He talks about my not having had responsibility and yet he won't leave us to do anything on our own. I am considering calling Hunter today to wangle a move and E and I are both going to ask Osler for a move and tell him why. The only things that deter me are (1) I don't want to leave London while the parents find my 30/- per week useful and (2) it is humiliating to think one can't stand anyone and I want to be quite certain it is due wholly to him and not even partly to an ordinary district organization. Well enough, thank heaven it's Sunday tomorrow!

Went to the Vic with E last night to see *The Kingdom of God, The Two Shepherds* (Sierra) and *Hippolytus* (Euripides). I watched the District Ping Pong match with Finchley and kept him waiting ten mins and so we had a hasty dinner at Craig Court and got to the Vic just in time. Luckily there was heaps of room.

The Spanish trifle, about an old priest and an old doctor who were dismissed in favour of younger men, perfectly suited Morland Graham as the priest. The setting was attractive. The Greek seemed even to me incongruous with modern lighting and illusion but apart from this the production was impressive and the play came over effectively. How marvellous for Euripides to be admired and understood after 2,500 years. Yet his life was unhappy. I just begin to follow the saying 'he that shall lose his life shall save it'. In sorrow lies wisdom and development of the spirit, I am afraid. May I in sorrow have strength to do right even to my own loss.

Monday 25 February

Have felt a little better today, mainly because the great 'I AM' has only called to give me yet another typed form (for CI arrears) and because I have got through some work quite well. Waffled with E – he has been rather nice (and quite detached). He read me out a long extract from Hardy about the barn, from *The Woodlanders*, and shearing. He thinks it is one of the finest prose passages in literature known to him. He said he would learn it by heart. There is a fineness and genuineness about it which is most satisfying. I must read some more Hardy. We talked a little at tea and almost decided that the most satisfactory thing is to concentrate and really get to the bottom of one thing. E said two things, with one predominant – an art and a science, and one of them connected with the country. The difficulty is to choose – it mustn't be too small, like knitting jumpers, or too big like world literature.

Wednesday 27 February

A perfect winter's day yesterday, sunny and cold, and today the worst kind of winter's day – cold, wet and a strong wind. It snowed hard till 10.0 and then rained without ceasing till 4.0. Yet in spite of this I have been so happy.

Met E at Guildford. I had doubts whether he would be there, but there he was in his grey woolly suit and mackintosh. We had coffee and it then became clear that it was impossible to walk so we rushed back to Waterloo. We went to the Haymarket and saw *Barnet's Folly*. It was better than I expected, especially Muriel Aked and Jan Stewer. Nicer than all, the gallery was half empty so we had the back of it to ourselves for Acts 2 and 3. E held me tightly and once he put a small warm kiss on the back of my neck.

Tea and scones at the Thistle. He is on leave tomorrow as well and I said at Charing Cross I hoped it would be better. He said, 'It might be a finer day but it couldn't be better.' Oh, marvellous to mean so much to each other. It must be too good to last, and yet now it is almost 17 months since he told me.

Thursday 28 February

Our friend Bertie* has been almost unbearable today, but we will not dwell on him in case the thought banishes sleep. I had a poem last night about us, just simmering below consciousness – all the feeling and almost the concrete expression, but I fear it has fled. E had a lovely day for leave.

Friday 1 March

Re-posted my letter to Hunter today and while Margot and I were at skating he rang up. I spoke to him when I got back. He was very nice and surprised to hear about Goldstein. His son – a fat boy – is in John's form at Whitgift. He told me to ask Osler for a move and then he (Hunter) would be able to fix it up. I felt a bit mean not to do more for E, but I am bad at asking favours. It is at any rate clear that the Inspecting Officer's recommendation is the thing to get. Hunter told me not to make any fuss about Goldstein – a girl doesn't get a square deal. It looks fairly certain I shall get a move in May anyhow and Hunter will try to keep me in town. It shouldn't make much difference to us.

Tuesday 5 March

I have reacted to Goldstein with spiteful dislike. He put on AB Davis 'Keep in touch with me' so I fixed an interview this afternoon and practically

---

* Nickname for Goldstein, new Inspector in Charge.

agreed to drop the case. What will he say? He is making E miserable –
keeps raising footling points. I hope he gets a move.

Another lovely sunny day. We lunched at Mandes and walked back
through the Park. He has been feeling rotten but I think I improved him. I
don't know – how I should love to bring Goldstein low. It would be
doubtful and dangerous – humiliating if unsuccessful and dangerous if not
– or provoke him to slap my face – safer, but not so effective.

Wednesday 6 March

It's a poor thing I am! Again I have cried in the bath. It has its
conveniences, i.e. privacy and the disposal of tears is easy. I think too much
of E. I must find something else to think about. He went to the Queen's
Hall about seats for tomorrow's concert. There were only orchestra and
side stalls so he got none. I don't know how much he wants me. He likes to
talk to me, to feel that I am in the office as a sort of background, but he
makes practically no effort now to do things with me. It is probably just
inertia. Goldstein makes him dismal, I know, and he has heaps of work. He
has been working at home all the week. I suppose I'm suffering from a
conflict between love and pride. I wish I knew, tho'. Heaven preserve me
from becoming another Hippolyta!

Friday 8 March

A fine triumphant day with moments of sweetest happiness. We had a very
hasty lunch and a small discussion of Ibsen and hurried back to the office as
we both had appointments at 2.30.

E decided to come to the Westminster with me to see *Happy and
Glorious*. Just before the curtain rose he said, 'You've been a tremendous
help to me this last fortnight.' Just ten words but I've glowed with
happiness ever since. It's not that I have tried to be or even that I may have
been a help, but just that he knew and felt. It was like struggling in the
dark as he seemed not to be aware of *me* at all. God, how I love him.

Tuesday 12 March

A hectic day at the office signing claims, seeing a woman accountant re Magnet BS and issuing Schedule A duplicates as Goldstein had a whole day interview re the United Dairies. At Psychology we did the Time Sense experiment and I found I was quite accurate – could tell one fifteenth longer or shorter than 2 secs. Typed draft of E's appeal.*

Thursday 14 March

An unpleasant day – cold and dark with an overhead fog so that I developed a headache. Had a brush with Goldstein. I knew I should have to see him and shivered and wobbled at the thought. He took the attitude that his harassing was not criticism but helpful advice and instruction with future reference to a Special Inspection. I got a blow in about (1) working lists and (2) his PS in manuscript to my letters – told him in 2 cases this week he had added what I had deliberately omitted. I should be glad if he would discuss his amendments with me first. Felt much better afterwards.

Sunday 17 March

Today has broken the chain of concentration on Goldstein. I am so happy that I have that power. We took the train to Groombridge. He pretended to be thrilled to be on a line new to him. We found a private road and footpath nearly all the way to Crowborough. Lovely country, characteristic of the Sussex/Kent border – low point of hills showing blue in the gaps wooded to the top, green meadows and oast houses, streams and primroses and pussy willows. We had a very small picnic lunch in a field by the road and loved for half an hour with a lark singing with abandon just over our heads. So sweet to feel him awakening till he said, 'Now I'm all stirred up I want to try everything with you, even perversions.' I said, 'I'm glad you still like me.' He said, 'I shall go on

---

* Against the decision not to promote him to Higher Grade.

always. The sex side has been quite quiet the last few weeks but still I liked you. That proves it.'

Wednesday 20 March

In the Park at lunchtime every day. Three days of tension and dramatic clashes at the office – the General Inspection and our attempts to persuade Osler of the position. On Tuesday morning I asked him for a move, keeping to the reason that I wanted experience. He agreed. Today E asked him for a move for personal reasons. He agreed, but said it was unlikely we'd both get moves. Rimmer told Osler clearly what had happened. Civval asked for a move, Miss Hale is going to. Goldstein looks uneasy and had grown quite polite and genial. Osler seemed quite overcome and went home at 3.0.

Thursday 21 March

The first day of Spring and the loveliest 21st March I remember. Brilliant sunshine, a cloudless blue sky, very warm, the daffodils dancing in the Park. Lunch with Reen,* Glasson and E. Then took Mrs Potter's file up to Osler and talked to him about Goldstein and he quite vindicated me. E is quite confident about his promotion to Higher Grade Inspector of Taxes and he quite liked me.

Saturday 23 March

Major Barbara at Vic last night. We had been going together when K phoned to say she was coming so we had dinner at Craig Court and I went alone in the gallery. I didn't mind when the play began. In fact I forgot all about E except in the intervals. Shaw is so stimulating, but this morning I didn't like him till lunchtime. We picnicked and then he said, 'Just 2 minutes; I feel like loving you – much more than last Sunday.' So sweet,

---

* Doreen Hosier.

tho' not quite perfect. Before we went he said, 'I shouldn't care what you said to me because I should know that underneath you loved me.'

I rushed home to help to entertain Aunty Katie⋆ and the Benbows.†
Quite an amusing evening. I thought how aghast they would all be if they knew that a few hours before I had been in the arms of a married man! I was sorry for Aunty Katie. She was nervy and feels the responsibility of the family and the house. A rather heated discussion with Mr Benbow on art. He thinks Epstein is wicked – art must tell the truth!

Monday 25 March

Wore my zig-zag blouse tucked in with Rosa's belt. E liked it and said, 'You fancy yourself in that, you can't hide your feelings.' Picnicked in my room and then waffle and coffee while he explained the Wheatstone bridge to me again. I told E that if it were not for the parents I should like 2 – just 2 – babies. We discussed the effect on Establishments and at length he said, 'Just let me put my cheek against yours.' He is better. I signed the post today. Goldstein said it would be good experience for me!

Tuesday 26 March

Just a note of the medley of happiness in my heart. There was no lecture at UC so we tube-ed to Golders Green and walked over Hampstead Heath from 6.05 to 7.55. A lovely red sunset, a small silver star in the blue sky which grew larger and brighter as darkness fell; cool breeze blowing over the top of the trees, sleepy birds twittering below in the trees, then across the road towards Kenwood and looking across to the east, myriad of lights, and by a great tree we loved. I thought of Keats (the letters still fresh in my mind). We must have been near the Nightingale wood. And Ella‡ beginning a whole month's holiday but with no E to love her.

⋆ Her favourite paternal aunt.
† Neighbours.
‡ Another friend from college days.

Thursday 28 March

So quickly can events alter one's feelings. I can hardly realize that it is only 2 nights ago we were at Hampstead; 2 crowded desperate days since then. Yesterday E heard that the Promotions Board were not giving him a hearing. We did not know what this meant; a complete turn-down or quite hopeful. I phoned Reen and Glasson but got nothing conclusive. An Appeal meeting this morning – Goldstein and E went. E got back at 12.15 and said Goldstein is quite ineffective at Appeals.

Saturday 30 March

Colder today – dull, and chilly wind blowing under my brown hat. Woke up with a headache, still left from yesterday when it developed from rage due to E's bad luck and powerlessness over promotion. We went to *Frolic Wind* at the Royalty and, in spite of all, managed to enjoy it. A peculiar play with odd characters, poorly constructed with numerous scenes, but perfectly acted and cleverly written. It had sufficient truth to make an illusion. E kissed me in the second interval, rather unexpectedly, as we were most dejected and at the same time full of impotent fury earlier. An odd evening, surprisingly happy in spite of his circumstances.

An unpleasant morning. Office harangue on Osler's Inspection Report – AG and E argued and I merely indicated my agreement with E. Did no work at all. E is going to ask for a Special Inspection. He kissed me and then went home.

Saturday 6 April

I haven't been very happy and pleasant and light and brave this week. Have felt a little resentful to E, thinking he doesn't make much effort to do things with me, but today he gave me half his lunch and said, 'If you like I could go for a walk with you.' We decided to go to *Hamlet* at Streatham. After lunch he said, 'Now I'll just kiss you and then wash the orange off my hands and then we'll go.' I love him so. I hate K. We stood in the gallery for *Hamlet*. It was packed. It is odd how superlatively good it is when it is just talk with no action and how it fails when the action begins. The Gravedigger's scene is a perfect example of this. E said *Lear* is a beautiful stormy winter sky and *Hamlet* a dancing stream on an April day. I didn't agree. *Hamlet* has more sheer nastiness than this simile suggests but it does suggest the continuous glint and flash of intellectual play.

Monday 8 April

How unsatisfactory I am – I feel quite ashamed of me. I think far too much about E. I have worried myself into a state of nerves simply by thinking about him – what he will do – whether he likes me – what he wants of me – when and what he will arrange to do etc. I *must* get interested in other things before I get quite neurotic.

Wednesday 10 April

Just finished my bath, during which I cried salt tears of self-pity. 'There's nothing either good or bad but thinking makes it so.' This is, of course, true, but how to control one's thoughts? I think E loves me still – I am sure I help him and console him in his dismal position at the office. I also know that his weaknesses are the inevitable outcome of his good points – might almost be called another aspect – which is no advantage to me – of his virtues: self-control, sensitiveness, delicacy, subtlety, the things most characteristic of him, the things I love in him. Yet it is these same things that drive me to despair – almost to a regret that the car which only just missed me *did* miss me. It isn't that I want him as a husband, or even that I want more sex contact than we get – but just that I want his companionship in quiet, unhurried leisure. I want to comfort him and to be comforted, to be free. Well, perhaps I shall never have more than I have had already. Maybe the only thing to do is to fix my eye on the people worse off than me – people who have never loved or been loved, who are poor, or ill, or stupid, or coarse, and just count my blessings – a secure job that isn't too uninteresting, a nice family, a pleasant home with most luxuries, enough money, a tolerable heart to perceive beauty in nature and in art.

1935

Friday 12 April

A queer mixed day. Still fairly elated, altho' E definitely said it was useless to refuse to go on the cruise in the hope of having 2 weeks with him – one, perhaps, but not till October at earliest. I am going to talk to him seriously tomorrow. I must *do* more, if not with him then without him. Goldstein came in for a few minutes this afternoon. His wife is very ill and depressed – has to have an operation for a cyst. He was pathetic in his helplessness – he told me all about it.

Monday 15 April

A full and most exhausting weekend with summertime in the middle. As a result of these two circumstances we all overslept this morning. No one awoke till 8.30. On Saturday I gave E a homily on his recent way of life – he had done nothing but sleep and work for 3 months. It was not merely that I was bored, but bad for him. Accordingly he read Tomlinson's *Snows of Helicon* and started Jenks' *History of England* and talked to me about surface tension all through our waffles and coffee.

Saturday 27 April

A long gap since I last wrote during which E and I have done nothing except go to Westminster Abbey at lunchtime on my birthday. I hoped he would want to do something, if only a walk or a show at Easter but he said nothing and I decided not to suggest it. Finally I enjoyed Easter more than I expected, mostly walking with Margot. By Wednesday evening, however, I had become hopelessly depressed and almost decided to write E a letter to tell him how unsatisfactory it was for me – my love depended on him and I could not be inactive. Doing things with him is essential, otherwise my love just curdles in me to bitterness. It grew on contemplating and doing things with him – my best moments have been when we have both felt something to be beautiful, e.g. the Mass in D, the violin concerto, *Lear*, Linley Hill, Long Mynd, the moonlight walks, the kingfisher. I felt dismal on Thursday morning (my birthday) but he made an effort – had put on his grey suit – and at lunch we went to the Abbey. E had not seen the tombs before so I made the most of my knowledge. I felt better by the time I returned for an appointment at 2.30. We loved for twenty minutes in the office. He also read Goldstein's letter to me about his wife's death and said he had often told me to marry a SI,* and probably I could get a chance there. He said it would be a good thing, the idea should cross my mind because 'no one could walk across the stage so unconcernedly as you – it is a main element of your charm'. It is not that the possibility doesn't enter my head (it had), but I dismiss it, bury it and think only of the moment. E quite liked me today and I loved him so much, tho' I felt sad underneath.

Friday 3 May

I feel curiously light-hearted. I wrote E a long letter last night and gave it to him this evening. It endeavoured to make clear how I feel, i.e. the most important aspect (to me) of our love which has declined this winter. I felt doubtful about giving it to him, but now that it is done – tho' it may have spoilt our whole relationship – I feel better, as tho' it had to be.

Thursday 9 May

I am much happier and much more settled now. E replied to my complaint on Saturday in a letter which made me cry – said his hopelessness was the only reason for the loss of vitality in our relationship. He has been, I think, better this week. We loved this evening in my room – long and passionately. We had just stopped when Ridout came in – an awkward moment, but E said I showed admirable sang-froid. I feel as if I had resolved a difficulty. I do hope I shan't start straining and wishing and wondering again. I feel happier about E than since Sept.

* Senior Inspector, one rung above Higher Grade in the promotions hierarchy.

Saturday 1 June

At the AIT dinner last night Osler told me in confidence I was going to St George's so I was thrilled to know we should not be far apart. Quite enjoyed it, tho' I talked to no one but Wilson, Cook, Butler and Osler. E came to Waterloo Junction with me and kissed me in the train – 'Short but quite nice,' he said. I felt sorry for him but liked him better than ever by comparison with everyone else there. He has an indefinable attraction for me – his subtle intelligence and his truthfulness and clearness are the things I admire most consciously in him. Duff Cooper – a little man with an expressive face – made a bright speech for the guests.

Tuesday 4 June

Our love has flared up to ecstasy again. Now I am alone and weary and a little sad. I had not been able to prevent myself from looking forward to Whitsun, thinking we'd go away together. While we were having coffee E told me that K wanted to take her mother to Brighton and would probably not go unless he went with her, so it is very doubtful whether we can go. Still, we love each other completely. I feel that it can never die. I am so proud to have the power to make him feel so. It is not that I crave the sexual satisfaction, but it is a thermometer of his love and of his health – an indication that he is turning outwards from his sorrow. I feel that I have called him back to life if not to happiness. We went to see *Yahoo* done by the Irish Players at the Westminster last night. He kissed me fiercely in his room and I – I loved him so. I felt shaky at the knees and my heart thumped. I said, 'That was too much.' He said, 'Why do you do it then? You are terribly sensual. It's gorgeous to feel you working up.' We had dinner at Zeeta's and bickered about the time and the food and the route to the theatre. In the 2nd interval we went down the stairs. He just kissed me once so hard that it hurt me. Then, while we waited for the music to stop he said, 'Your face is not very pretty.' I said, 'No, not a bit' – he, 'But it's marvellous, simply gorgeous, when your soul looks out of it like that. It's just a measure of what is behind it, the poorer it is, the lovelier your soul.' So rarely he says a thing, it is an effort as he is inarticulate – it was so sweet, so sweet to hear. I am writing it down here so that I may not forget, or if I do, so that years hence, when I have lost the attraction that youth gives to any face, I may be reminded that the man I loved thought me beautiful on June 3rd 1935.

Wednesday 12 June

This is a new diary which I bought at Woolworths today. I am just beginning to write before going to bed – my face is throbbing with sun blisters and my lip is stiff from kissing and I have neuralgia in my eyes and I am tired – but I must begin to remember all that has happened since I finished the last diary.

Last weekend was Whitsun and we were together from 5.30 on Saturday until 5.30 on Monday. It looks so bald and prosaic written down like that – yet these two days were a lifetime of experience. When we loved on Saturday night E said afterwards it was for 2 hours 10 mins. Our love grew till it filled my whole universe. I felt we were the only living beings in the world and we were almost at one. It was the best time we have had – I was unafraid and unashamed. I did not really lose consciousness of him at all – when I felt I was growing misty I turned on the light and looked at him. Although I find it almost impossible to recall my feeling or to remember what happened I think I was more conscious than I have ever been. It seems so remote now but then at any rate it was clear. I can never reach greater heights of passion with him or anyone, I know. There is an absolute quality about this union which we may re-capture but I am sure we can never surpass. On Sunday night we were too tired for any love-making – besides, I felt it would be an anti-climax if we tried. On Monday morning there wasn't time. On Sunday after lunch we lazed on a tumulus in the sun and loved a little – but quietly – sweetly, and a little remotely – reminiscently, as it were – so much for the physical.

We walked on Sat evening through East and West Hagbourne – two lovely villages, especially East, with a lovely church. E is so satisfactory as a companion quite apart from our love. We like the same things if in different degrees, and, although he knows more, I do know some things he doesn't. He likes the actual architecture and can talk with some knowledge

East Hagbourne

of buttresses and arches, capitals and periods. I like wood carving and old glass and queer names and grotesque heads. We both like birds and wide views. He hates red roofs almost to frenzy, and bungalows and dumps, and loves barns and old cottages. I like flowers and trees and clouds and odd people. On the whole we supplement each other's likes and laugh at each other's dislikes.

Monday 17 June

This evening I sharpened this pencil and made notes for a novel – just the skeleton of the plot. It is to be based on the life of E, but will not have any obvious connection. The character of the hero will to some extent be modelled on him. I feel the idea is beginning to grow. It was an effort to put anything down in black and white – it is queer, the repugnance I have in actually and objectively making a start. It is not simply indolence; I think there is some psychological conflict somewhere. I feel like Jacob wrestling with the angel. It is only by driving myself that I ever do begin. Once started, however, the fact that there is some material objective scheme spurs me on and the thing grows. I feel that so few novels are really worth writing, however well written they may be. I don't want to make a clever or even a just beautiful novel. What I want to do is make a character as a perpetual memorial of E, with rare gifts of mind and spirit and conscience – his only weakness being some lack of force and a too great trust in reason – set in the London of today.

Monday 1 July

For the period 21–29th June Margot and I were on holiday at Chester and Capel Curig and I kept a separate diary.

I returned to the office today still with a red nose and peeling arms but hoping for the best in my new plaid silk blouse and best stockings. It was very hot with a thundery heaviness in the air. I had looked forward to seeing E. I re-read *Jude* all the holiday and he is so associated with the book that I felt him as a background all the time. He looked nice and much better, but altho' we lunched together and talked quite a lot and bickered I felt a bit dismal by this evening. He said, 'It's too hot to go traipsing round the Park.' It was quite true and sensible but how different from 2 years ago.

How will it end? I do love him so. It is strange he should feel such an affinity to Jude – ominous and tragic. He said he thought Sue was more like me than any character in a book. I don't like her – even less now than the first time. I think I deceived him in the early stages of our friendship and it was as if I was driven to play up to him, to give him the entertainment and stimulation he asked for – and in doing so I gave him a false impression – that I had more intelligence and sparkle and vitality than I had. I have felt this all the time and on many occasions tried to undeceive him but it was too late.

Tuesday 2 July

Not so bad today, tho' I have had dismal moments. We had a small brawl over something – I forget what. He said, 'You fight with a tiger's fearlessness but fortunately not with a tiger's strength.'

1935

Wednesday 3 July

Today I said farewell to Paddington and go to St George's tomorrow. I bought two Dundees and 2 walnut cakes for tea and gave Miss Hale 'Texts and Pretexts'.

I was rather tearful this evening. It is awful to be naturally sentimental and emotional. Williams, Ridout, Civval, Rimmer etc. all came to say goodbye and E loved me for 25 minutes in his room and I cried. On the whole I feel much less dismal. We got a taxi to Victoria – 'A bad precedent,' he said, but it was hot and there was an awful crowd at the bus stop.

Saturday 6 July

I have moved to St George's. Thursday morning I listened to an interminable speech from Cheel handing me over his cases till my brain was in a whirl. I had a headache by lunchtime which was 1.45. E had given me up so I had a salad and he had an ice at Lyons. I was so tired by the time I got to Mac that I could hardly steady my fingers and I went to bed at 10.00 and turned the light off at 10.15. Since then I have felt a little better, but it is terribly slow work – every case takes ages as I have to wade through all the correspondence. So far as I can judge the stuff is bigger and more varied and therefore more difficult but good experience, and not the volume of work there is in Paddington.

This morning I felt rather dismal; I felt we were drifting apart, getting swept in different directions, but at 12.15 I took my Wales snaps to show him and we went to Victoria together with the new love bird (budgerigar) (Miss Muffett, yellow and lovely lime greenish). He said, 'You seem to get a lot of dismal patches these days,' and a minute or so later, 'We must arrange to do some shows, and I might be able to go for a walk next Saturday.' At the station I said, 'I don't want you to scratch your head just because you think I'm looking dismal.' He was, I think, quite surprised that I should have connected the two things – anyway, he was quite moved and emphatically denied any connection. I'd been thinking about it the whole morning. One is queerly made – I felt much better after that exchange.

Tuesday 9 July

It has been too hot today but in spite of the heat I have felt better. Only two callers and I have tackled two of the sticky cases. Between them they took me the whole morning and part of the afternoon. Lunch in the Park with E, who was nice. I told him I should be grumpy and edgy. He told me about a Chinese book he had just begun. We have almost decided to go for a walk on Saturday to the Chilterns. This evening quite suddenly he kissed me and said, 'You're quite thin, you know.' I said, 'You are funny' – I suppose I must be very sensual – I loved him to kiss me. Yet apart from the physical pleasure I think the more important thing is that I like to feel he wants to – that it gives him satisfaction – that he still likes me *actively*. He said, 'Someone's got to begin – we should wait a long time if I waited for you to begin.' I often feel like it but I really think he prefers to think he has to 'warm me up'.

Thursday 11 July

Lunched in the Park with E who had brought the Chinese book (by Bramah) to read an extract to me. It is satire on England – quite amusing – there was a skit on the Shakespeare craze with 3 quotations, the third one of which I placed when E read it to me. *Romeo and Juliet* came into my mind, but I couldn't think where it was – 5 minutes later I looked at the paraphrase, felt the context was on the tip of my tongue, gave it up and said, 'It's in one of three places – *Romeo and Juliet*,' and I was just going to add, 'or *Othello*, or the Sonnets' – when the line leapt like a revelation to my mind, 'He jests at scars . . .' It was a perfect example of an unconscious solution to a problem – the 3rd neogenetic principle of Spearman!

I don't dislike my new boss, Johnstone. He is finicky – meticulous to the point of mania, but one feels he does it for the aesthetic satisfaction of seeing a file look elegant. 'Don't put big ticks and crosses all over an a/c.' His writing is pretty (and difficult to read). He makes quite an effort to be genial – enquired how Muffett was getting on.

1935

Red-letter day Sunday 14 July

On Friday night I met Ella and we went to the Russian Ballet at Covent Garden: *Cotillon* and *Aurora's Wedding* were lovely. I had two verdicts about them. Neither was great – they were concerned with little things – the jokes, fantasies, trillings of the imagination – fairy tales, dances, light-hearted and captivating just because they are not real. *Scheherazade* was a contrast. It made me feel mentally sick. I just felt disgust and distaste for the whole gorgeous spectacle so elaborately staged and set and dressed. I thought the skill expended on its design and performance was wasted. My feeling of distaste was so strong that I suspect it must have 'touched' a complex – but I don't know. Again a fairy tale – from the *Arabian Nights*, but there was not a single pleasant character – the episode of the negroes and the harem women seemed to me the most obscene I have ever witnessed – not 'subversive of morals' but calculated to evoke one's most ascetic feelings. Horrible! It affected me so much that I felt I could not bear E except at a distance.

And yet in spite of the heat and in spite of this feeling we loved for three quarters of an hour yesterday in Hatchet Wood. It is a measure of my love for him and perhaps the effect of a different environment that I could so soon overcome my disgust. I have rarely experienced so many and such varied feelings in 24 hours.

I went from Paddington and he went from Marylebone (for greater discretion) and we met at West Wycombe station – a blazing sunny day at its hottest with hardly a breeze. We walked through the village which is lovely. It had been bought and given to the National Trust. There are small dark shops in one of which we bought two oranges and some lemonade from a slow-moving, gruff old woman who said to a customer asking for a loaf, 'I suppose you can go and take one for yourself.' The shop was a higgledy-piggledy collection of stock and she seemed not to know where anything was.

We were anxious to find a shady spot to rest and lunch so we turned off the road without exploring in the village and climbed a steep sunny hill. When we finally reached some beech woods we found that they sheltered horse flies that so worried and bit us and got on our nerves that we went on as quickly as the heat would allow till we emerged in the sun. This persecution by horse flies lent a sinister atmosphere to the day. The sun

West Wycombe High Street

blazed remorselessly, impersonally. It seemed like the noontide counterpart 'Good things of day begin to droop and drowse' – one of the most sinister speeches in *Macbeth*.

However, we plodded on hot and thirsty to Boulter End where the expedition changed its character and became successful. We found the Old Peacock Inn in a lovely position at the top of the hill, viewing the Thames valley at the crossroads from Marlow, Oxford, Wycombe and Henley. We looked through the open window of the bar parlour and beheld Mr Keppel reading the local paper and trying to keep cool. He was a little deaf, strong-minded but slow-moving and he said we could have tea – they didn't hang out a board as they hadn't room for 15 or 20. A huge bowl of Canterbury bells and lilies was on the table and a row of chairs around 2 walls which to me always makes a room look as if it is waiting for relations to come and hear a will read. The tea was excellent – brown and white bread and butter, blackberry jelly, chocolate cakes and Dundee cake, 1/- each.

We set off at 4.45 and found it cooler – we were aiming at Marlow indirectly by way of Fingest, a fascinating name with a soft 'g'. A lovely mile or two by path dropping gradually through corn fields to the village. The corn seemed more developed, already showing a tinge of gold; poppies, scabious and corn-cockle provided splashes of colour.

Fingest church is old and most individual. Inside we found a guide and pottered all round. Then, just by the table of the affinity, E put his arms round me suddenly when I had my back to him. It was almost the first time he had touched me and I loved him. He kissed me and I could feel his heart thumping. I have never done or suffered anything with such a conviction that it was right. To do this in that lovely old church made it seem sweet and sanctified. I had not told him of my disgust at the *Arabian Nights* ballet but if I had he could not have done anything more effectively to wipe it away from my mind. After about a minute someone came with some flowers and a maid and we went on.

Went to church this evening, I in my Jerusalem frock. The psalms were lovely – 'The Lord is My Shepherd' and 'The Earth is the Lord's' – especially the second – E's psalm 'Who shall ascend unto the hill of the Lord and who shall rise up in his holy place? . . .' The Magnificat just fitted my mood and so did the Nunc Dimittis. I felt blessed and unworthy. I felt that unless I made my return – gave back something for my happiness – I should sin. I must strive humbly to be worthy and thankful and perceptive and when the flash comes and I feel the glow of happiness and see the reflection of beauty – make it into something that others can feel.

Sometimes I am transported with happiness, and it is good. I can perceive beauty – it is good. Oh, may I not become blind to these things before I can learn to make something of them – where much is given much is expected. I *must* not fail.

Wednesday 17 July

Cooler – a breeze, and even about 30 secs of rain – heavy, beginning and ceasing suddenly, like a watering can poured over the roofs – then billowy clouds and sunshine.

Inclined to be dismal. I am a miserable creature – 'Oh, you are full of self love . . .' Just count your blessings, woman – a good job, a nice family which helps me and needs my help, someone to love who loves me, quite a good selection of friends, a glimmering of intelligence and a glimpse of insight – why sigh for more love – just more love-making in time and amount, and a baby?

I want to make E a verse for his birthday . . . (I didn't).

Sunday 21 July

A perfect day – bright sunshine with cool breeze. I met E at Clapham at 10.30 and after I had bought half a pound of cherries and an orange we caught the 10.53 train to Three Bridges. I had had misgivings – wondered if he would be prevented from coming, would not wake up, or would have had to go to Sheffield – but there he was as I was looking out of the window on the bridge at the trains. I felt gay and light-hearted and full of energy. We talked about the resemblance between the Polyphemus story in the *Odyssey* and 'Sinbad'. A lovely walk through Worth Forest – pines, silver birches, oaks, beeches, bracken and baby partridges and one big jay. After lunch we loved and for a few seconds I was afraid of him. Then I liked him, his soft fluffy hair, short and washed. I felt so proud that he liked my body – his hands as he stroked my bones, then I felt gay and laughed at him. He said, 'It's a nice thing to take someone into your arms and then jeer at him.' We were not long – ten minutes perhaps – but sweet. We walked to Cowdray Arms for a lovely tea – bread and butter, China tea, jelly, raspberries and cream and cake – one of the best teas we have had. A perfect day of happiness (with only a few mosquitoes and half a mile of cars on the road to emphasize the beauty), snatched from destiny – ours for ever, so long as we remember.

Saturday 27 July

I have gradually reached a comparatively detached state – I feel less actively in love with E since about Nov 1933. It is a kind of calm serenity, a pleasant freedom from the gnawing longing for him when I wasn't with him and anxious desires when I was, which made the last year or so tense and which have made me miserable as often as happy. I have so often resolved not to think so much about him and failed to carry out the resolution. I can't think how it has happened now. I suppose it is partly sheer weariness, partly because last weekend and the weekend before we loved and I am physically satisfied, partly because I have had other things to think of – holidays, St George's, the Wyndham Lewis book. Last night I was dismal in a detached way – almost decided to finish things when I can no longer see any point in them – which for me means beauty. Decided to tell E how I felt and ask him, sentimentally, if he would like my diaries! Of course, I didn't.

Tuesday 20 August

A long gap during part of which I spent a queer week with Nancy* in Derbyshire. It was a strain. I find her terribly narrow, tho' refreshing in a way. It was not altogether her fault that she got on my nerves. Till the second Saturday I was in a state of uncertainty and conflict – didn't hap – was 6 days late – didn't know if I was having a baby and whether I should keep it or not if I was – a wretched state of indecision and suspense – was relieved to find I wasn't on Sat. What made me wonder most was that I had lost all desire for E from the week after our Sunday at Worth Forest. I liked him but didn't ache for him, as tho' he had satisfied me. K is at Eastbourne all this week. Last night we went to *Noah*. He just gave me one very small kiss. I loved him a little. I liked the play better than I expected – I nearly cried at the end of Scene II, Act III where Noah prays that the Ark be overturned as his sons are so hopeless.

Wednesday 28 August

I am a pig – I wish I could be better. I hate K. An intellectual appreciation of a person does not alter one's feelings to the smallest degree. I am just obsessed with the idea that she has prevented me from having children. I told E a little how I felt and then felt ashamed. It makes it bigger and more

* A friend from childhood.

alive to have spoken of it – and to have said nothing all this time – I might surely have held my peace for a day or 2 more. It isn't jealousy, tho' it may be envy. I said to him, 'You shouldn't blame people for their natures but you can't help disliking them for them.' Oh, how will it end?

Saturday 7 September

A lovely day – cool, in fact, cold this evening but sunny with a slight mist – a perfect Sept day. I did no work whatever this morning thanks to a long visit from Hyde (a colleague) who stayed from 10.05 to 11.45 just chatting. He is quite nice but completely lacking in subtlety.

I have been rather depressed. I have almost ceased to love E. I don't know why. I almost feel like giving him an ultimatum: I have given you my utmost and you have given me all you could in the circumstances. But I can't go on. You must either give me up or K – you can't have us both. He would keep K, tho' he might suffer, I know, but I feel that I should soon get over the loss, especially if I worked hard. He will have to strive again to get me back to the point I had reached. He did nothing really for months but I kept our love going after Shaw's death. It is his turn now.

Thursday 19 September

I had a queer dream last night which was almost a nightmare – thought E and I were sleeping together in one bed – that was all. I felt tired and heavy and couldn't concentrate clearly – I just slept and he did too. Then K came in and saw us. She was full of righteous indignation and went back to her room with hardly a word – just a look. I tried to rouse myself and kept putting on my teddy bear dressing gown and then finding the sleeves were inside out or I'd taken it off and hung it on a hanger – a long period of confused struggling with the dressing gown before I succeeded – I don't know what E was doing – rather think he was asleep. I was determined to follow K and have it out with her. When I reached her room I found she was in bed with a man, who was simply repulsive and hated me. He simply gnashed his teeth at me with loathing – I didn't know him and yet at the same time he seemed to be E. He was as-it-were a hideous opposite of E

– the back of the portrait, distorted and horrible. I just looked at him and was appalled and then awoke.

Sunday 6 October

Now, in contrast to the last entry – a lovely day with E. He came back from his cruise on 27th Sept and I got back from Germany (the Harz and Köln with M) on 1st Oct – last Tuesday. He was glad to see me after 31 days apart. He had given me up on Tuesday – expected me on Monday and waited for my train on Tuesday morning and then resigned himself to wait till next week. He didn't come down to see me – I wondered why but waited till 1.25 and then just looked in. He got quite a shock and was glad to see me. I said I supposed he didn't care when or whether I came back and we started again to bicker and talk and argue and love. We lunched together every day – he decided to come to Birkbeck to Philosophy with me Mon and Wed. I was surprised at this, and divided – in a way I would rather be independent, in case we have to stop – also he makes me nervous with Joad and the others. However, I couldn't bring myself to say 'No'. I knew I should regret it.

Thursday 10 October

I have been a bit edgy today – possibly because I went to bed late after seeing Greta Garbo in *Queen Christina* and because my sleep was disturbed by the film. It is queer that from this afternoon I have been a little dismal after being almost quite happy for a week. I was quite content and thankful to love this morning yet by this evening I disturbed E by asking him if he told people when he didn't want them. He finished reading his diary. How I do hate K with her placid unselfishness and sense of duty spoiling 3 lives. If he still loves me – and I believe he does – I wish he'd tell her and settle it one way or the other. Why doesn't he? Is it consideration for her? – for me? – kindness, or selfish fear and weakness? I don't know, but he won't. Unless a miracle happens we shall drift on. I must try to be patient. I am tired.

Monday 14 October

After a laborious weekend a good day. It has been dull, milder – slight rain, wore my brown shantung blouse and costume and brown felt hat and best shoes. Worked nearly all day – hard and concentrated – got quite considerable satisfaction out of it. A pleasant lunchtime at Vianne's with E – he told me about Eddington's new book, *Pathways of Science*, and I told him about Powys' *Autobiography* and a good bit of shop – tricky things. We went to University College and did Pitch Discrimination and Intensity Discrimination and then to Joad on Plato and the change when ice melts. He liked me today. He said, 'You look nice tonight – I suppose it's the brown hat,' on the escalator at Warren St. We hadn't time for tea. It was sweet to argue with him and disagree and agree. He is subtle and can see what I mean. He thinks the main hope of finding design in the Universe is that water expands instead of contracting – an anomaly which makes life possible. There is nothing sweeter than intellectual clash and duet with someone you love – even the ecstasy of sex contact.

Friday 18 October

Elsie Fisher called this afternoon. We couldn't be quite frank as Miss Cameron and Miss Hunter were working in my room. I was a bit dismal. I told E, but not much. Really I am proud that he doesn't think me weak but now and then I get discouraged. It is a necessary measure of his love in a way – he makes me suffer as he would make himself suffer. Yet how I long for peace and security. I saw two nuns this morning and almost envied them – so restful to surrender one's will and not to have to think for oneself.

Saturday 19 October

I went to the Vic to see *Peer Gynt*. I half wondered whether E would come, but I didn't see him. A queer play – poetic, visionary, obscure, tremendous – well produced – the effects get better and better.
    Oh, I want E so much. I *can't* go on sharing his time and energy with K.

It is impossible to go on like this. Why did he marry her so heedlessly? Yet he pitied her, and I pitied him at first and my love grew out of pity to the overwhelming feeling it is. I suppose he loves her in a way. Oh, if one of us could die, I don't care which. 'Give me the patience. Patience I need.' I must not blame him for his nature, still less for his weakness. Heavens, if I could *do* something, but I must always keep my tongue silent and fold up my misery in my heart.

Sunday 20 October

Better today – I feel rather a pig – thankless and grasping instead of sitting down quietly and thanking whatever arranges the Universe for giving me someone to love, who loves me. Why don't I feel sorry for K? I don't, and the only wrong we do her is in deceiving her.

Monday 21 October

I am better – much more tranquil. We liked us – bickered a little. I told him at Waterloo that I had had a bad day on Friday and Saturday and said that I believed that if I could get over it I should ultimately be better than if I had been lucky. He said, 'Do you think you're unlucky? Why?' I said, 'Because I can't have all I want – having a positive lot of one thing doesn't fill a negative void – in fact it makes it worse.'

Saturday 26 October

I am 29 and a half now. It seems quite impossible that in six months I shall be 30. I don't really mind because I am not standing still. I have so much energy now. I don't get so thrilled and excited as I did but I get disappointed less. I am more discriminating and I don't (much) try to do things because they are done.

A queer day – last night asked E whether he was always honest with me or whether he sacrificed honesty to kindliness (as he had confessed he did with most people). He said he was, though I should probably find it difficult to believe him. It is a barrier between us that I can never quite overcome. I expect it is as much my fault as his. I have an intense yet just selfish pride. It flares up and makes me say things which must be quite misleading. He said today, 'I must start going to theatres again.' Now I was really very glad as I love going to plays – I love doing anything with him. But all I said was, 'Why?' – at once suspecting (as he guessed) that I had jumped to the conclusion that he proposed it because *I* wanted it. It is stupid – even if he had it would have been sweet of him. In addition I find it almost impossible to confess to him what I mean. I have to grind out every word. It is partly because I can't express exactly what I mean and I shall give the wrong impression, but it is also due to some emotional block. I must try to get rid of it. It is unfair to him as I grumble when he doesn't say what he feels and I always expect him to guess how I feel. He agreed that it would hopeless if he couldn't read my face. He was nice.

Monday 28 October

My changes of mood almost amount to dissociations. I got up this morning light-hearted and gay and completely in love. E came to talk to me and I wouldn't listen but frisked and interrupted till he pretended to be cross. We lunched at Stewart's and I bickered and chirped altho' he complained of a liver. We walked back. I was still lively at University College until after doing Visual Acuity and Colour Vision I suddenly felt I must sit down – felt completely done.

Read Mary Butts' book on Cleopatra in the train. I feel an overwhelming attraction to Greece and Rome. I can't resist a book on them and they get me like a spell even now.

Wednesday 30 October

To Joad's lecture – Plato again, after dinner at Craig Court. E was sweet. We talked of us. I can talk much more easily now. I am not so emotional and worked up. I told him I had lost the terror I had last year at the uncertainty and precariousness of it all which used to spoil some of our loveliest moments for me. I am learning to take things as they come and be thankful for any happiness without grieving that it doesn't last. I asked him if he would have liked me as much as a man. 'No,' he said and I pretended to be cross – really was in a way. He said we get this perfection because we're complementary to each other. Of course, he's right. He has been wearing his fine new brown suit all the week and a green shirt and tie that make his eyes look green.

Sunday 10 November

I have just been meditating in the bath, starting from the thought that E was married 11 years ago today. Not dismal and weepy – not even hating K – but calculating and bitter and mercenary. Made an imaginary speech to him – 'Do you ever look ahead to the day when either I can't go on as we are, or K finds out and says, "I can't live with you if you go on being unfaithful," and you won't leave her and so give me up? You think I should soon get over it – catch another man, marry, have babies and live happily ever after. That is a convenient picture, and you see yourself pining in silence for the rest of your life. Well, it's not true. Even if I didn't lose balance at the beginning and take an overdose of aspirin, you can't make a woman love you and then expect her to throw away that love like an old pair of stockings, and buy a new pair – either in the shape of a "man" or just "other interests". The older I get the more difficult it is. It is convenient for you to go on as we are. You don't do badly – you have it both ways – someone more or less efficient to keep your home – *your* house (you have the pleasures and privileges of a householder), the approval or tolerance of your relations and hers – and the pleasures of love in your spare time. Before we loved you had the worst of it, I grant you that. I don't doubt it was hideous, but now it is I who suffer more. You simply have the discomfort of deceiving K. Don't you think I am a fool? The only explanation is that I love you so much that I should not get over it to the end of my life (even if I go on living).' It would hurt him if I said these things. Does he think of them? I don't know.

Thursday 14 November

Dismal on Monday – 'calculating' I told E – but really just hopeless. Slightly better on Tuesday and yesterday – we had dinner at Museum Garden. E explained Eddington (Time) at lunch and dinner.

There was no lecture last night so we went to the Vic to see *The Three Sisters*. It was almost empty and we were in the second row of circle. The play was exceedingly well done – produced and acted. I have learnt to understand Chekhov plays since I first went. The first time it just passed over my head, making practically no impression – little more than 'about 3 sisters who wanted to go to Moscow'. The beauty of his artistry, the truth of his observation and the profundity of his view of life – the sorrow, the pity and the humorous detachment in his approach – the cunning counterpoint of his literary symphony – the power and weight and significance he can throw into the simplest and most trivial conversation. *Uncle Vanya* (Croydon Players) was the first I began to appreciate, then *Seagull* and *Cherry Orchard* and now *The Three Sisters*. I think it is the saddest of the four, or perhaps I was in a mood to be moved easily to sadness. I could hardly bear the 3rd Act. The first is so full of hope and youth and ambition and selflessness – the third is old and weary and disillusioned and hopeless. Olga – Nina – (the only bright thread is Masha's love for the Colonel and that merely accentuates the hopelessness of her love and the despair of the others) – the Doctor (whose drunken despair made the audience laugh – hideously) – worst of all, Andrey, disappointed but reconciled to the loss of his academic ambitions – disillusioned but still deceiving himself about the failure of his marriage. I wanted so much to cry – as it was I did my best, not very successfully, to deceive E.

Saturday 16 November

In the middle of dictation E came over to say he had had his move – to Finsbury 2. It was really better than I had hoped. I was afraid it might be Wimbledon or Hounslow. At any rate he will be in town with a reason. We have said we will lunch together on Tuesday and Thursday, and with lectures on Monday and Wednesday it won't be too bad.

He was unexpectedly free this afternoon so we went to *Romeo and Juliet* – the last 2 seats in the gallery, right round at the side. It was well done on the whole, tho' I didn't care for Laurence Olivier as Romeo – a hopeless part. We thought Peggy Ashcroft good especially at the beginning. Edith Evans and John Gielgud as Nurse and Mercutio better than the lovers – both gorgeous parts. An unequal play with some marvellous lines. Tea afterwards at Lyons in the Strand. I said, 'I do want a baby like you – if it were not for the parents I would have one.' He said, 'You *can't* go to Moscow' – referring to the sisters. I love him so much, but it doesn't plague me so much. I just glow all through with love – to be with him colours a whole day so that I feel nice to everyone.

I must cease to dream idle dreams and be thankful for all I have got. He said, 'I can never forgive a woman for just not wanting a baby, though I understand her not having courage to have one.'

Friday 22 November

We talked about Free Will at lunch – he gave me a lecture about it. Tonight I loved him terribly. I do wish I could express to him how dear he is – he looms up and grows enormous – he fills the whole of my mind. All my dismalness and discontent just fades away and I feel that just to be with him for that short time is worth anything. In a way it is nicer not to be able to complete it – to have to keep apart and alert. I know more how much I love – I see and understand and feel into his mind. Being in love makes one feel that everything is worthwhile – that there is something to live for. Dangerous, because precarious, but splendid and transcendent.

Saturday 30 November

We lunched at Mandes and walked back thro' the Park. I was a little gloomy. It is hateful to break with the past – Kensington Gardens and Hyde Park are full of memories – almost every tree. For 3 summers we lunched, read plays, talked or just lazed – the grass and the leaves, the trees and the slopes, the water and the ducks, pigeons, sparrows and squirrels, Epstein's *Rima* and the Speke obelisk – they are all bound up with us. Even if we go back together it will not be the same as the regular routine of bus and rush, then an hour of leisure, E's stern decision to go back and my grumble.

Sunday 8 December

Yesterday K had a ballet rehearsal and we hoped to have a good long afternoon – then Elsie (E) decided to have her half day! It is like getting at him through iron bars. If it isn't one obstacle it's another. Altho', as he said, Elsie doesn't have much of a time and it is cruel to grudge her. Still, if only she would find someone or something else to amuse her if she must have Sat. As it turned out it was thick fog – like night. He hadn't to meet Elsie till 4.0 so we went to see the Chinese Exhibition at the BM. It was interesting and there were some lovely things and a few funny things, all giving the impression of highly developed civilization – nothing could be less primitive – all elegant, formal – you couldn't imagine them being at the Anglo-Saxon stage – or Homeric. The weakness being that the manner mattered more than the matter.

Wednesday 18 December

Bitterly cold but no wind. Slight mist and a red sun which melted the frozen grass at midday. A perfect day for a winter's walk. Met E at Victoria and he just said, '10.25 from Marylebone.' We went separately for discretion and caught the train to High Wycombe. It was very slow. We didn't get there till 11.45 but we didn't mind as far as Gerrards Cross as we had the carriage to ourselves. We loved gaily and vigorously – parting to sit respectably in our opposite corners at each station.

    A good route by footpath to Hughenden – we bickered and smacked (or E did) and admired the birds. Just inside the Park a flock of yellowhammers – we had never seen so many at once – were dipping and splashing in the thawed puddles of the path – then flying into the trees to dry and wipe their beaks. Lovely! Hughenden church with a row of fifteenth-century cottages apparently only half occupied. We walked all round the church observing the graves of Disraeli and his wife. Inside the finest thing was the font – like a stone tub but beautifully carved round the top, and one of the panels had a lily – why didn't the mason put something in each?

Hughenden church

In a shadowed corner E held me in his arms and kissed me. This is the third church he has loved me in – Church Stretton, Fingest, Hughenden. There is something so beautiful about doing this in a silent church. It sanctifies it, as it were – makes it sweet and holy and purifies it of connection with Eastbourne Terrace or biological mating or suburban respectability. It makes it as-it-were an offering – a tribute – a testimony to the creator who could imagine his creatures rising to such heights of feeling, which transcend so completely the material ends of the activity and signify so much more than the poor manifestation which is, after all, rather absurd and inconvenient. In his arms in that quiet church I loved him so much and, because of him, the whole world. I have never felt more complete and fulfilled and at the same time less self-conscious or self-concerned.

Tuesday 24 December

I dreamed last Thurs night an appalling dream. I went to see K. After a nightmarish muddle of buses I found the house – a box-like suburban villa. She was cold and disagreeable. It was like beating one's hands on a stone wall. E seemed to be there, but just vaguely uncomfortable on his own account. Then, altho' neither of them told me, I knew she was going to have his baby. I just felt hopeless – absolutely knocked out – utterly desolate. A hideous dream!

1936

Monday 6 January

Epiphany – Twelfth Night – the day of adoration and promise. Rarely has it lived up to its past, but today has been a day of joy. My heart sang. At 12.0 E rang up and ordered 3 tickets for the play for Mrs Shaw and said, 'Lunch today?' We went to Hills – a lovely gay hour. I grumbled at the parents – said we had inherited both sets of bad qualities – irregular features, weak eyesight, big feet. He said, 'Where did your rich colouring come from? And your skin? And the poise of your neck?' We have arranged to go to the Prom on Wed and for a walk on Sunday. He said he had wanted me badly – couldn't sleep last night and had made up a low limerick. I forget it but he told me on the station. He said he couldn't write poetry. I felt like a creature newly created. I trod on air. The sun shone for me – Oh, my love, how my heart sang!

Wednesday 15 January

Over a week since I last wrote here – the omission is due to (1) the weather having turned bitterly cold making it uncomfortable to sit up in bed writing (2) my having been very late from Sat till last night.

On the whole it has been a good period, and should be noted in detail to counteract low periods which are often noted in full. On Sat Margot and I took 6 of her Brownies to *Hansel and Gretel* in the afternoon – interesting in itself, and I have never seen it so well done so it was beautiful just to hear.

On Sunday I met E in the tube for Euston and we caught a hiking train to Castlethorpe. It was a perfect day – no rain, no wind and sunny – you could feel the warmth of the sun on your back. It was cold in the evening but the stars blazed.

We had a sweet, gay, glorious day and I didn't get depressed at the end partly because we found a good place for tea and I got interested in the woman who lived there and didn't think of me, partly because E tentatively sketched a plan to have a long weekend walking on Stane St from Dorking to Chichester next month and I began to look forward to it at once. We bickered and argued and fussed as we walked. In fact E said that 2 little girls walking sedately hand in hand along the road ahead turned round hoping to witness a violent quarrel. We kept to the road and made for Salcey Forest (shown on E's new map). We climbed a little and found the country refreshingly unspoilt – up and down enough to break the monotony with trees (mostly ash) tracing their winter pattern against the sky. Lunch (not very extensive) on a gate in the sun. The forest was not too wet and we picked our way in through brambles and loved leaning against a mossy tree. We found a place for tea where the proprietress, Mrs Lay, welcomed us bringing an oasis of custom in the desert of the winter slump. We talked but it was almost time for the train. A lovely day, complete and satisfactory all round. We were both quite lively and serene.

On Tues (last night) the Rowes and family came to play games. I like the vicar but not Mrs R who is Bedford and very grooved and Victorian. I should like to spring my double life on her and watch the effect. My feelings would be quite incomprehensible to her but I don't think they would be quite to the vicar.

Monday 20 January

Since Friday the King has been known to be ill. Everyone seemed to expect that he will not recover – it was taken for granted that there was no hope. There is a gloom and hush as if people are holding their breath to wait for the news. This evening the bulletin said his strength was ebbing away. I have never heard anyone say anything serious against him. There seems to be a real affection for him and sympathy with him in his difficult job.

This evening E. We dined at Museum Gardens and bickered. I scolded him and argued with him. He said I was a whole evening's entertainment

– it was quite sweet and funny. Joad is ill so there was no lecture. Before we left the fire he said, 'I have never kissed you at Birkbeck,' and did – just a little warm kiss.

Tuesday 21 January

At midnight last night King George V died. Today the flags have been flying at half mast and all cinemas and theatres are closed. The gun in Hyde Park was fired 70 times at minute intervals. The shops are showing black only – even the exclusive lingerie shop in Park Lane showed a white nightie and a negligee of white satin trimmed with black lace.

Wednesday 22 January

A significant dent this morning – Wyndham said, 'I see your friend Bertrand Russell at 63 has married for the 3rd time – his secretary of 25.' Rosa said, 'Is that the man who wrote that book you told me to read? I've no time for him. A man who has made a hash of his life is not worth reading.' She is simply iron on that subject and yet quite broad on others.

Tuesday 28 January

It was George V's funeral and the office was closed so I met E at Clapham (avoiding the mad crowds in town) and we went to Bookham. We set off for Bagley Hill, leaving some hideous new houses and bungalows behind. Over a field full of flints we heard the first lark of the year, and then 2 or 3 at once. The wind was too strong for them to stay up long, but they persevered. The country grew broken and wooded till we climbed up to Ranmore, lunching scantily on his lunch only and then indulging more fully in each other. We loved for an hour, sweet and fierce, walked over the common and down to Abinger. Bus to Dorking for tea and then home. A lovely, quiet sweet day with some fierceness in our love.

Abinger Bottom

Friday 7 February

I set out this evening to go with Margot to *Murder in the Cathedral* but was turned back at Charing Cross owing to feeling sick. We caught the same train back and at E Croydon I leaned out and was sick on to the line. It has been bitterly cold and I suppose it is just a chill. I hope it is but wonder whether it is a baby in spite of E's precautions. It is too soon anyway, probably, to make itself felt. I hope it is and it isn't. A lovely full moon and Sirius twinkling fiercely in the freezing air. We were both frozen when we got home and surprised the parents.

Monday 24 February

Joad's lecture thrilled me. He was just winding to the close of Aristotle – his idea of God. It has been difficult and rather dull, a contrast to Plato, partly because Plato is more understandable, partly because Joad prefers him. Aristotle seems so mechanical and merely logical – dry, analytical, uninspired – with none of the leaps you meet in Plato – just a plodding, practical, classifying scientist. Yet now that we have struggled with him I got a glimmering of satisfaction, a thrill from the efficiency of his intricate machine. The jigsaw fitted so perfectly, the whole scheme suddenly came to life as a marvellous creation of a human mind. I felt its fascination and could imagine the compulsion it would exercise over a mind different from mine. For me it is too mechanical – merely the skeleton of the universe, not flexible enough to be living. However, it was a good lecture.

We had dinner at the Armorel, near the BM. Over coffee at Birkbeck I told him he ought to use his mind to do something solid. After the lecture he said that I had chosen a bad time. He had been depressed since Saturday, humiliated by the Chinese Art. I think he is mistaken. He considers that the Lohan at the BM shows the Chinese view of the universe, detached and supercilious, looking at nature without the power to alter or understand it or enjoy it – helpless but superior. This is one element of the humiliation. Another is that he feels he is lazy and indolent – the Chinese industry and application and patience are a reproach to him. I can understand this and I feel the same.

Sunday 1 March

This is Sunday evening after my bath and I have decided to resume this diary. I intended to write a good account of last week – full and vital – for a permanent record. Hence I have written nothing. It was a good week – one of the best we have had, not up to Shropshire perhaps, but good – a week to remember and to look back on with thankfulness, a gift from the gods which can never be taken away whatever evil or unhappiness there may be ahead. On Tuesday we had half a day's leave. I met E at Chancery Lane. We had a long leisurely roll+cheese lunch at the ABC and then went to the Chinese Art exhibition again. E knew his way around it and decided what he wanted to see and insisted on me seeing it too whether I liked it or not. He said it was slipshod to look at only what I liked at first glance – I could never get a connected idea of the whole if I did not look at, say, everything in a room. Eventually we had been there for four and a half hours and I was dead tired. E made me walk

through the Park to Zeeta's for dinner. I was so weary that the traffic
scared me and I could hardly drag one foot after the other.

Saturday 21 March

A good day completely. The first day of Spring, and for the first time I
remember a worthy introduction. Sunny and mild, the only clouds a few
misty white (ones) high up against the blue sky. A soft slight wind from the
south, exactly 'thy azure sister of the spring shall blow Her clarion o'er the
dreaming earth' from the West Wind. A perfect day to be remembered
when the inevitable east winds and frosts return. All the morning I kept
glancing at the window guessing that by 12.0 the sky would have clouded
over. The forecast was 'unsettled and showers later' so I wore my brown
costume and took my mac quite unnecessarily. Met E at Waterloo which
was swarming with sporty people whose goal was either Twickenham (for
the England–Scots match) or Sandown Park races. He said, 'Get a ticket to
Effingham Junction,' and we caught the crowded 12.45 electric. We were
not left alone till Bookham, when he seized the opportunity to kiss me. I
bought an orange near the station which we ate walking along the road.
We turned off the road along a path by a stream. We consulted the map
and I sat on the tiny parapet of the bridge. E sat down too and we loved
and laughed till he said, 'Let's do it properly.' We went further on and lay
among some rhododendrons in a grove of pines. I lay watching the tops of
the pines etched black against the blue sky, swaying gently in the wind. I
have always liked pines but I have never felt them to be so completely
beautiful. My love for E and enjoyment of his body fused with the beauty
of the trees and their movement to make one of the most overwhelming
experiences I have had. It was, as it were, a double mingling of form and
motion. This is quite inadequate to convey the happiness I felt at the
harmony of everything but I think this was one of the significant and clear
experiences which will remain in my memory and make itself a part of me,
as tho' I shall be different in some profound way because of it. In 10
minutes I heard a dog bark nearby and the spell was broken.

1936

Thursday 2 April

A too eventful week again, which can just be catalogued in the 5 mins before we turn the light off. Monday a rehearsal which went quite well. Tuesday – hectic morning, lunch with E in an ABC basement with an uneven floor, dress rehearsal at Cripplegate – ham, cakes and tea and bread and butter with the crowd (jolly, with West on one side and Scales on the other), an airy walk round the city looking at Smithfield and bits of London Wall with Williams and West – the show.

Yesterday lunch with Nancy and met E at 6.15 – a hasty meal at Lyons Corner House and then *Things to Come* at Leicester Square cinema. 'The best film I have seen,' said E afterwards and I almost agreed. I felt quite proud of my official association with London Films. It is a film in a hundred – a gamble commercially, but what courage to spend thousands on a film which would be banned in half of Europe and might not be popular in the other half as it is wholly concerned with ideas, has no sex, no humour, little story and no pretty scenery. Yet a breath of fresh air – a subject that matters and a translation of Wells' spirit with no distortion to another medium.

Friday 24 April

This is the last time I shall write in my twenties for tomorrow I shall be 30. When I lunched with E today he teased me about it – was ready to pounce. I don't mind it and I don't regret the years that have gone. I think if we hadn't loved I might have felt a panic, as tho' life was slipping away and I was missing something vital, but as it is I feel humble and unworthy of the riches that have fallen to me in the 30 years of my stay on this queer world. I only regret that I do so little, that I render back nothing in return.

Now for the 30s.

Monday 27 April

It was mild today, tho' less mild than I expected. I wore my black costume and new jumper, full of vanity and pride.

Met E at the top of the escalator at Tottenham Ct Rd where he waited for me after passing me on the stairs. 'How do you expect me to recognize you in those clothes?' he said. We had dinner (celery soup, mushroom omelette, cauliflower) at Bertorelli's and a small bottle of Sauternes. There was a sparkle and gaiety about the dinner (even before we had touched the wine) due either to my new clothes and pleasure that he liked them, or to being in a new place. We bickered and teased and he said when our glasses were filled, 'May you soon be 40!' Sweet. It was as entrancing as those first picnic lunches in the park. Joad on Spinoza and we were late – didn't leave Bertorelli's till 10 to 8. Afterwards we walked over Waterloo Bridge and he said, 'What a pity we can't go to bed together.' How weak it is to be exhilarated by new clothes. Still, I wear my clothes for him alone.

Thursday 30 April

Yesterday Joad was not lecturing so we went walking. Got to Ashtead at 5.45 having picnicked hastily first. We set out, leaving the big new houses behind, towards Epsom and walked in a circle one and a half to two miles from Headley and Leatherhead. The country was surprisingly unspoilt. Within sight of the grandstand we passed a farm crouching in a little fold of the land surrounded by corn fields, just green with larks singing over them. Not far away we heard the monotonous sobbing note of a nightingale, and earlier a cuckoo called idiotically. A perfect evening. I felt quiet and tranquil as if I were passively inhaling the perfection to store up for ever in my mind. Completely satisfied and happy, yet when E sat under a pine tree in the dusk and kissed me I could do nothing but cry. For an hour and a half we loved, and off and on I cried and cried from too much love, as if I could not hold it. There was a clear beauty about the evening which uplifted and intensified my love and made it at once grave and joyous.

I lunched with him at Letley's today and felt quite different. We might not have been the same people except for an added affection in his look at me, or perhaps affection is not the word – depth is better, as if he had found more of me, delved further and added this deeper knowledge to his ordinary everyday superficial idea of me. We talked shop and about Margot going to LSE and provisionally arranged to go to *Figaro*.

Sunday 3 May

Yesterday we went to the Vic matinée of *Figaro*. The opera is lovely – the better one knows it the better it seems, and shorter. In some ways I enjoy music with him better than anything because he hears only the best, and music he knows, so the only criticism is of the execution. I can enjoy a thing more whole-heartedly knowing he is enjoying it too. To plays or films or pictures he gives a much more 'all or none' reaction than I do. I can usually find something to enjoy in any serious thing. I have, as it were, various planes of appreciation, while he is always in relation to the absolute standard.

Monday 4 May

An almost full moon shone clearly from a dark sky over Waterloo Bridge as we walked over it after Joad's lecture. We went to UC and did the psychogalvanometer experiment. I make a good subject but a bad experimenter in this. I can't think of suitable stimuli for E. I get somewhat inhibited. I wore my red frock and he looked at it properly for the first time and liked it. He held me to him for half a minute before we emerged. We had dinner and then went to hear Joad on Spinoza at 8.30. We bickered a little but with a strong underlying and almost emerging affection. I said something foolish and he said, 'Just what a woman would say.' I said, 'I can't help that' – he said, 'No, poor thing, failing to be a man you are a woman!' I said, 'I don't mind, I quite like it. I'd rather now.' He said, 'I might see that as a compliment.' I said, 'On the reverse, now I know what a man's mind is like I'd rather have mine!' Then I said, 'How, as a compliment?' After I had pressed him he said, 'Perhaps now you've experienced the satisfaction a woman can feel – now I've shown you – you feel it's worth it.' I said, 'Yes, and more.' A small, light conversation but it shows so much – how we laugh at each other, how we bicker and tease and fight, how we read each other, how satisfied we are, completely and firmly and fundamentally when it just comes out simply expressed like that, as a matter of course – only put into words because I made him put it. We both knew just what we meant before.

I am reading a queer Russian historical-philosophical book by a man who was imprisoned for liberalism by the Czarist government and for religion by the communists. He thinks Europe is breaking up – in politics, economics, religion, art. His dissatisfaction with now accords with my feeling. I have almost wholly lost my optimism as I refuse the things that seem good more and more. I grow to hate the 'goods' of this age – speed, noise, glare, short cuts to everything, synthetic and canned foods, clothes, amusements, arts. Perhaps all roads lead to the same place if you plod on – the road to beauty, the steep ascent to truth, the painful path to goodness.

Tuesday 12 May

Lunched with E and we had a long and vigorous discussion on pacifism. He had read Huxley's booklet and disagreed while I agreed, in theory at least. His view is that peace must rest on force and the non-resister over-simplifies the problem. I felt oddly depressed over him, as tho' this difference between us is fundamental.

Thursday 14 May

Perhaps I shall remember today all my life and especially when I am dismal, just to remind myself that I have been lucky with a happiness perfect and unsought and undeserved. I can do little to record even the concrete ingredients of this day because my mind is drowsy with fresh air, my face is glowing from the sun and wind and I am tired and sleepy. The *Telegraph* announced 'Rain: rather warm' on its front page, but at breakfast the sun shone too brilliantly into my eyes and the cuckoo shouted from the hedge. I set off in a silk check blouse, no hat or mac and brown check coat. It was a perfect Spring day – sunshine with a cool breeze, just right for walking. We walked from Reigate over Colley Hill to Walton Heath where we picnicked, then on to Box Hill and Bookham, all footpath or lane except 2 miles of country road from Walton to Box Hill. We loved on Walton Heath among the gorse bushes and violets, short and sweet. We looked into Bookham church (and missed the train).

Walton Heath

My knees suffered in the descent from Box Hill. We could see Chanctonbury quite clearly. We hardly bickered at all as E pointed out on Bookham station, but we were completely happy and at ease and satisfied, I certainly and he almost as certainly. There was an extra sort of bond between us connected in some obscure way, I think, with our argument about pacifism – not that we talked much philosophy, tho' we did spasmodically, a little, mostly at tea. It is odd that I did not dwell on, and look forward to this as much as I have to some days, and yet on the whole it has been one of the loveliest days we have ever had.

Thursday 21 May

Went to Adler's lecture at UC. He is short and tubby. He spoke fluent English with merely a few queer pronunciations and reversed order and one or two odd mistakes. An alive man with expressive gestures. A strong sense of humour especially in looking at himself and his individual psychology. Not a trace of pompousness. He is a practical psychologist before everything, with a tremendous sense of responsibility, a hopeful faith in evolution of mankind, a wide view and an artistic outlook, as impressive for what he is as for what he says. In fact, his effect depends on both but more on the man. He is a missionary preaching salvation of society. He knows where each has gone wrong as a child – the feeble anti-social with vanity who becomes neurotic, the active anti-social who compensates for inferiority feeling and becomes delinquent and criminal.

Tea with E who told me that K's mother is in hospital so he will have to stay home for Whitsun. In any case he may have to go to Sheffield as his mother is sinking. So we are fated. If only Whit had been a fortnight earlier!

Friday 22 May

Still cold, tho' the wind has dropped. This evening I heard the swish of heavy rain on the elder tree while I was eating a solitary dinner. The sky was solid grey. When I poured away the tea leaves there was the lovely dusty smell of rain on the dry earth. Margot came home at 10.0 so I had an evening mainly with *Lady Chatterley*. So far I like it better than any of Lawrence except perhaps *Sons and Lovers* which seems good in another way. *Lady Chatterley* is less feverish and unhealthy. There is more simplicity and repose in it. It is more detached and impersonal, almost like a will. The writing, tho' careless in places, has marvellous vitality and clarity and vividness. The concreteness of intense vision, less abstract morality, less 'fluff' and unrevised soliloquy. Possibly the improvement (to me) is due to taking a woman for the main character. This necessarily forced him to be more objective.

Lunched with E at Hills. I was rather dismal and didn't bother to conceal it as I could have. This was mean as he has more to worry about than I have.

Tuesday 9 June

I am weary with longing for him and desolate for lack of him. I looked at myself in the bath and thought, 'What waste!' If he could have come to me tonight my weariness would have fallen from me like a vest and I would have battled with him and accepted him with joy and power. As it is he is alone in his bed and I – I am waiting for Margot to finish her bath. I have no jealousy for K. I have not seen her, but how I hate her in her quiet, persistent intercepting of us. A discipline, perhaps, to score my love deeper with pain instead of dissipating it in an unrestrained procession of physical ecstasies? I don't know. If chance, in blind cruelty, should free him when I am too old to have a child I could not marry him. The irony of it! I do not know why I should be so dismal tonight (except from just denying physical desire).

This morning Margot and I had heard that we can go on the *Voltaire*. I had a glimmering of excitement which I fostered till at lunch with E. I gloated too much, not quite unconsciously.

Tuesday 16 June

A queer thing happened tonight which I must try to write down before it fades completely. I felt rather yawny today at the office after 3 days on the Isle of Wight. I went to UC at 5.15 to do practical with E and after a while we did the ergograph experiment – the finger pull, and he did it. There isn't much to do as experimenter and I got rather bored at the end of an hour. At 7.0 we went to Lyons for a coffee. I felt (as usual) rather aggrieved when he talked about his holidays without mentioning me, but on the way to Goodge St I resolved not to sulk but just to let go – to give him what he wants to the best of my ability and expect nothing in return – 'whosoever would save his life shall lose it' floated through my head. This is just to indicate my state of mind.

I was hardly aware of him till we were in the lift at Strand. He said, 'Are you walking over the bridge?' I said, 'No, I don't think so, it's so windy,' but he went on down Villiers St and I followed him as if I were dreaming. The Embankment Gardens looked pleasantly green and were full of people. We climbed the steps and passed through the dark gallery on the bridge, smelly and a little sinister. Looking on to the Embankment we saw the trams held up by the new traffic lights – arrested as if by magic to allow pedestrians to cross. We walked slowly over the bridge, out into the middle over the slow dark river. The setting sun still illuminated the south bank and half the bridge and touched the higher buildings leaving the water and the lower buildings to the north in deep shadow. The air was unusually clear and the sky quite cloudless. I saw the whole scene to the east as a unified picture, beautiful even in its ugly details – the lead shot chimney (which E explained to me), the waste paper works, the skeletons of the piers of old Waterloo Bridge, the sluggish dirty ripples on the mud, the ponderous clumsy masses of the buildings jumbled against the sky. They all fused without losing their individual characters into a vision of beauty in which the ugliness was not less a part than the loveliness of Wren's spires and the dome of St Paul's resting against the sky. It was an experience of unusual poignancy and intensity which left me quite dazed. To myself I expressed it in words and thoughts which were quite inadequate. I felt it was a flash of insight into our civilization – the conglomeration of efforts which is London, so sure and safe and calm and clear and yet doomed to destruction soon or late, to be survived by an effortless river which has flowed for aeons and will still flow when all London is desolate. I was left dazed, to struggle against a crying which I couldn't control. I could only say to E (who with his usual discrimination left me in peace), 'It seems like the end of the world.'

Nothing I have written here is truer to me or more vivid or more real than this vision from Hungerford Bridge. Explanations have occurred to me: I had eaten nothing from 2 to 8.30 except coffee and biscuits; I had been reading Gerald Heard's book *Source of Civilization* which is broadening to the mind; I had sublimated my personal feeling into aesthetic sensibility; I was just posing to impress E. I don't know, but I don't believe any of these. I do believe in the reality of the beauty I caught a glimpse of and I felt I must note it, preferably in poetry, but anyway here.

Sunday 21 June

I reached Waterloo yesterday after an uncomfortable steamy squash in the tube for 10 mins. E got my ticket while I had a cup of China tea to fortify me against the heat. We found the train to Horsley. We bought some fruit and set off in the shade down the woody lane by the railway. We had lunch in a cleared patch by the path. We did not walk far, just past Horsley church up the path to the hills. E chose a beech tree with a massive round grey trunk splitting into fantastic coils of branches over our heads, shaded from the sun but stirred by a breeze, which was blowing in our faces at the beginning but in our backs when we left two and a quarter hours later to return to the station. We loved for a while, distracted by mosquitoes which left me with 6 bites requiring constant douches of ammonia.

Afterwards we talked for long about pacifism and war. We disagree about this and I wanted to know why he thought England's only possible course was to re-arm. He thinks death is preferable to Nazism dominating the world and out of the destruction might rise a better race, and tho' it might, and probably would, have to re-tread much of the ground covered would ultimately make a better society. Life and human life would survive even another war, tho' we shouldn't. He said, tho', that he had too much fear to make a good judgement. His opinion would be either too much dominated by fear or over-compensated intellectually against it. He waved a hand to the land we were passing, quite an ordinary view – the heavy green trees of full summer, a field vivid green with growing corn, a brown field beyond reduced by perspective, setting off the green – the whole slightly dimmed by a heat mist and yet clear in the yellow evening sunshine. 'It looks good,' he said. It is the feeling for that kind of thing which you can see from one end to the other of England that is at the bottom of everyone's feeling for England. This passionate disinterested love of the land about which the talk under the beech had made him unusually articulate never fails to move me since I first met it in Shakespeare and *My Magazine*. He is discriminating and uncapricious but he is too afraid of sounding sentimental to express it often or at any length.

Friday 26 June

Lunched with E – not very satisfactory. He is going to a wedding tomorrow so I don't see him till Monday. I have been reading Huxley's *Eyeless in Gaza* – Tues, Wed and Thurs and finished it in the bus this morning. Consequently it has been dominating my mind. I was struck again and again by the resemblance of E to Anthony Beavis, who was the main character – neither so bad nor so good, but still a near resemblance. It depressed me. I have no right or power to judge him for I know my feelings sway my judgement but I find myself doing it, calling his prudence weakness, and at the same time taking advantage of it. The truth of Huxley's analyses of motives fascinates me and the necessity of analysis seems overwhelming, but I find it exceedingly difficult to dissect myself, let alone him.

Tuesday 30 June

We went to the National Gallery last night and to dinner at the Oak and talked about Huxley's new book which he had read from Friday evening to Sunday afternoon. He thought it was good and we discussed it all through dinner. What would Huxley say to my wish that one of us – K or I – might die? I suppose I am just seeking my own pleasure and that is an aim unworthy of consideration and should be inhibited. So easy to say but so hard to do.

Wednesday 1 July

Felt better. Lunch with Reen who told me about the Birmingham women's meeting. Apparently at least 2 AIT women are living with their lovers rather than marry and lose their jobs. Moreover, one has had a baby – worked till a week before and then had 3 weeks' ordinary leave. Reen said it was an epic!

Tuesday 21 July

11.30 after a bath but I must just make a note of my happiness today. I lunched with E today and he said he wanted to write a poem last night and tried to for half an hour. He had the inspiration but lacked the technique and craftsmanship. It would have been about snowflakes. I scolded him for not persevering and he told me what it would have been about – Waterloo last Saturday – swirls of people coming and going and then a look of recognition which, like a 'silent explosion', lit up the universe, and the last line was, 'I said, "You are one minute late."' So small a thing, and yet since he said it I have felt it as a glow of happiness warming me, suffusing other ordinary things with its radiance. I suppose I like to be flattered but I do so passionately want to please him, not entirely for the satisfaction of my own vanity but also to touch him – to reach him, to give him pleasure and value.

Monday 27 July

No rain today tho' it is still cool. Lunched with E. He went straight to the point: K's mother seems to be better enough to enable her to have a holiday on the 9th and so they will probably both go to Malvern – so much for our hopes of a week in August. Still, we may have a week in Sept on the Roman wall, and a midnight walk this weekend and a walk tomorrow evening. He was rather sweet – so full of plans, necessarily tentative, but I don't mind. I told him I hoped I wasn't grasping – he had called me grasping. He said he hadn't meant it. I am not sure. I try not to be and to have patience. Sometimes I think our love is finer for being confined, as it were – controlled and limited by circumstances, like a good sonnet confined within its form. This may be true if only I can succeed in accepting the limitations and working within them. A bad sonnet is still bad but not so widely bad as bad free verse; but you can make some sort of free verse when you can't even begin to fashion a sonnet. If I could make our love a Shakespearean sonnet – every line taut with significance, every word shining in its place like a jewel, sound sense and rhythm combining to make a whole of truth and beauty.

Wednesday 5 August

I have worked hard and fairly well and interestedly today. This morning Hyde was away. DJ is away all the week. Mac was away with a cold so I had everything to do. I have missed seeing E. He went home on Friday and yesterday morning there was a note from him waiting for me. Somehow I was not surprised. He said his mother was dying. It was a short, incoherent note, wild with grief and horror and my heart bled for him. I could tell by the extravagance and effort how he was suffering. Then, in the afternoon, a wire from him – 'All over – better than expected' – a queer way to announce her death. I was relieved to hear because all the morning I could not shut out from my imagination the lingering pain and helplessness of her illness. Afterwards I managed to work quite connectedly.

Friday 7 August

No letter from E. I felt about as cheerful as the dark grey sky but I didn't give him up till 12.0. At 12.10 he phoned – his long low clear 'Hullo' with its faintly north country intonation made my heart jump. I lunched with him. He told me all about his mother and how the family had reacted and what he had felt. He was suffering from the reaction after the physical and emotional strain and was limp and edgy. It was good to see him. I would have given much to be able to comfort him and soothe him and give him all my vitality but I felt helpless and useless. Still, he said he was glad to have seen me so perhaps I did a little.

Saturday 8 August

I want to say some more about meeting E yesterday. When I got to Chancery Lane he was waiting, wearing a new mackintosh which somehow made him look pathetic and childish, and his green Vantella shirt and dark green tie. I saw reflected in his face the rush of feeling when he saw me. I chattered foolishly about nothing because I felt ill at ease, cut off from him by the experience he had suffered, which seemed like an emotional wall between us – impenetrable, palpable. When we sat down he began to demolish the wall. I asked very few questions. He gave me a detailed account of what had happened and how it had affected him. Quite simply, tho' he had at times to make an effort to control his feeling, he let me see into his mind. I don't know whether it was an effort or a relief to him. I only know that I felt complete at-one-ment with him again. It was an extraordinarily strong feeling. I remember that my mind was so concentrated on him and on 'constructing' his experience that once or twice I perceived with a small ghost of surprise the ABC where we were sitting and the roll I had been eating. I felt almost happy when we said goodbye. Perhaps it was the unconscious fear of finding him a stranger whom my best effort would not quite reach that made me feel so desolate before he spoke to me again.

Monday 17 August

The heat wave continues. I set off in brown and white frock, white sandals and white gloves. Lunched with E and thereafter spent the afternoon in a state of dismal stupor. It is all very well to count my blessings, which I know extend to everything of importance with the sole exception that I happen to love a man who is about as tied as he possibly could be and yet loves me. There is, as it were, a nice calculation in my misfortune worthy of a celestial Louis XIVth. Had he been better or worse, or had K been better or worse, more or less intelligent, or were I better or worse – more or less scrupulous – the situation is fixed in a delicate but unbreakable balance. My eyes are heavy with the tears I can't shed. All this tirade being due to K's misfortune in falling off a bicycle last Friday and dislocating her collar bone. She is helpless for at least six weeks and E has to look after her. He is even enjoying it – tasting the satisfaction of a perverted sort of maternal instinct. Miserere me.

Thursday 20 August

I have felt happiness since lunch in spite of having a headache, all because E after complaining of feeling queer said on the way back to the tube, 'I feel better. It's always good to see you even if you're not sympathetic.' It would be worse – immeasurably worse – if he ceased to love me. I feel it, as well as just know it intellectually. Yesterday I felt that nothing could be worse.

Monday 24 August

Lunched with E in an ABC whose atmosphere was like a laundry's – steaming heat. I gave back to him Dorothy Cheston Bennett's book on

Arnold Bennett including some of his letters to her. She does not write
well but the interest of the subject kept my attention fixed and the letters
are well written and fascinating for the portrait they conjure up. It is an
oddly attractive, boyish, vulnerable Bennett – surprisingly attractive. On
the whole he makes a better impression than Dorothy's. He must have been
maddening with his meticulousness, but this seems to have really been a
defence mechanism (I am reading Freud now). His cable to her after she
had announced that she was to have a baby was delicious 'very sorry . . .
very glad . . .' Many small unexpected points – he suffered from insomnia,
he had financial worries, he couldn't undertake an expedition without
planning every point, he had surprising gaps in his knowledge of history
and classics, he played regularly with Virginia (the daughter).

But the real reason for my gusto is not the fine weather, or my new
knitting, or any of the books I am reading, or the growing up-to-date-ness
of my work but the hope, which will keep growing, like a genie let out of
a bottle, however much I stamp on it, that (I will write small in the hope
that Heaven will overlook it and not punish my assurance) we may, after all,
have a week in Sept. Ha! Ha! *Haah.*

Thursday 24 September

Over 4 weeks since I wrote anything here, not because nothing has
happened which I wanted to remember but because too much has
accumulated. On 5th Sept (Sat) I met E at Paddington and we went to
Chirk. We traced Offa's Dyke from 3 miles south of Wrexham to 4 miles
south of Knighton, about 87 miles.

Friday 25 September

We finished assessing yesterday, so today was an opportunity to pick up
loose ends, such as getting instruction books up to date. E was due back at
Finsbury. At 11.45 I was just wondering whether I would not go to
Chancery Lane if he did not ring up when the phone went, and he asked
me if I was going to the concert. My heart just jumped with surprise and
pleasant anticipation. I felt quite affectionate to the telephone afterwards

– it looked so kindly in its shiny black. We lunched and talked hard. He had the Offa's Dyke photographs and the Jones book on the Welsh Marches. We met again at 6.10 and had a leisurely dinner at Flemings (too big), bickered and chattered and then went to the Prom. It was steamy. Overture to *Fidelio*, a fat soprano in some Weber, then the Concerto with Szigeti which was what we had come for. Beautiful! The better one knows it the lovelier it is. It is surprising how differently it affects one. I liked the first movement best tonight. The violin is lovely even where it seems just for effect and the orchestra re-enters so quietly yet inevitably dragging the music back to earth.

It was sweet to see him again and he still likes me too. He would wonder, probably, at my writing that – he would repeat that he knows his love will last. But I still have a little shock of happy surprise when I find that he is pleased to see me again. It still seems like a dream from which I may awaken one day, that just me, my mind and body, just as they are, should have aroused his love.

Thursday 1 October

Last night we had dinner at Slaters and went to the Bach Prom. On the whole I enjoyed the concert better than last Friday, perhaps because it was cooler. The 6th Brandenburg and two violin concerto and the Suite were the loveliest things. It is perhaps nicest to go with him to a concert. He is less critical or the standard is higher – I can't judge which. I can enjoy it therefore unreservedly. He 'specializes' in the bassoon and jerks me into noticing it. A good evening, too soon over.

Friday 9 October

At lunchtime I went to Lyons for a hasty meal and then set off down Bond St with my cheque book in my bag. Having reached Asprey's I found St Christopher in the corner. I walked in almost unconsciously and asked the price – £4/17/6d. Bought it, wrote a cheque and came out with the elegant purple box. A new experience – probably unique – to shop in Bond Street. It is a lovely thing and I knew Rosa would appreciate it. Having definitely rejected the Hellenic cruise next April it is not an extravagance. It was good value in itself and even more for the pleasure of seeing her open it and exclaim.

Monday 12 October

Still cold but this evening it was definitely milder. The *Sunday Times* yesterday said it was the coldest first 10 days of October for 24 years. The weather makes such a difference to me. I am hypersensitive to it compared with other people, like the tactile sense of the person with a temperature. I always look at the forecast before anything else in a paper and read every word of the *Sunday Times* weekly review of the weather!

I began my Budget letter this morning because I was so straight! This unusual state did not last long and I ended with an account (Isobel Ltd) unworked. Went to a meeting at 29 Marsham Street. The women inspectors had been invited to meet the committee of the Women Civil Servants Association. They were to give us tea and arranged to meet us at the door. I knew Reen had accepted and also Miss Plunkett, but I was the only person to turn up. It was a little wearing since I know next to nothing of Assocn politics and could hardly begin to answer their questions, nor could I tell them how we regarded them. It was quite informal and they were all most friendly.

Tuesday 20 October

Now for half an hour I have the house to myself. Wyndham is up north; he went to Liverpool yesterday. Rosa has gone out. Margot has not come home from Brownies. I can do as I like – cry, laugh, read poetry aloud or go to sleep. It is a relief, quite different from being solitary in a crowd (as in a train or restaurant) when you feel the Eye of Society on you to note and disapprove the slightest deviations from the ordinary.

Yesterday I felt completely worn out, so weary that to breathe was an effort. I have been reading Middleton Murry's *Shakespeare* in the course of which he has some remarks on *Macbeth*. For the first time, and with appalling clearness, I saw my own attitude to K reflected. There are times when it is only lack of power and not of will that prevents me from leaving her to what I should regard as worse than death. If E was prepared to abandon her I should have no scruples at all. I suppose if we did we should be no happier than Macbeth and his wife after the murder. I said to E at lunch, 'What should Macbeth have done?' He said he should just have stuck to his job. He said also that women had no social conscience and that accordingly I could never answer the question. I don't know whether he knew what was in my mind and how truly he spoke. Probably not.

Possibly the best thing I could do would be to chuck E and start working hard at something. After all, he has probably saved me from a peke and parrot obsession in middle age and that is all you can ask of any man, even a husband. Anyway, I shall not be able to go on indefinitely at this tension – the struggle to subdue my feelings and cope with them secretly and solitarily will end either in death for me or my love for him.

Friday 23 October

Lunched with E. I declined to meet him tomorrow for coffee. I am going to ballet with Margot at Sadler's Wells. It just unsettles me to see him. I always hope against hope that he will want to do something. Yet this is the first time I have of my own will refused an opportunity to see him for however short a time.

I don't know what to do. I feel emotionally exhausted. I love him but I must heave myself out of this cul-de-sac – this vicious circle of love and hate. To do this I must either divert some of my energy from him (so that the little he wants or is able to do is enough for me) or, if this is too difficult, he must be completely sacrificed. Pervading temporary fluctuations of feeling I have a conviction that I shall die before I am 40. This conviction first became conscious in 1935. It was also an element in the depression which made December 1934 so hideous. This is curious because now it doesn't depress me – if anything it adds intensity to happiness and there is release and peace in the thought. Still, I would like a baby first to make a testament – and well, we shall see.

Tuesday 3 November

A wet dismal day which varied only with the change from drizzle to heavy rain. I wore my new skirt and jumper to liven me up. They are successful but too warm for today, tho' at times comfortably cosy. Lunched with E. We talked towards the end about Pasteur and chemistry and the structure of substance and he said, 'I am glad to have found something to wake you from your torpor!' He pronounced my jumper quite cute and observed, 'You do like to lay mines in people's paths, don't you? If I hadn't noticed and remarked that you had a new skirt and jumper you would have given me a silent black mark.' This had an element of truth, tho' I didn't admit it.

Wednesday 4 November

Dinner at a new place, Red Lion Restaurant, with E. It is a quiet place with candlelight only, a pleasant change from Flemings and Bertorelli's – about the same price. I told him the analogy I had prepared to explain my 'torpor' – if you have a fire and no coal and you want it to burn long but not fiercely, you heap wet newspaper balls on it. He said I was livelier, having pinched me (merely as a test).

Sunday 8 November

I lunched with E on Thursday and as we were going down the escalator he said, 'I'll take you to the Science Museum on Saturday afternoon – quarter to one at South Kensington.' We went first to the Science Museum. It is surprisingly interesting. He took me up to the very top to representations of Pasteur – tartaric acid and bismuth crystals, a model of a distillery. On the second floor, clocks, mathematical objects with string and plaster models as for drawing, electric machines; 1st floor, steam and sailing ships from an Egyptian boat from a tomb to the *Queen Mary*. On the ground floor railway engines and a pendulum to show the twist of the earth. In the basement, most fascinating to me, the children's section with things to work. Outside we passed the Museum of Practical

Geology which is not so bad as it sounds. It has a magnificent entrance and E went straight to some fine photographs of Shropshire. We didn't stay there but went on to the Natural History Museum to see crystals. They are beautiful but most complicated, so fantastic and yet regular in structure and colouring. It seems impossible that they are just natural and effortless. It was nearly 5.0 so we went to Victoria for tea. I was so tired I could hardly stand in the underground but E was quite satisfied. He appears to judge the success of an expedition by the degree of fatigue it occasions. I enjoyed the afternoon which is the first we have spent together since Hereford 8 weeks ago today.

Monday 16 November

Just a short entry because the last few days have been full and unexpected. On Friday Mr Zimmer★ came to dinner. He was more expansive about Germany than he has ever been. Beneath his discreet remarks you can see he dislikes the 'extreme' policy of the government. He thinks it will become less extreme. May he be right!

On Sat I met E at Waterloo and we had coffee – at least he had coffee and I had China tea. We stayed longer than we meant talking of rearmament and Baldwin. On the way back to the station he said, 'What about going to Eastbourne tomorrow?' I was quite staggered but couldn't believe it.

Yesterday I waited by the phone for 20 minutes round 10.0 for E to cancel the expedition. He didn't and I found him at East Croydon. It was fine, tho' sunny only in gleams and was blowing very hard from the west. At times the gusts almost swept me off my balance and it was hard going against the wind. We walked straight up to Beachy Head and over the Seven Sisters. On the Second (from Birling Gap) E's cap blew off and trundled before the wind towards the edge. I was horrified to see him run after it – my heart almost stood still. On Crowlink we looked at the thorn bush which sheltered us before – the occasion of the second poem I wrote about him.

★ A German business associate of her father's.

Crowlink

On the Fourth Sister I lay down for a few minutes' rest from the wind and immediately felt sleepy. E said I must sleep there in sight of a house (the coastguard cottage which seemed to be inhabited as smoke circled from the chimney).

Tuesday 17 November

[continued]
I toiled up and down the Fifth Sister and nearly at the top of the Sixth E, who was ahead, found a sheltered spot behind a gorse bush and we sat down to rest. He kissed me most deliberately and I was surprised to find almost immediately I was almost aching for him. It was simply a physical pain. We loved for a while, I don't know how long – there on the Sixth Sister, with the grey sea on one side and the grey sky overhead and the west wind roaring around us. We went on to Exceat Bridge and by road to

Seaford where we had a big leisurely tea, walked along the front and caught the train back.

Tuesday 24 November

A whole week since I last wrote, and a full week.

I ought to have happed last Sunday week – 15th – and haven't yet – the latest I have ever been. I have felt strangely tranquil about it, tho' it was only this evening that I decided not to have an abortion if it is a baby. I should manage and I do want one tremendously at bottom. This feeling of certainty and acceptance is quite independent of E, whatever he may say or do, or not do. If only I could be sure of my health and my life I would have no qualms about doing it deliberately even if this is nothing.

Thursday 26 November

This morning I had a poem just beneath consciousness on the theme of the Sixth Sister – grey sky, wild sea, west wind and strong earth – the sowing of the seed, gay and full of joy, no one but ourselves in the world; the one small seed falling where it could grow – his gift to be cherished and fed and warmed and rendered again as a new life. So it murmured in my mind emerging a phrase here, a line there, forging itself a rhythm beneath the typists' chatter, the crackling of the fire and the smell of paint. Then before I had put down a single word, the hope that had stimulated the whole feeling was destroyed. Still, tho' no opportunity comes now I know my mind, if it should come. I'll not refuse it. I'll not do anything to prevent the seed from growing. And perhaps – this is tentative – next Sept I'll ask E to give me one deliberately. I should have a baby when I was just 32, not too late maybe. I shall save up. He said £150 but I think £100 will be ample. It is a long time and I will not think of it again except for a minute now and then.

Sunday 29 November

I met E at 12.20 yesterday for coffee. We talked hard for 35 minutes. He had to catch the 12.59 as K's aunt is still very ill – it seems only a question of waiting for the end. What a year! I feel unpardonably impatient about it. My own good health makes me callous perhaps. But still, how simple and more satisfactory to have a nurse. The main reason why she won't is that she wants to leave more money to K, which is not a reason to impress me. However much she gets won't make any difference now.

Tuesday 1 December

I met E at 6.15 and we dined (largely) at Bertorelli's and had Barsac to drink. It was a pleasant meal and I liked him. I heard more about the aunt (who now has a nurse) and we talked about Macartney's *Walls Have Mouths* which he found interesting and has just finished. Joad was lecturing again, mainly on Russell's views. I caught the 9.27 from Waterloo as usual. As I walked along the cliff I saw a red glow in the sky and thought 'looks like a fire, but it's probably the Astoria's neon lighting'. At the end of our road I happened to look north and saw an angry red glow. When I got home Rosa greeted me as if I had survived an air raid – 'I'm so glad to see you . . .' etc. The Crystal Palace was on fire. It had been burning since 7.30! The 6 people in my carriage hadn't noticed it as we passed so close to it! You could see from our garden a huge red glow with flames shooting high now and then, clouds of smoke and the tower dark against the light. It was a magnificent sight especially in its contrast to the other parts of the sky. I suppose I should have been horrified to see from near, but as we saw it it was beautiful. There is a splendour about fire which compels admiration. It has strength, power, remorselessness, beauty and purity and a certain inevitability. I can understand the Parsees and other fire-worshippers. It is a fine symbol of the absolute.

1936

Thursday 3 December

Mild and sunny, a pleasant day. Everyone is talking about the dispute between the King and the Government about Mrs Simpson who has apparently been his mistress. It was a bombshell – all this morning's papers wallowing in it and all the placards shouting it. I can't imagine why it has been allowed to appear. It is of course impossible to judge without knowing his motives. I am sorry for Queen Mary and Baldwin, for that matter. Poor old man! He is having a rough passage on the whole.

Sunday 6 December

I had coffee with E yesterday and felt rather dismal. The aunt still lingers, and may for a fortnight. He said he tended to like people with high cheek bones (arising out of a discussion of the King and Mrs Simpson) and said mine were. I then had some lunch and went to the National Gallery to look at the Rembrandts. I felt absolutely hemmed in with immediate frustrations – everywhere seemed black – home politics, foreign politics everywhere, business, the office and relations with E. I thought perhaps in the calmer, less disturbed atmosphere of the seventeenth century I might find peace and sanity. The pictures were beautiful. I found the difference between the self portraits at 84 and 54 not so depressing as before. There is an arrogance about the younger that has given place to an understanding and wisdom in the older.

I got to the Vic at 2.28 and got a seat in the gallery – *As You Like It*. I went almost entirely to see Edith Evans' Rosalind. I didn't like James Dale's Jaques, tho' the character is refreshing – he is the vinegar that brings out the flavour and keeps the whole thing from over-sweetness. William Devlin's Duke was quite unusually sinister – an undiluted villain. Edith Evans was delightful. Her voice is not good – in fact, it is cracked and unmusical – but her vitality and invention are gorgeous. Her Rosalind just flattens one out. She roars with laughter or rolls on the floor of the forest and produces the daring and ingenious remarks with complete spontaneity. Moreover she conveyed a belief in her love for

Orlando. She makes all the incredible ingredients of the plot seem natural or unimportant. I have never seen the gay vitality of Rosalind so adequately expressed. It was perhaps because the play was a comedy, a withdrawal from reality, that yesterday it did not succeed so well as Rembrandt's pictures in making me forget myself. One should be in a gay mood to enjoy the comedies to the full.

Thursday 10 December

A cold, dark, gloomy day, depressing, but no fog. Everywhere a sense of expectancy waiting for the King's decision. It was in the papers at 4.45 – abdication. A pity. A sorry business from every angle.

Wednesday 30 December

I am feeling not dismal (tho' I could) but edgy and nervy with the effort not to be dismal. I lunched with E after not seeing him for a week. Yesterday morning he phoned to say he couldn't meet me till today as the aunt had died an hour before. He had had an awful Christmas, just waiting. Today he was tired, worn out. He told me about it. He also talked about the P&O cruises. It needed all my self-control to prevent me saying things I should have regretted. He will probably go for a cruise next year – I hate the idea of his enjoying himself with K. This is mean and ungenerous and jealous but there it is. If only . . . it isn't as if K has a particularly happy time – I can't prevent myself from hating her. It is only cunning that prevents me from railing at E. Heavens, if it were only me or her that was going to be buried on Friday.

Thursday 31 December

Lunched with E. He was less tired. I didn't feel so abysmally miserable about him this afternoon. I decided I would wait a fortnight and then tell him I must either do more or not see him. I wish he would tell K and take the chance of having to stop altogether. I might just have a baby and be able to get over the break.

On the whole this year I have been better – less extreme, not the same heights of ecstasy nor the depths of despair.

1937

Sunday 3 January

I did not begin earlier mainly because I felt dismal. Now, having
listened to *Much Ado* on the radio, I feel livelier. It is the first Shakespeare
I have heard in this way for years and it was by chance I heard it today.
Following it with a book I think it is the best way to hear and understand
the language. You can follow it undistracted as you cannot in the theatre.
A lovely play, tho' Beatrice's bickering rises to rudeness at times. Still,
so completely light-hearted and subtle too – almost a parallel to the
music of *Figaro*.

Saturday 23 January

Lunched with E and arranged to meet him at King's Cross on Wed for half a
day's leave. He left London at 2.0 for Sheffield today. I have read Suttie's
book on psychology – *Origins of Love and Hate*. It is interesting and original.
He admires Freud as a psychotherapist but disagrees with his theory.

In spare time I am indulging in daydreams about a baby, but they are
practical and not dismal.

Tuesday 26 January

I dreamt last night I had a baby – for the first time to my knowledge. It lay
in my arms as I nursed it with a big pale serious and almost sad face. I was
so happy in my dream. Oddly, it talked like a grown-up sensible person
and discussed things such as the time it should be fed. Its conversational
style resembled M's.

1937

Sunday 7 February

A long gap due partly to lack of time between events, partly to a slight upheaval which I felt I couldn't write down.

On Monday evening we had dinner at Flemings and E read to me his reply to my Budget Statement* for 1936. I copied it to keep. We talked about it on Wed evening but without reaching any decision. He doesn't want me to have a baby but I am not sure I shall accept this. We arranged to have a day's leave on Friday and intended to go for a walk and continue to talk the situation over. It rained and we stayed in town and I did not talk again. So it is still unsettled.

Wednesday 10 February

I met E at Chancery Lane. He had a chill and seemed in low spirits but I felt quite lively, possibly the anticipation of a day on Friday with him.

On Monday he was wearing a new overcoat so we went to Bertorelli's and had some Barsac. There was no lecture so we talked there till 8.30 and then walked to Waterloo. We discussed the situation till he was sick of it (I think) and I had said more than I meant. Still, I feel more strongly than ever that I want a baby and I did my utmost to persuade him. K is of course the difficulty. She has an extraordinarily tenacious hold on his mind – quite unconscious on her part.

Friday 19 February

A red-letter day to open a new book. Now, while I am waiting for Margot to finish her bath before I have mine and while my head is aching and my stomach feels sick *I* am rejoicing in the thought of this day. And the main reason for all this emotional flag-waving is simply that E felt sufficiently stimulated by me and his ductless glands to enjoy a little love-making. Perhaps I should feel humiliated that such a

---

* Doreen's Budget Statements were end-of-year accounts of the state of her life as she conceived it at that point.

physiological event could elate me. But I don't. I just loved him and
rejoiced that he loved me. It was precious after all our heart-searchings
and discussions and arguments of the last few weeks. We had arranged
to meet at Guildford this morning. By the time I got there and found E
waiting for me it had almost stopped raining, tho' the air was wet and
the sky still grey. We decided to walk and I bought some chocolate
wholemeal biscuits before setting off up the Portsmouth Rd. We turned
off the main road to the right, along Sandy Lane. This took us to the
Pilgrims' Way which we followed to Compton. The path, tho' wet, was
not very muddy except in patches. We paused under a holly tree to look
at it and E kissed me. When we reached the road we turned left to
Compton village to look at the church which we had both intended to
visit for years. It is most fascinating and took one hour and forty
minutes to explore.

Thursday 25 February

In bed at home again and I must just note some events of this unexpected
week. So, briefly: on Tuesday it was cold but sunny. I met E at Clapham
and it was so fine that we decided to walk instead of staying in town as we
had planned. We went to Shoreham (Kent) which is in the Downs and far
enough away to be quite unspoilt.

We walked to the hill top and, keeping to the tiny roads, followed a
twisty course. I am hazy about exactly where we went, except that we
reached Kingsdown and passed a Youth Hostel. We picnicked on the road
sitting on a fence and almost at once turned up a steep narrow lane with
banks through beeches. The path led eventually to Wrotham but a mile
from there we turned back. Before we left the beech wood E loved me till I
felt quite dissolved away.

Yesterday morning it was dry and we caught the train to Steyning. It
was raining slightly when we reached Steyning. We first explored the
church. It was unheated and we felt frozen in it. In spite of this we looked
at it carefully as it was old and good. It was raining harder when we
emerged and we were cold. E then had the bright notion that we should
have a hot lunch in Steyning before starting to walk and keep our

sandwiches for today. We did – a very good lunch at a guest house. We warmed ourselves by the fire and had excellent roast beef. We felt warmed and revived.

The bridge at Shoreham

Monday 1 March

[continued]
We could see that the top of the Downs was shrouded in mist and we very soon reached it. When we walked along the edge of the Downs we could not see how far below was the valley. We consulted my compass when the path disappeared but we were never lost and in fact walked in a direct line for the trees on the top of Chanctonbury. The first indication that we had reached the ring was suddenly coming up against the very distinct 2 circular banks of the outer rim of the camp. It was dramatic in the mist. A few minutes later we reached the trees. It was very wet beneath them as the mist was dripping off their branches in heavy cold drops. From this highest point we gradually descended keeping due west

to Washington village where we were wet and uncomfortable and it
looked as if it wouldn't cease to rain before morning. We cast an
appreciative eye over the church. E sat down in a pew and gave forth a
paean of misery. His shoes were full of water; he was cold and wet; the
rain had come through on his shoulders, he thought (it turned out later
that it hadn't); he had developed neuralgia (later it became clear that he
had just had one twinge, but it *might* have been the prelude to hours of
agony). He consulted his 6-year-old bus timetable and we waited till 4.30
and then made a dash in the rain to the bus stop to catch one to
Storrington. It was raining harder than ever and we had 5 minutes' walk
against the wind. By good luck, at the bus stop, there was a telephone
kiosk in which we sheltered until the bus came.

It was still raining at Storrington and we didn't know of anywhere to
stop. We were just having a look round when I saw the Old Forge Tea
Room. It had a good fire and looked inviting so we went in and asked
whether they could put us up. They couldn't but the proprietress told us
of a Miss Joys who might take us. We found the house but Miss J was out
and a forbidding old lady eventually opened the door 3 inches and told us
the rooms were let. We went back to the Old Forge for tea hoping they
would enquire our luck. They did, and then the proprietor told us to try
the Old House guest house and eventually telephoned to them and fixed us
up while we had tea and warmed ourselves at the fire. It wasn't raining
quite so hard when we emerged for the 5 minutes' walk to the guest house.
The woman was expecting us and we were as comfortable as we have ever
been – a gas fire in the bedroom, hot water, a big log fire in the dining
room and another in the lounge, which had a wireless. After supper E read
one or two of the essays in *The Olive Tree* (Aldous Huxley) to me and at
10.15 we went to bed. We had two pennyworth of gas fire which was
comfortable and we sat in front of it for 10 mins. Then we went to bed and
loved for 40 minutes, E told me at the end. I loved him altogether so I can't
remember what we did. I can just remember feeling as I put my hands up
and down his back how the five and a half months since we slept together
last vanished. It was odd to feel how still the warmth and cool of his back
varied in the same way and had done ever since last September. Afterwards
he said, 'I suppose it's all right,' and I hoped inside that it wasn't and I
should have twins, although I don't sensibly want them next Nov. I shan't

have any money and Nov is a horrid month. E told me to try the tube Dr
Malleson gave me. I did, because he said so. It was warm in bed and we
both slept well, tho' the traffic awoke me in the morning.

Thursday 8 April

More than a month since I wrote here, most of which was occupied by a
Hellenic cruise. We got home exactly a week ago and since then I have
been to three rehearsals of *Jonah and the Whale*, done a good deal of work at
the office, lunched with E four times and had coffee with him on Sat. He is
busy preparing to move to the aunt's house where he will have a room of
his own for a study. It irritates me to hear him on decorations, stoves,
boilers, gardens etc – I suppose because it arouses my envy and I loathe
feeling envy. Still, I liked him today. Without knowing how I love it he
read me just a page of Shaw's *Village Wooing* which I like best. I haven't
finally decided about a baby. I want one (or two) so much, and for such
mixed reasons. There is an element of just wanting *my* baby, pure and
simple (this is offset by knowing what a nuisance and bother and tie it will
be), an element of wanting *his* baby – something of him I should have the
right to love and look after and help, an element of wanting to make
something concrete out of our love which will last longer than either of us
– a challenge to try for this thing, so much more difficult and painful than
anything I have ever tried to do – perhaps, too, a suspicion of rivalry with
K, to do something which she wouldn't do even in her much easier
position for doing it, and connected with this a desire to show him it can
be done. Finally and impersonally the belief that our baby would be worth
producing, i.e. it would at least not reduce the baby standard and ought to
be above average. Against all this is to be set physical pain, sacrifice of time,
freedom, money, opportunity for things I like doing, comfort at home, the
esteem (such as it is) of other people and the possibility of alienating them
and, worst, the upsetting of the family. Well, I don't know, but how I long
to surrender to a desire which grows stronger every week.

Sunday 11 April

Jonah last night. I didn't feel nervous until we were waiting behind the curtain for 'God Save the King' to finish. Then I felt my mouth go dry. Everyone is friendly. The show seemed to go well. I watched Act 1, Scene 1 and Act 3 from the front. The lighting and scenery are effective and sometimes beautiful. It is a play which has grown on me.

Tuesday 13 April

It has been cooler – not cold, but a slight east wind. Lunched with E and gave him my Pros and Cons re a baby. I was unreasonably depressed because on Friday he said he would come to *Jonah* last night if there were to be no lecture. Yesterday he phoned to say Joad began next Monday but he was tired. He had been messing about all day on Sunday with this confounded move and then had sat up writing till 12.0 and was too tired to come. 'He would like to come but thought it would be foolish!' I felt cross and injured – unreasonable perhaps, but natural! It isn't the particular fact but the condition of which it is a symptom. Today he suggested going to *Anna Christie* on Wed to make amends.

The show went better on the whole; the Prologue (I think) and the first Act certainly. The second act was slightly dashed by Bilshan's mistake. He changed for the third act and forgot his entrance at the end! The hall was fuller but not so discriminating, tho' more expressive, which assisted the players. BR had to do the whale as Stuart Bull had a professional engagement at Eastbourne. He sent a telegram – 'Love to all. Good luck brother whale. A whale.' I enjoyed it and was glad to be distracted after feeling so dashed by E.

Sunday 18 April

I didn't meet E yesterday as he is moving on Tuesday and is busy this weekend. He is sacrificing the spring to it but perhaps it will be worth it. We went to *Anna Christie* on Wed night. The play was better than I remembered except for the last act which seems wrong.

We discussed (in bits) the question of a baby. He had read my Pros and Cons. He admitted that I had stated them reasonably but he thought I underestimated the cost. Anyway, he wasn't prepared to face the cost. After some amount of questioning it appeared that the cost for him consisted of (1) knowing the cost to me and not being able to do anything active, (2) having to tell Kathleen or deceive her. This (2) was the decisive factor. I pushed him about this perhaps further than I should have done and he accused me of being coldly logical when it suited me. Still, I had to know what was in his mind. It made me dismal for 2 days to realize that the chief obstacle is not due to consideration for me or for the baby but simply to his reluctance to tell K that someone else is prepared to do in more difficult circumstances what she was afraid to do. It is extraordinary how in his attitude to her he contradicts his most serious principles – he makes a kind of emotional exception of her whenever his feelings about her conflict with his principles. I was so unhappy at seeing the true position so vividly that on Thursday I didn't mention the question at lunch. We were both conscious of it between us and waited for it to crop up, like a wild animal dozing.

On Friday I felt better. It is as if I am driven on, knowing that I may, by my own act, destroy what remains of our relationship, but indifferent to anything but this unconscious concentration of energy. I said, 'Do you think I am right – for me?' He said, 'Yes.' I said, 'Do you think I am right abstractly, apart from me and you?' He said, after half a minute, 'Yes.' I said, 'Why?' because I wanted to see what was in his mind. He said, 'Because I believe that the most promising need of the world is for good babies.' We left it at that. I think he meant these answers. If he did, he must be suffering from a clash of 2 opposite wishes. I felt sorry for him, but even if it were certain that my action were to turn his love to hate I could do nothing else. He said on Wednesday, 'You are so restless, a sort of divine restlessness,' but he resents my placing him in this dilemma he has so successfully avoided up to now. I believe he should have faced it 3 years ago but when it affected only me I had patience and yielded everything to K. But I can't do it when the life of my child is at stake – how could I? How can he weigh the two and decide for her? 'My intellect and my feelings pull different ways.' I was surprised when he explained that his feelings led him to sacrifice the baby. I feel hard – cruel on Thursday. I almost lost faith in myself – it is difficult to be so sure when everyone would condemn me. But if I am prepared to put up with the suffering it will bring I haven't really much compunction if she is told what only her own lack of imagination can have prevented her from realizing years ago. I think that this lack of imagination should also prevent her from suffering unbearably. I suppose he would say in reply (or think more likely), 'It is only your own blind selfishness that prevents you from realizing how much she *would* suffer.' It is true.

Sunday 25 April

31 today – well, it is less of a landmark than 30. Yesterday E and I went to Three Bridges, Worth church and round via the inn where we had raspberries and cream back to Three Bridges. It wasn't just an expedition, tho' it was that incidentally. I liked showing him the church. After Greece the pillars of the chancel arch looked quite Doric.

What we really went for was to get E's attitude to a baby quite clear and after leaving Worth we adhered to this subject right till Purley station on the way back. He made a great effort to explain how he felt. Briefly, he is in a dilemma from which his one hope of escape is that I may come across someone else and have his children. He feels unable to face the 'emotional responsibility' which he would feel if I had his baby. K is an insurmountable obstacle. He thinks she ought to be told but he fears that if he tells her it will make everything impossible. He admits that if I don't have a baby he sees no alternative but just to peter out. Last night I felt quite worn out with wrestling with him, and almost hopeless. I must admit that if I feel it should be, and he feels it shouldn't he is as right as me. We have both only our own feelings to judge by. I felt the same this morning till about 10.15 when I revived. His feeling has not the same authority as mine. It is negative, and is the outcome of lack of faith – he foresees only difficulties he couldn't face. I don't see why I should have to start at the beginning again. I love him and always shall. We are suited to each other. Apart from and above physical attraction our temperaments harmonize surprisingly. We ought to have a satisfactory child. I shall attack him again tomorrow.

Wednesday 28 April

Such upsetting fluctuations of feeling (mainly due to physiological causes). On Monday I felt incurably despairing – almost frantic. I could have torn my hair like the people in the Bible. I met E for dinner before the lecture and gradually felt better. Yesterday at lunch almost tranquil. This evening we resumed discussion. I told him I thought it unlikely I could love anyone else and I didn't feel like trying. He said he would like three months isolation 'if K had to be approached'. He has definitely and finally decided that she must be told if I have a child. But he is still as much against it as ever.

E gave me a photograph of himself at twenty-six which he had come across. I shall have to give him his three months' peace – which may develop into always.

E aged twenty-six

Friday 30 April

Lunched with E yesterday and today. We did not resume discussion. I merely asked him when he wanted to begin his 3 months' peace. He said, 'Not here and now. Shall I see you tomorrow or Monday?' I am feeling weaker about the position. I fear that I shan't have the strength of mind to do what I feel is the right thing against everyone's judgement including his, and I shall just yield to the easier way. Yesterday he said, 'In Christie's words (from *Anna Christie*) "I think I go mad!!"' I don't see how I can force this dilemma on him. I wish I could get a sign from heaven!

Monday 3 May

I might have known I should pay for my joy yesterday with sorrow today. We had dinner at Beta and E was quite sweet. We talked about gardens and birds and pictures and he incidentally made 2 announcements which reduced me between them to the depths of misery – (1) Marjorie* had a son yesterday morning at 3.0 am, (2) Elsie proposes to come up next Monday for a coronation holiday, but 'next week is as good as any time'. My fatal mistake is to be incurably hopeful. The thwarting of my quite unjustified hopes repeatedly plunges me into depths of gloom. I know this as my hopes emerge but it never saves me from disappointment. I just wished I was dead and at peace. I used to feel uneasy at my good luck in so many things, feeling obscurely that it couldn't go on and I was bound to suffer somehow. Well, here it is.

Wednesday 12 May

This is Coronation Day so I have some leisure to devote to this. So far as I am concerned the coronation has merely been an inconvenience. The gawping crowds in Oxford Street have impeded my attempts to get along and the sight-seers have made the tubes worse than they need have been. The decorations are on the whole poor achievements. We listened to the beginning of the service, which was effective. I feel sorry for the King who spoke excessively slowly and with obvious effort. I resented unreasonably W's turning up the wireless to hear him better. It felt like looking through a magnifying glass at someone's deformity.

Lunched with E yesterday. We are going to start our 3 months separation when Joad finishes Hegel or from 1 June. I feel the sooner we start the sooner we finish, but how hideous it will be. I must do something concentrated. I should like to write something.

* E's sister.

Friday 21 May

In the morning I went to see Dr Malleson. On the physical side she poked about inside me and asked a few questions and then said, 'I can promise you as healthy a baby as any woman could hope for.' On the practical side she thought K ought to have been told before – anyway, she should be told before I begin a baby. E probably had neurotic reasons for avoiding the unpleasant task but 'your life is as much involved as hers', she said, when I suggested that telling her was for him to judge. She thought I should lose my job if the department got to know and this must be considered, but with luck I might be discreet and it would never come out. She would give me a vague certificate for 6 months – 'a gynaecological condition requiring rest', tho' if they specifically asked for details she would have to give them. It would be expensive running a place of my own but on £350 p.a. I ought to do it easily. The cloud at home would blow over – she knew heaps of cases where it had, even with a most conventional family. Conclusion was – it would be a pity for me to be deprived of a baby just through 'this jam'. And the cost of this moral support was a guinea, but I felt decidedly a step nearer.

Sunday 23 May

Met E at Waterloo yesterday and during coffee told him the result of my interview with Dr Malleson. He made no comment. After he went home I had some lunch and then to the National Gallery for half an hour, then to the Queen's Hall before 3.15 for the concert with Solomon. It was good. After the concert to Piccadilly Monseigneur News Theatre and saw the coloured and uncoloured versions of the coronation film. The Abbey pictures were interesting. It all looked a stupendous make-believe. I felt sorry for the King – at the end he looked an over-dressed idol – quite inhuman. The odd incidents were amusing – the Archbishop twisting the crown around to find the front, the Duke of Kent nearly over-balancing as he knelt to do homage, the King wondering where to wipe the ink off his finger after signing the oath. He looked very sad all through.

Sunday 30 May

We have had a week of summer only broken by a thunderstorm on Wed evening.

In spite of the heat I have had a full week. We have said nothing about our 3 months' separation all the week but it has of course been in my mind. I expected to feel very dismal, rather as I felt just before E went to Finsbury. Oddly enough I have felt quite cheerful, possibly because now my mind is made up. It has been a kind of Indian summer. I have seen him a lot and we have done a variety of things – a kind of epitome of the last 3 years. On Monday I met him at 6.10 as usual and it was obvious that he was feeling miserable. We went to Flemings for dinner. After a while he talked and although he was more upset than I have ever seen him, I think, I couldn't help feeling a little happy. For the first time it was clear that he looked on the baby as I do in at least 2 aspects. From the public standpoint we ought not to waste my good machine; if he can't do it he would always feel he had failed, had been unable to face a challenge. This is what I have wanted him to feel. Now I think if I give him time and leave him to fight his battle in peace he will eventually reach my position. Still, although one part of me rejoiced I pitied him – he had suffered appallingly. He said, 'I feel like Macbeth, as if I had murdered sleep,' and he looked like it. He said, 'I feel quite inhibited from any sexual approach to you.' I said that if that was how he felt and continued to feel there was no point in nerving himself to tell K and in upsetting her unnecessarily – and more on this subject. Joad gave a good lecture on Hegel. Afterwards E felt better, looked better, and said he felt better. We walked over Hungerford Bridge and the moon was rising, a pale yellow-silver in the south. We stopped to watch it behind a puffy light bank of cloud which was faintly luminous with its light and he said, 'The cloud-capped towers and gorgeous palaces.' Then the moon's disc emerged and the spell was broken. As I was going he said, 'I like you tremendously.'

1937

Wednesday 2 June

Well, Goodbye for 3 months. I had to say it quickly before I cried completely. I suppose I'll feel better in time. I wonder, does he feel the same? And only an hour and a half of the 3 months is gone. So far just a hideous attempt not to drown in what he would call a 'complete revulsion'. I did quite well, though, till I'd finished my cigarette.

Thursday 3 June

One out of 96 days till I see you again. This obsession in my mind is like a child's toy railway, the one thought running round and round till I can see nothing, hear nothing without thinking of you. *Figaro* (Act 3) from Glyndebourne this evening. It was foolish to listen but it is so lovely and I thought perhaps you would be listening too. The scene before the battle in *Julius Caesar* runs in my head. Shakespeare has such rhythm and can fit any situation.

> 'For ever and for ever farewell Brutus
> If we do meet again we'll smile indeed
> If not, 'tis true this parting was well made.'

Friday 4 June

Better today definitely, for 2 reasons – (1) I have been busy – a lot of post, running round for DJ, 2 hours' lunchtime with Reen, IRSSA committee, (2) I am beginning to take in emotionally the fact that if I am going to have a baby this 3 months is probably the last period of comparative leisure I shall have for years. Therefore (a) it is a pity to waste it in groans and tears anyway, (b) it is a final opportunity to write something.

Tomorrow will be bad and Monday will be worse – 2 out of 96, 1/48. It isn't so bad for him going away for a fortnight next week. He will have got used to it anyway before he notices it.

Friday 2 July

I got Ella *Jude* for her birthday as she said she had never read it all. It was foolish as it made me think of E, as always. In any case I have wanted a baby very badly today. If I'd had time this morning I would have tried to make a verse on the contrast between making guns and tanks and aeroplanes and making a baby.

Monday 5 July

An unsatisfactory day – a hurried, hectic morning and then a hasty small lunch and then to meet Rosa at Charing Cross. She gave me as a holiday present a green cotton Hungarian frock with silver buttons, tight bodice and full skirt. In spite of all this I *couldn't* work up any enthusiasm. I know now that the interest I took in clothes was almost entirely for E's sake. I do want him. I feel lonely and dull and unenterprising and bored and boring without him. It is humiliating to feel it and I suppose it is just temporary but there it is. I don't care a hoot for anything. It isn't exactly active pain or unhappiness but emptiness.

Tuesday 13 July

After close and heavy clouds the sky cleared to a lovely golden evening – cloudless and lofty with a pale new moon in the west. I finished *The Porch*★ yesterday evening and sent it off to E with a note at lunchtime.

Reen has got a move to Maidenhead. She rang up yesterday and it gave me quite a shock. I was sorry. She has grown on me over the last 12 months. Still, she is anxious to keep in touch with London beginning with a lunch tomorrow.

I feel surprisingly cheerful this evening – why? Perhaps because I worked hard till 5.40 without noticing the time. Perhaps because I have imagined E reading *The Porch* with interest, and through me! 5/12 of the

★ By Richard Church, a former colleague of E's.

time yesterday. '40 days and 40 nights'! 6 weeks tomorrow since I saw him, 7 weeks next Monday till I shall. So it passes.

Wednesday 14 July

Still cheerful, perhaps because I have looked nice. No spots, nails not chippy, hair manageable without being greasy. DJ showed just a suspicion of personal interest – oh, nothing to notice – just a little responsive to persistent nagging, even a suspicion on his own, e.g. I said (on some small point), 'I agree, I daresay you're right.' He feigned surprise – 'No, that's not like you! What's the matter?'

How I want E – not dismally at all – but just to bicker and laugh at and irritate and then (in spite of the heat) to love a little and then to have a baby. Ooh! I could just put one finger on K and squash her like a mosquito, quite calmly and almost disinterestedly, as a blot on the landscape! How fortunate that I can't do anything!

Wednesday 21 July

I have felt increasingly if obscurely dismal today. Why? (It is always a healthy exercise to find concrete reasons – it reveals the rickety basis for most emotional states) (1) Perhaps because E has not sent back *The Porch* yet. (2) Reaction from a week's liveliness culminating in yesterday when, to celebrate the arrival of halfway through the 3 months, I took a day's leave and went to Seaford with Rosa and Margot.

We climbed on to Seaford Head and lunched in the hollow where Ella and I lunched last month. Rosa was as enthusiastic as a child. We went down to the shore and paddled. The tide was out and I have never seen the Cuckmere such a tiny trickle – you could almost cross it in shoes! There were yellow sea-poppies growing on the shingle. We walked along the embankment finding teazles and purple sea lavender by the path. It was a lovely day and a harmonious expedition. I looked at Rosa and Margot and thought: is it evil in me to be preparing for them such disturbance? Why don't I leave them in peace? Accepting (with oddnesses) the ordinary conventions. Giving them more than they expect or ask or will accept

The Cuckmere river

without hesitation but being what they think is right, and the best for me. I don't know. It *is* evil if suffering is unconditionally evil. I only know it would seem as much a sin for me to refuse to have a child, if E is willing, as it seemed wrong to Sue to go on living with Jude. Perhaps it appears a mistake and silly to others as Sue's attitude seems to me. It is appalling to be in suspense, to have a choice taken from me after I had chosen.

Friday 23 July

This is going to be one long gloom. E sent back *The Porch* this morning and with it a letter – quite long – consisting of (1) comment on the book, (2) description of his cruise, (3) a few notes of 'family' movements including that he is going to Malvern the 3rd week in August and (4) 'I am afraid I cannot give you much consolation.' The cold-blooded 'thoughtfulness' of (4) has blackened the whole universe for me today. This is not an exaggeration. Everything I did or tried to do – read or tried to read – was spoilt. I suffered the whole spectrum, as it were, of evil feeling which I have come to know so well. Hatred of the woman who prevents me – I didn't know it was possible to hate anyone with the gusts of hate I feel against her; bitterness with E which almost curdles my love. He has the final say. But how convenient to stop loving me just at the moment when I asked him for the only material thing I have ever asked him for. Worst of all, the moral paralysis which filters into my mind, almost like a voice of the devil himself. 'You were wrong – you should be more calculating – make sure of what you want and go all out for it – ask for what you want from life, and take it; pay as little and get as much as you can; it is only a fool who gives without considering the cost – it leads to emotional bankruptcy as surely as complete charity leads to material bankruptcy. *She* knew what she wanted and took it. He gave it to her – all, more than she asked. And the result? She has a permanent hold on his affection. Harden your heart, cut your losses, leave him his peace and an occasional sentimental memory, have your hair waved and go out for all you can get.'

Finally, better, but heart-breaking and I *could* cry. Regret, remorse. It is my own fault. I let the opportunity slip by because I was afraid. If I had had a boy at Shrewsbury★ he would be two now. If I had taken my last chance in Feb he would be alive inside me now, I could feel him move instead of the hard emptiness beneath my heart. This is only my fault and it is the bitterest thought, tho' it is not evil. At least – there is the richness of experience. Nothing – no pain, no misery, no frustration can take that away. I must reflect on that and resolve not to waste the smallest opportunity again.

Wednesday 28 July

I am having an orgy of reading. All this week 2–300 pages a day – too much: Keyserling's *Art of Life*, Gunther's *Inside Europe* and *Mathematics for the Million*. I went to the library today and got Trevelyan's *Grey of Fallodon* and Heard's *Third Morality*. It is a kind of gluttony – almost like drink. I read so as not to think. Still, I *do* think. Today I wonder whether perhaps he will have the courage. My hope is like the bindweed in the lupin bed; I pull it all up – roots and leaves – there is not an atom left apparently one day – 2 days later it is sprouting a whole new shoot complete with tiny leaves and if I don't destroy it again quickly it leaps up and strangles everything else. The advantage is that while I hope I am happier. The disadvantage is that the

---

★ She is referring to a blissful week's holiday in Shropshire with E, taken in September 1934 and mentioned in her diary entry for 13 September of that year.

more I hope the more cruel is the disappointment. At bottom I suppose it is a matter of temperament – simply physical ingredients, like a cake.

Sunday 1 August

For a week I have done little except eat, sleep, work, play the piano and read and reflect. You would think that time would pass slowly. At times it did, notably when I was working on something not interesting in itself but not dull enough to be done without thinking. Meanwhile I have accidentally improved in relation with Rosa who approves of a quiet life. This adds to the pleasure of the moment and incidentally will be an advantage in the future if I should have to explain that I want a baby and why.

The *Mercury* yesterday contained the best journalism on the Spanish war I have seen – an account of Guernica by Geo Steer. It was unexaggerated, concrete, and one of the most moving articles I have ever read. It is terrifying to think that Guernica is merely an experience in miniature of what most of the big towns in Europe will suffer in the next 10 years unless a miracle happens. The blind futility and clumsiness of war is tragic. They suffer and die for nothing – no one is any better off. The incentive and principle for which the war is fought is utterly remote from them. To an uninterested spectator it must appear as nothing but a possession of the mind by an evil kind of insanity. I don't know what to do. Pacifism seems to be the only intelligent and logical view to hold but I have 2 misgivings about it: (1) should I have the courage to hold it (a) against other people or (b) if there were any possibility of the whole of England going pacifist ((b) means – is it possible to be a pacifist and enjoy the shelter for everyone by non-pacifists?) (2) Is it merely sheer terror of war itself that makes me a pacifist? I shouldn't choose any other course if material things only were at stake (I think), but there are some ideas and principles for which resistance might be worthwhile. Does my inclination to pacifism depend on fear or laziness in resisting evil? I don't know. There is of course in addition to these 'theoretical' misgivings the question of my job. Can one be a pacifist and work even in a small way for a government which isn't? Gunther's book *Inside Europe* is journalism but it is interesting. It shows Hitler as a neurotic – he never reads, never listens to anything but Wagner's music. He has one passion and one aim which he follows with the strength and concentration of insanity. The fact that this passion (for German nationality) coincided with a strong but frustrated emotion common to all Germany gave him his power. It is appalling that peace depends to a large extent on the neurotic whims of one man.

Thursday 12 August

Lunched with Hip.★ I quite enjoyed it. Peta is growing into a lovely child, very fair hair, dark blue eyes and black lashes. Intelligent and very happy. I explained that I was trying to keep a clear head, hence I had not intended to see Peta. She thought I would be asking for trouble to have a baby. I should hate having to work and leave it with a servant. Having made the break she thought I ought not to go back to the old relationship but cut it out and start afresh. She thought I should meet someone else. This is all quite sensible. I would if I could but it takes me ages to get on close terms and it is such trouble; also, how can I trust myself, in any case? I would have believed E more than anyone both for his present feeling and his judgement of the future and (to put it quite neutrally I won't say his love died) less than 3 years after we first loved he ceased to feel any particular wish to be with me. I *couldn't* endure marriage with a man who didn't actively want my company anyway, and no one could want me more than he did 4 years ago. Whatever another man said or felt in the heat of love I should be certain it would not last. A child? Well, being independent even with that would be preferable to keeping an unenthusiastic husband tied to one.

During the last week I have been better. I don't love E less – if anything more – but I have reached (temporarily, I suppose, only) a new feeling – almost tranquillity and serenity, less worried and stirring. The difficulty is to sustain a kind of detached quietness and passiveness without just relaxing into sloth or sorrow. My attitude to him of a year ago seems utterly remote now. It seems, as I look back at it, to have been

★ A friend from college days.

made up of a collection of fears and wishes (a fear of him, of having a baby, of people finding out, of his love waning or waxing, of mine for him leaping up or dying down, a wish to see more of him or less of him, to do particular things and spend my time in particular ways and to evoke similar wishes in him), always looking ahead except for the short times when I was just shot through with ecstasy. I can see where I was wrong at the beginning – I could not trust to my love for him, I was afraid. I ought to have known and to have insisted on K being told then. It would have been worse at the time and might have finished our connection but I am certain it was right and if we had all survived we should have been happier and much more peaceful.

Wednesday 25 August

Nearly 2 weeks since I wrote here. I had a completely 'cold' letter from E this morning asking me for the address of the eye place. It was unexpected and made my heart pound for a time. I wrote at lunchtime and (I think) kept just as cool. I hope so.

I shall have to begin a new book next time.

Sunday 29 August

There seems to be little point in doing anything now. For the moment I feel quite finished. On Monday night I had a letter from E. The 3 months had had no effect – he was worse, if anything. I felt quite hopeless but I wrote to him a reply. Another letter this morning which proved what I have known – that my effort had been wasted. He is quite out of reach. He can think of no one but Kathleen. To her he can sacrifice his own sense of right, and the child, not to mention me. What is the secret of her power over him? She is like some vampire spreading death and desolation. So small a thing would satisfy me. What can I do? It is so lonely. People pass like shadows in the sunshine. I talk to them – joke, work, grumble, while all the time my self stands apart desolate and cold and broken and bitter – pushed down lest its unhappiness leap up to desperation. How can I distil some meaning from it? Break the evil circle of hate and misery?

Thursday 9 September

I was dismal but managed to get submerged in work to such an extent that I was oblivious of time from 11.45–1.45. This lack of time sense is rather frightening. I had the impression that 20 hours or 20 days or 20 weeks or 20 years might just as easily have passed and I had done nothing with them.

It is odd that I can concentrate on other things quite well. Everything seems a dismal grey but (possibly because there is no conflict in my mind – I have the peace which E needs – much good it does me!) my mind seems empty, bleak. I find no delight in anything but music.

Friday 10 September

I felt today at times as if I was just beginning to un-numb, to feel what has happened. Instead of being quite pleasant at home with no animation I found myself impatient and edgy. One goes on thinking automatically on the same lines long after it has become useless, e.g. I began to economize and save up, have small lunches etc. Now, when there is nothing to save for, I still go on. Partly habit, partly because I have no desire to do more now. Is it a desperate, forlorn hope that things can't be as bad as they seem, that after all, the bottom hasn't fallen out of the world, that the point of life has not been broken, that the machine has not gone into reverse? The irony of it is as exquisite. Almost I can endorse *Lear*, 'As flies to wanton boys are we to the gods.' What is so unbearable to me is the inaction, this suffering in quiet, in which all I must do is to ensure that no hint of its existence should be conveyed even by expression.

Sunday 12 September

I had a long letter from E yesterday (15 pages) which made me realize it is hopeless. Then I went with the parents to see *The First Legion* which is a play about the Jesuits, the psychological effects on various men of a miracle. It is much to its credit that it held my attention. This afternoon I wrote to him – rather a last will and testament – but I was calmer than I had been at all. I knew what I wanted to say. I had been pondering over it ever since I read his letter yesterday morning. After I had posted it I felt better, very clear-minded, light-headed as it were and perhaps a little exalted. I felt a peace which comes of feeling that nothing can be worse, that you have touched the lowest point, that all your fears are realized and yet you still live. I even thought, 'I will write a Te Deum, a dedication of praise and thanks.' I would remember only the happiness, the joy, the ecstasy – keep only the good things which he gave me. So I felt until I had a bath, until I was confronted with my own body, that body which he only among men has seen and touched. Then with the swift suddenness of a hailstorm I was swept with physical desire. I would have faced torture for the mere comfort of his physical presence, to feel again his hands, his lips on my breasts, the smooth coolness of his back beneath my hands, the touch of his hair, ruffled by my fingers, the pain of his coming in to me. The calmness so carefully imposed by my will just vanished in a gust of physical passion.

What can I do? I am afraid, terrified, I don't know how to keep my soul in this dark place, where is no thing and no one to comfort me, to guide me. I cannot see where to put my feet, I can feel the wings of evil, the evil in my own mind beating terrifyingly around me. It would be a good thing if I could pray with faith.

Monday 13 September

I have felt dead and numb all day. I made great efforts not to let my mind rest on E. This deadness is an anaesthetic, preferable to the violent pain of feeling, safer at this stage. I have never felt like this before for so long, a sense of unreality, of remoteness, with just this perpetual ache. Like a nightmare. I feel I *must* awaken soon and find things have come right. It is awful having to stop habitual trains of thought, ways of seeing things. I seem unable to grasp all at once and all of me that it is finished; he is dead to me, dead by his own will and choice. It was easy (comparatively) to make my resolution; today comes the harder task of keeping it. I will try to finish this day without crying – it can be done.

The only tiny compensation is the peace which comes of suffering the worst I have feared for years, of knowing there is nothing more. I have never been so free from fear. I didn't have the slightest shoot in the thunderstorm. I remember thinking it was odd that I had never been able to overcome it before.

I am so thankful that I can sleep. I even slept last night, tired out with feeling and thinking. If only there seemed to be the slightest point in waking up.

Thursday 16 September

I had a letter from E this morning. It made me happier. Not that he said anything to suggest even the faintest ground for hope. He is clearly grateful to me for resolving his conflict but he is still completely obsessed with his duty to K. He reminds me of a cross between Abelard and Sue in *Jude the Obscure*. I thought Hardy was incredible in his picture of Sue's gradual loss of intellect to emotion. I couldn't believe that Sue, being intelligent, would have abandoned Jude just when he needed her to satisfy her conscientious scruples. I can believe it now. It is almost parallel with E. The shock which jolted the conscience into irrepressible action is even similar – the death of his mother in E's case, the death of her children in Sue's. It is quite extraordinary. I always felt the ominous similarity but I saw the parallel between Jude and E, which ran like a motif through all our relationship. I didn't see myself as like Sue (tho' he could perceive a similarity). It never occurred to me that he would end by a revulsion like Sue's. We never discussed the parallel. I never told him how I felt about it from some obscurely superstitious feeling that it would strengthen the omen to put it into concrete expression. It was he that said I was more like Sue than any other woman in literature, as long ago as 1933. It is odd.

Friday 24 September

An interview with Russell (my plumber Enquiry Case)'s Accountant, Buckmaster. He called at 11.0 and went at 12.20 and not before he had told me his life history, with emphasis on the fact that he was a bachelor but would marry if he could afford it. He had already said that he knew the first time he had seen me that we should think alike on a lot of things. He wound up with, 'Take care of yourself.' He did not say anything direct and he did nothing – didn't even shake hands with particular warmth but I am pretty certain I could marry him if I gave him any encouragement. This is all very odd and most unofficial. He has had a roving life, never made any money, looks a bit as if he drinks (watery eye) and is stone deaf in one ear. Well! Well! I can't deny I have thought of him. It gives me self-confidence to realize I can hold a man's attention, but how I long for E. I sent a letter to him today.

Sunday 26 September

Today I must decide what I am going to do this winter. The following are possible: (1) cut off amusement and cram for Psychology finals next June. The advantage of this would be (a) I should work hard, (b) I shouldn't have time for repining, (c) I should have something tangible to show at the end; (2) go to Joad's Ethics lectures at Birkbeck. He is stimulating and I should do more work for him but the associations would be heart-breaking; (3) try some left politics; (4) try Mass Observation,* or a combination of 2, 3 and 4. (1) Psychology (seriously) would be good if I go on feeling there is no point in anything without E. If I can survive without drowning my sorrow in work it will be better to do one of the other things, if only because I should be less solitary. Solitude, beyond a moderate amount, becomes a habit and can be unhealthy. On the whole, perhaps Ethics and Mass Observation is the best. I shouldn't have to have dinner in town.

Monday 27 September

Oh, I am so weary of trying not to think of him and of trying to think sensibly about him if I must remember him. Love is like a disease or like an evil mist which seeps into one's mind, is in every breath one draws, is part

---

* Mass Observation is an organization founded in 1937 and launched by Tom Harrison and two colleagues at the *New Statesman*. It invited members of the general public to send in information about their everyday lives and also developed a National Panel of Diarists, of whom Doreen was one.

of everything one thinks or sees or does. It is 3 weeks since he first wrote
to me, 17 weeks since I saw him. How long will I go on like this, if I do go
on? If it has a physical basis perhaps I shall recover when my ovaries wither
in perhaps 10–15 years. With him physical desire was the driving force;
when it waned he seemed not to want me much or so much. But with me
it has never been insistent. Still, it seems the only hope. Now my mind
feels poisoned – with love for E and hate for K. I wish her dead but that
would not, in reality, improve things. Our love – spoilt, all the spontaneity
is gone.

Wednesday 29 September

What can I do? There is no peace. Always I see with my mind E as he
was. I can hardly believe he is as he is. If I could but forget! The country
is the worst place of all now. He quickened so immeasurably my
appreciation that now it is not merely that I can feel no more zest than
before I knew him. It is an active want. Before, I didn't miss what I
hadn't known. Now I feel a perpetual and conscious want. I am better if
I don't go. I wouldn't want anyone to feel as I feel, not even K. What is
so hard is to know that she wouldn't anyway suffer just what I suffer
because she has never enjoyed that quality of companionship. He has
given us different things.

What can I do? I know I am mentally ill. I cannot make my mind look
forwards or even consider only the moment, I can only look back. If only
I could amputate him from my mind I should be better. At this moment I
would not keep even the memory of happiness with him. 'If thine eye
offends thee, pluck it out.' The thought of him obsesses me, paralyses me,
comes between me and everything. It is a disease and I don't know how to
control it. That it should come to this – I didn't think his love would wane,
I believed him. It was inexperience. I would still believe him over any
other man. I would never expect another man to go on loving me. I
suppose it was a subconscious realization that the life had gone out of his
love that made me want a baby last Nov, as a substitute.

Thursday 30 September

A great amount of work had accumulated in one day's leave. It was just as well – I tackled it with concentration from 10.0 till 1.30 and from 2.20–5.30 without pause. Another sunny day but this evening it seemed colder.

Went to Joad's lecture on Ethics. It required some effort and I felt haunted by E all the way from the office till I got home. In a way I resent my feeling for him. It tyrannizes over my judgement. I can see he is not worth feeling so miserable about. There is really not much to be said for a man who satisfies his physical desire and as it dies discovers his conscience (that is what it comes to, however nicely one can put it), who refused the only thing I ever asked of him, not because he thought it would be bad for me but because he simply didn't want it. Yet, tho' I can see all this – and the realization of it will perhaps save me from letting pity and inexperience lead me to such an emotional cul-de-sac again – it has no effect at all on my feeling, knowing all this.

Friday 1 October

I don't know quite what to do. I had an appointment this morning with Russell (my plumber enquiry case) and his accountant Buckmaster. The main point was to form an impression of Russell and to give him the white paper. He was a solid, rather repressed-looking man who said he was over 60, wore a quite good quiet brown suit but a dark blue tie with white spots. He seemed the old-fashioned, independent Victorian type – shrewd, opposed to all new-fangled methods. I could imagine him resenting having to pay tax. He said he had been ill off and on with asthma, catarrh, stomach trouble, kept going with doing three men's work. The deposit was his last savings. Running his business he was an asset to the country and so on. Buckmaster naturally had little to say. I felt a bit nervous at the beginning but settled down to the job not too badly perhaps. The interview lasted an hour.

At 1.0 Buckmaster rang me up to know what I thought and to say how he had admired my handling of Russell and more of that strain – what an interesting set of books, he had enjoyed himself, perhaps he could borrow a book on Buddhism. It would take him perhaps a fortnight to do the accounts but if I wanted to see him before he would be only too pleased to come. He concluded, 'Goodbye, little one.' I don't know what to do about him. It is of course soothing to my vanity to realize I can impress a man. It gives me pleasure to think that here is someone who, however superficially, is interested in me. I am inclined to flirt a little. I haven't encouraged him at all unless failing to choke him off completely is encouragement. I have answered his comments, made non-committal comments on his unofficial remarks and, so far as my attitude went, kept strictly official. There are 2 points to remember: (1) I dislike mixing official and personal relations. It was bad enough with E, it is worse with an accountant handling a BD case. On the other hand I shall be bound to keep on more or less friendly terms till the case is settled; (2) I don't like him as a person. There is little danger of my feelings being involved. I don't know him sufficiently to know whether his might be. There is always a risk of hurting or being hurt. In this case it isn't worth the risk.

Monday 4 October

I found a letter marked Personal at the office. It contained a cutting from a Sunday paper of an article on Charm with underlinings in red ink and a little note on the back of a card from Buckmaster explaining how the article applied to me. It made me a little sad. It is obvious that he must be thinking about me from the mere fact that he couldn't keep his mind off me even while he was reading the newspaper. Poor thing! I hadn't the faintest notion I had impressed him the first time I saw him. It is useless and can only lead to disappointment and sorrow. I shouldn't marry him – there would be no point. I shouldn't want his child. In any way and in both senses E has spoilt me.

Wednesday 6 October

I was comparatively successful yesterday in refraining from remembering that on the 5th Oct 4 years ago E in desperation told me he loved me. I have not been so successful today. I have thought of him and wanted him persistently. It seems so stupid just to waste the elaborate understanding we built up in six and a half years, at least it seems so to me who wants it to continue and not just to disintegrate. I can never realize that the understanding was valuable only in so far as both of us wanted it. Now that he does not it is useless to regret it. It has already disintegrated. There is nothing to waste. It must be chiefly vanity that refuses to let me realize that in spite of all he said and did, I have failed to satisfy him and his love has waned. Perhaps wanting the child was a last desperate gamble.

Thursday 14 October

I have got behind with these notes mainly because I went to stay with Ella at her flat in Richmond on Friday evening and came home on Sunday before dinner.

On Monday evening I went to hear Russell at LSE. Afterwards, with an hour to spare before Joad, I had tea and missed E as much as I have ever missed him. I felt utterly desolate, absolutely alone. How he would have talked of the lecture, picked holes in it, enlarged on it. I am trying so hard to extract value out of the things I do by myself. There is no reason at all why I shouldn't but my mind somehow won't kindle. It is like a fire of damp sticks. I get less than half what I got with him. I liked Joad, and the other people are friendly.

On Tuesday Buckmaster rang up. He had looked me up in the Civil Service list in the library and was much impressed – said I might get anywhere if I was keen but was I ambitious? If not, what did I want? Still, he didn't want me to become a blue-stocking. He had thought of me every day. Well, strange as it seems, after he rang off I found I had got quite stiff with sheer physical stimulation. I thought – I suppose some people would think they were in love. But what a complete difference. I felt bitter that E should expose me to such humiliation.

Tuesday 19 October

I wrote to E on Sat to ask him if he would like *The Years*. Had a letter this morning. Quite chatty and unconcerned. He advised me to listen to Bach till I feel better. This complacency annoys me. How simple! As tho' one's problems could be solved by aesthetic contemplation. If it did work it would simply be a drug – lose oneself in the music. I know how unhealthy that is from my own feeling. It is just another form of intoxication – I might just as well take to drink for all the good it would do. I am surprised that he should consider it. But I suppose I don't know him now. People are always changing, and more rapidly than usual in an emotional crisis. The E I knew and loved, and still love is dead.

Thursday 21 October

This afternoon Buckmaster rang up about Russell's accounts for 32/3 and 33/4 and added some personal chit chat, including what did 'D' stand for? Would I come out to dinner tonight? I refused at once but not before a whole medley of reasons rushed through my mind of which a few were (a) I had on old clothes, (b) I had promised to be home for dinner which was steak pudding, (c) I didn't want to be rushed and felt in a panic. But I didn't discourage him – said I would some other night. I told him we couldn't fix an appointment about Russell after Monday till the following week. He asked why and I told him I was going away. He enquired where and said if it hadn't been so far he would have come down for a day. Asked if I minded what he said – didn't want to give me a shock etc – I had to say to him, 'I hope you won't be disappointed in me.' I don't know what to do – it is inevitable that one of us will suffer for it if I let it go on. I suppose I shall, as usual, drift into a position from which it is difficult to emerge. I distrust my interest (such as it is) in him – how can it be real when I want E so much?

Tuesday 26 October

I have felt as if I were living in a dream – the same feeling of unreality, the same sense of compulsion, of moving inevitably, involuntarily on a pre-destined path – the same sense of suffering rather than acting. Buckmaster (B) came yesterday 11.05 and went at 1.50. A large proportion – quite large – was devoted to Russell and the rest to how he felt. He told me if he could have his way he would like to live with me in the country. He didn't use the word 'love', but he made it clear. He said he felt it before I said a word, at the first glance, but he wished me to understand it was not simply physical desire, tho' he was only human. He told me of his work, his struggles to live, his poverty. He had nothing to offer – he didn't know how he would do next year. He even still owed money he had borrowed to live. He has nice hands – big, clean, well cared-for, firm. Before he went he held my hands, my elbows. I was surprised to find I was trembling and very wobbly after I had said goodbye. In the afternoon he rang up about a visit to Russell and then asked if I was all right. Was my heart weak? He had noticed my lips turn quite blue just before he went. I can't understand this; one would think I would be used to it. I was as upset as the first time E kissed me. I recovered in the afternoon but after going to Russell's lecture at LSE I was dead tired.

I was reasonably pleased to have an acknowledgement of my Mass Observation from Madge, thanking me for a model report on Oct 12th.

May it be fine for the rest of the week. To Dorset with Ella tomorrow. I am glad of the breathing space and to get away from the office.

Friday 5 November

On Monday morning B rang me up and asked me to dine with him on Thursday. I also found a letter from E saying he had told K all that had happened. She had forgiven him but hadn't really understood, but – a surprise – had offered to have a baby. Between these two things I was quite upset. By lunchtime I had a headache. I couldn't work or think or decide what to do. I felt quite helpless. E said, 'Our life together must end,' but he saw no reason why we shouldn't meet now and then and write.

Sunday 7 November

On Thursday I met B at 5.30 outside Flemings and he took me to dinner at Regent Palace. It was big and certainly palatial. We went to the superior of the 2 restaurants and he had Chablis and coffee afterwards. I felt rather unworthy but I told him a little about E. He seemed rather dashed but I thought I owed him honesty at least, even if only as explanation of failure to encourage him more. He had first accused me of being a brick wall. There is something about him I like. I told him I wanted babies. He told me his view of marriage as companionship and the sanctity of the oath. I liked his independence of mind, his lavishness and attention and enjoyed his compliments and care that I should catch my train. He taxi-ed me to Charing Cross and kissed me twice on the lips. I didn't mind – in fact, I liked him physically. At the station I had a fit of trembling and shivering – again, I can't imagine why. He rang me up on Friday morning and I sent him a note of thanks. I can't make up my mind what to do with him. If it is only the difference in manner it shouldn't matter but so far I can't trust myself to him. It isn't for anything he does or says or looks. I suspect it is just because he is different from E. Perhaps because he has an irrational, mystical streak which makes him incalculable. If so, it is foolish because everyone has this streak. E certainly has. I also had a letter from E on Friday.

Tuesday 9 November

Yesterday I went to Russell's lecture which, so far as I was capable of judging, was one of the best yet, on Power and Opinion. Very sane and unimpassioned. I didn't go to Joad's lecture and came home with Margot. I found at the office a long letter from B, rather severe. I spent a good deal of the morning replying. In view of the fact that he told me conclusively he could not marry I feel his attitude is unreasonable. However . . . !

Thursday 11 November

A hectic morning. I found a letter from B which I read till 10.15, dictated till 10.45. A letter from E came while I was dictating so I began to read it. B phoned at 10.45 till 10.50. Interrupted at 10.55 by a message that von Marx had called to see me; arranged to see him after the two minutes' silence, spent them vainly trying to concentrate on the problems of peace and war but my mind was filled with B and E. Saw old von Marx, returned to E's letter, interrupted by James' discussion of a point on copyright royalties of

Berlitz School of Languages and Miss Cameron about claims. I decided I must write a note to B and began to read his letter again. Before I'd read a page he phoned again and talked till 2.15. I promised to meet him on Sat at 1.25, went to lunch at 2.20 till 2.45, did the claims (9), saw a girl accountant from E Watts about Yevonde and had a general discussion on women and jobs, signed the post, did a little work of my own and finally DJ came down quite pleasantly to see how much had accumulated.

My mind is in a muddle. I don't know what to do. It is, as Elsie suggests, a turning point.

Friday 12 November

I have done – on impulse – what may be a decisive thing today. It was cold but the sun shone brilliantly from a pure pale blue sky this morning and I felt as if things *couldn't* be wrong. In the bus I decided to lunch with E, partly because I couldn't bear the dismalness of his letter, partly because I thought I could manage it without getting emotional. I read his letter through again and dialled his number without thinking again. After a lot of trouble I got through and was very surprised to find my voice had almost disappeared. I could just about croak the appointment. He said, 'Usual time and place,' without comment and we rang off. I felt overwhelmed – all sorts of feelings just chased each other round my mind; the beating of my heart almost choked me; I didn't know whether to burst into tears or roar with laughter. I thought I must calm down and to do that work is the best thing. I did the claims, powdered my nose and set off in the sunshine in a dream. He was a few minutes late. I am glad I managed well and did not dry at all. I was, on the whole, better than he. We just talked as we used to during lunch, filling the gap in facts and only discussed the situation at the bottom of the escalator for 10 minutes. The joy of seeing him and hearing him and getting at once back to the easy communication we achieved, the restfulness of knowing I would be understood and followed without mistake and complication. The bliss, the utter bliss of that snatched hour! I didn't feel the faintest throb of physical desire but I knew that whatever I did or didn't do I should love him utterly with my whole mind and feeling to the end of things. My love has gone through and beyond physical attraction and has become the centre of everything for me. All the afternoon I felt absurdly light-hearted.

Sunday 14 November

Well, I can't understand me. Yesterday it was very cold but brilliant sunshine and I met B at 12.05. Lunch at Flemings and we walked through the park to Victoria and caught the 1.48 to Merstham. I took him the walk through Gatton and over Colley Hill. It was warm walking and there was

Gatton Park

hardly any wind. The leaves had nearly all fallen. The curves of the downs along Gatton were lovely and he liked them. He doesn't know many birds and trees but is quite enthusiastic, pleasant to walk with. Under the beeches on Colley Hill he kissed me etc for three quarters of an hour perhaps. Surprisingly, I quite liked him and responded to the stimulus.

A robin came and hopped round us. Tea at Reigate for 2 hours and we talked. I don't know quite what will happen. I liked him better than before. To see him against a familiar background was reassuring and he survived it better than I should have thought.

Monday 22 November

E rang me up at 12.45 today and talked for a quarter of an hour. I was so surprised I could hardly believe it. He said, 'as guide, philosopher and friend' and wanted my advice as to whether to appeal against his failure to be promoted. I didn't mind what he wanted. It was the fact of his ringing me up that elated me. Said he was still scratching his head over my letter of last Monday. He is coming to the London meeting tomorrow. I shall see him if only in the distance.

Tuesday 23 November

A full day. I had tea with E and walked to Waterloo after the meeting. We talked about impersonal things – Russia, China, Japan, the Labour Party, the gas drill lectures, his chances of HG. It was such peace to see him and talk to him. He kept me at a distance, I think because he has not, and cannot yet, reply to my letter.

Sunday 28 November

This must be very short as it is bitterly cold. It is only because I have just had a bath that I can write anything. I met B yesterday at 12.05 and we lunched at Flemings. It was dull and inclined to be foggy so we did not go anywhere to walk. We just strolled round Hyde Park and Kens Gardens – not where E and I used to lunch but round the Serpentine. That was bad enough but I managed to be fairly callous. He kissed me hastily once or twice. At 3.30 we had tea at Stewarts and at 4.30 we went into Hyde Park again to amble till it was time for dinner. He found a darkish corner and held me and kissed me till it was too cold. I quite like him to make love to me. He is pleasant and very considerate and has nice hands. We had dinner at the Regent Palace again and he was lavish with wine and chocolates. I think Uncle Arthur Bates was there, tho' I'm not sure. Anyway, between this and the chocolates to account for I decided to inform the family where I had been.

Thursday 2 December

I am so tired with one thing after another – nothing much in themselves but most wearing. Tuesday Elsie rang up at 12.45 to ask me to lunch with her in Bloomsbury as she was having an interview for a job at 3.30. A minute or two later B rang up to ask me if I had misunderstood the letter I had from him in the morning. I was in the middle of replying to it. Poor thing! He was in a dismal state, a conflict between inclination and prudence. He wants to see me and make me love him but his conscience tells him it is not fair as he has nothing to offer me. I comforted him as best I could. He sounded quite desperate, was afraid the worry might affect his mind. Then I rushed to lunch with Elsie, came back and worked hard till 4.50 when I dashed off to catch the 5.10 home. Yesterday, at 1.50, E rang up to ask me the answer to a question he expected Smeed to ask him in the course of the Special Inspection he is to have. I didn't know the answer but said I'd see what I could discover and ring him at 2.0. I did and we talked again and he asked me to lunch tomorrow to tell me about the Inspection. So that will be lovely.

Friday 3 December

A hurried exciting day with nothing much done. Lunch with E was the best thing. I sat and listened to his account of his Special Inspection and hoped and feared and worried with him. Two talks with him on the phone this afternoon. He was in a nervy state – hadn't slept, had been concentrating too much, very edgy. He said he felt better as we went back. I hoped (with no grounds for hoping) that it was partly me.

Tuesday 14 December

A letter in the morning from B which upset me. He had misunderstood my last letter and was quite extreme in his bitterness. I decided I should never love him enough to marry him even if he *had* enough money. Such an unstable, uncertain character would be nerve-racking. For the first time I made a serious comparison with E's calm, rational temper. I wrote to him hoping to make him feel better (for he must have been upset himself) and this morning he rang up, the storm having blown over. I am dining with him on Friday.

Thursday 16 December

Still cold tho' not so wet and snowy. Lunched with E to give him Huxley's *Ends and Means* to read. He quite jumped at it. I told him I was dining with B tomorrow and a bit about him. I liked E so much. I don't know what to do. I felt dismal tonight.

Sunday 19 December

Still as cold and, this evening, fog. B took me to the RP on Friday. The waitress was inefficient and B complained with the result that we were given (in compensation) the most superb pêche melba I have ever seen, let alone tasted. I enjoyed the evening. He was quite sweet to me but I am more than doubtful whether a permanent attachment would work. I fear he thinks I am a hussy at bottom and his views are terribly rigid. His letter of last Sunday was in a way a blessing in an odd form. It revealed him in the cold clear light of day, shorn of the glamour shed by his admiration. Well, we shall see. At the moment I have just gone back to wishing K at the bottom of the sea.

Wednesday 22 December

I must have spent at least an hour speaking on the phone, first to B (who rang up to ask how my cold was and hear how my voice was); 5 minutes later to E (who wanted to verify Elsie's address as he was sending her book on with a letter about it. We actually discussed *Ends and Means* for some time. He liked it too); finally, at 5 to 5 Elsie herself (who just wanted to know how things were going).

Friday 24 December

I had lunch with B yesterday. I wore my cherry jumper and black costume and hat as it was very mild. He liked me and asked me to cancel my music lesson and have tea with him. I did, and afterwards we decided to walk through the Park. He kissed me and then there wasn't time to walk so we went by bus. He gave me 3 pairs of stockings and an enormous box of chocolates and another big box for M. The family were most impressed.

1938

Sunday 2 January

Now, while the family is at church, I will make the first entry of the new year. It has been misty, damp, chilly and dark for most of the day. After dinner I typed Mass Observation reports and wrote to Mrs Parsons to thank her for the cream she sent us. Today is the first quiet leisurely day since last Monday.

I have been much preoccupied with B this week. I have seen a lot of him, talked to him on the phone, written 2 or 3 letters to him and had 2 long ones from him and thought a good deal about him. On Tuesday I met him at 4.30 and had tea at the ABC and then he took me to dinner at the Regent Palace. It was nice and we had wine. Afterwards I caught the 10.29 and he came on the platform to see me off and, somehow, on the spur of the minute he hopped in and walked up the hill with me. The evening had a melancholy tinge because we had said it would be our last outing. The relationship must end because he couldn't afford to take it further. However, on Wednesday he was in town on work and rang me up to ask me to have tea. At tea he said he would go on seeing me till the end of the year. We talked on and finally we decided to have dinner together. We went (economically) to the Corner House and I caught the 10.44 home. On Thursday he was having an interview in the city and rang me up at 12.15 to have lunch. We went to Flemings and I had 2 hours for lunch. On Friday he rang me up saying he would be in town to see Russell's solicitor and could we have dinner for the last time? I had all sorts of jobs to do and thought it impossible at first but finally took half a day's leave and did my odd jobs. We had a pleasant, lively dinner at the Corner House and he gave me an Eversharp pencil. There was an atmosphere of subdued excitement. We caught the 10.05 and he came down with me – and kissed me again and again on the way. It took me half an hour to come from the station.

I don't really know about him. I like him in many ways. There are many things about his character I like: his generosity and lavishness, his frankness and honesty, his power of sticking to his principles. Intellectually I feel mixed. He is quick and intelligent in a concrete way (as one would expect in a person with his education and practical experience). He has an almost uncanny power of reading people's minds. He would be difficult to deceive. He is observant and quick at drawing inferences. He thinks I might be bored with him if he couldn't (or wouldn't) be interested in the books and plays I like. I don't know whether this is so. I haven't been bored with him yet. The main point on which I am doubtful is his attitude to me. He is considerate and gentle and would spoil me. This is the pleasant aspect of his attitude. On the other hand he might be jealous (to an unreasonable extent) and would probably be possessive, I am not sure if I could adapt myself sufficiently to this. Perhaps I could. He is prepared, in theory anyway, to give and take. I don't know. At any rate it probably doesn't matter for he is quite firm about terminating our relationship owing to his position. I have seriously thought of him. It is perhaps as well that his position makes him put the brake on for I might easily slip into marrying him partly because he would give me a child and look after me, partly because I am so weary of fending for myself. This wouldn't be fair to him however much I resolved to settle down and 'do my duty' to him afterwards.

I lunched with E on Tuesday. His prospects of promotion are not cheerful. He was rather dismal and lifeless. He rang me up in the morning and I suggested lunching because he sounded so miserable. I like to feel he wants to talk to me and that I can do something to cheer him up but I don't know that these meetings are really sensible, anyway until he has replied to my last serious letter. Heaven knows when he will. I love him still but he (or just circumstances) has killed my faith in the power and strength and right of my love. My faith and hope in it and him are dead. I just drift from one thing to another, or one person to another, with no will or purpose.

Tuesday 4 January

A horrid day – dull, dark, cold, north wind, thick drizzle at lunchtime. Not a pleasant day.

In addition I found I was missing B. He rang up (officially) yesterday morning. We almost had tea but just kept his resolution. I have thought of him and wanted him continually, and also thought of E with unmerited resentment almost. He hasn't replied to my letter of 15th Nov. Does he think it doesn't matter to me either way?

Wednesday 12 January

I don't know about B. I doubt if I could put up with him permanently. He is unreasonably sensitive and won't accept my statement of how I feel. He was huffy because I hadn't had time to read *both* his books – would hardly discuss the one I *had* read. I did my best but he was not mollified. I am afraid he jumps to conclusions, sees people through his own spectacles, either very rosy or very black, has no detachment or objectivity. We talked of foreign politics. He horrified me by saying he thought our only policy was to slaughter all Germans, Japs and Italians without exception. Realized this was impracticable but it was the only final remedy. Also inclined to jeer at my highbrow taste in literature – had lent *Ends and Means* to some man who read a lot – about 500 books – who said he had struggled through 4 chapters and found it heavy going. B couldn't read books that weren't practical – would only stuff up his mind. I suppose this attitude is natural in the circumstances. The more difficult it is to provide one's bread the larger it looms and the more important it is in one's mind. But, combined with his emotional corners, it made me rather dismal. I felt quite out of touch with him. I wasn't bored and the evening just slipped away but I felt far off and was surprised to find tears were running down my nose at Charing Cross station.

Lunched hastily with E who could only manage yesterday as his General Inspection began today. He went with Margot and me to the Friends' House to hear Joad on *Ends and Means*. It was so nice to be doing something with him again. Joad was good and we liked the Quaker

atmosphere. There were some extraordinary people there. I got back at
2.30 just in time to sign my letters before B called about Russell. Perhaps it
was the contrast that made him seem so unsympathetic. I don't think I am
intellectually sniffy, especially with people I like otherwise. Still, it is a
relief to communicate with a man moving in the same intellectual
atmosphere – E, or this evening, Mac, who told me about Scarlatti and
discussed the different types of introspection of Bach and Beethoven.

Friday 14 January

Yesterday was Rosa's birthday. Rosa took us to St John Ervine's *Robert's
Wife*. It is a play of which the main theme is: should a wife have a career?
But it raises incidentally the question of pacifism (there is a boy sentenced
to imprisonment for sedition parallel to the Phillips case), the church's
attitude to immorality, marriage, birth control, the dependence of 'good
works' on the whims of the wealthy etc. A good evening's mouthful and if
it didn't solve any of them one could hardly expect a mere play to succeed
where science, politics and organized religion and economics fail. Edith
Evans was a joy. Her zest, her artistic integrity and intelligence make her
one of the most interesting actresses I have seen.

This morning I received from B a letter and the papers relating to his affair
with Mary, which he sent to me to show me why he was suspicious. He rang
me up halfway through. The upshot of it was I had half a day's leave and
spent it with him in HP and tea afterwards. He was nice and felt better. The
letter I wrote him on Wed (in which I said truly what I felt, i.e. that I wanted
him to be happy but I could not do anything for him unless he could trust me,
quoting 'Perfect love casteth out fear') seemed to have pleased him. Anyway,
he liked me and accordingly I liked him. He said (in spite of all he has said on
the other side), 'If I had the means I would marry you tomorrow.' He bought
6 peaches and gave them to me as I dashed into Charing Cross station.

Saturday 22 January

My head is aching so that I can hardly see but I must note what has
happened since it may affect so much.

I lunched with E on Thursday and began to tell him about B and my doubts what to do. It was difficult and I had to go slowly so as not to cry so I hadn't said much when we had to go. I was in a turmoil for the rest of the day and couldn't sleep so I wrote to him. (He had said K was better or I wouldn't have talked to him at all.) Posted it yesterday morning and had a day's leave – went to Brighton with Rosa. The main reason was to avoid B. I couldn't face him or even talk to him on the phone as I was. This morning a letter from E – very upset. Also K was worse. I felt awful for having hurt him so and at such a time. Yet beneath all my misery, in spite of myself, my heart rejoiced for he said he would see me today if he could. He rang up and I met him at Waterloo. He was looking awful – hollow-eyed. Reminded me of the first few weeks of Goldstein. We walked round the station and I tried at first to be cool and matter of fact, knowing it would take very little to upset my self-control. He didn't say much. I couldn't say much. I didn't see anyone but I tried not to cry for his sake. We found a dark tunnel under the trains and in this place we walked up and down. I don't know what he said except to remark that this was where Whitbreads kept their beer and then found it was Black and White whisky instead. All I know is that my love for him just leapt up out of the careful wrappings I had tried to smother it in all these weeks and I knew I could never love anyone else with all my heart. I shall have to trust to my feelings. My reason and intelligence are useless and only mislead me.

Now I must tell B and that is hard. I am desperately sorry for him but it is better now than later.

Tuesday 25 January

I am so happy I want to sing the Magnificat from the top of a mountain. For the time, anyway, all the darkness has disappeared and the sun shines again. I can hardly think at all. I am giddy with joy.

So briefly, what happened was this: on Sunday morning the sun was shining. I had just arranged to walk over Riddlesdown with the family when E rang up and asked me to come to Clapham Junction at 11.30 as he had written something on the situation. I thought I would take him my diaries to read as they are a more or less connected account of the development of the position. He was better than on Sat; he had slept. He had managed to take a more or less objective view. I did not realize just how difficult it would be for him as I did not in the least imagine how jealous he would feel. But he had made an effort and talked the thing over impersonally. He said first that if he was B he would take me on any terms, for my lust if not for my love. He asked quite a lot of questions about him. He gave me a connected account of his own sexual experience including more facts about his meeting with K than he had previously given me. He said he was surer than ever of the rightness of her love.

Riddlesdown Common in winter

We walked up and down a muddy field for an hour and then I caught the 12.37 back to Purley. I read his letter in the train and cried, but I had made my mind up already. Yesterday morning I rang him up. He sounded dreadful, had not slept or eaten, being quite upset by reading my diary. I wished for a minute I hadn't given it to him but then was glad because it was better for him to know the worst. We arranged to lunch together. He gave them back to me. He did not reproach me for anything but not telling him the whole thing in detail earlier. He said, 'I feel all right when I look at you.' He had arranged to take half a day as he couldn't work. I went back to the office and asked DJ for half a day too and we walked in the sunshine in the Park. I don't know what we talked of. We went first to *Rima* and I sat down and looked at him. I felt like Isaiah's poetry – 'And sorrow and sighing shall flee away.' It was a miracle of happiness, a true Easter. We looked at a moorhen. Finally we had tea at Mandes and he had a huge scone. We took a bus back to Marble Arch and he pinched me – just that.

I met B at 4.45 and we went straight to the Park and I told him I did not and could not love him. He was very sweet and concurred lest I should be unhappy about it. He was, he said, used to disappointment. He was in a way relieved of responsibility because he could not afford to marry. He was very kind but dismal. He asked me to try to make a friendship. I said it must be on the understanding that I did not love him, that I must pay my expenses and he did not touch me. If he thought he would get any satisfaction or pleasure out of such a relationship I would try it. I didn't tell him of my newly living love for E, remembering how a man suffers from jealousy.

E rang me up this morning to convey a few 'notes'. He said he felt completely happy, happier than he had felt since Stow. His love was quite unaltered by what had happened and he was sure of the integrity of our love in spite of it. He quoted, or half quoted, St Paul – 'Not principalities or powers and things present etc shall cut me off from the love of God.' We arranged to go to the Friends' House to hear Catlin on Pacifism. We lunched at Lyons first. It was simply a long ripple of joy from the moment I saw him. I could hardly control my happiness. I felt my whole self quivering through the lecture and the glow of it lasted all day. He looked more solid and sensible but as I looked at him his mouth gave a little twiggle which said, 'Yes, I know.'

What will happen to us? I don't know, he doesn't. I shan't see him till K is better. But now I am riotously happy, with not even a shadow of precariousness. Now I could say the Te Deum with truth, or the Psalm, 'I called upon the Lord in my trouble and he heard me.'

1938

Thursday 27 January

A lovely, lovely letter (or rather 2 letters) from E this morning. I have read them about four times and nearly know them by heart. They made me so happy except for one thing – he had a sore throat last night. I tried to ring him over and over again today but couldn't get through as the line was out of order. So I don't know how he is today. He may be in bed. Perhaps he is ill and it will be my fault for worrying him into a low state. I wrote to him today. I must not think of him being ill.

Friday 28 January

I have tried not to worry today. I rang up Finsbury 2 this morning and learnt that E was away on sick leave. I felt so helpless and cut off. I told myself it was just a cold but whatever it is I feel responsible. I hope – I do hope – he will be better tomorrow.

A letter from B this morning, quite nice and sensible. It made me feel a pig.

Wednesday 2 February

2 letters from E this morning. He has tonsillitis and has been very ill. I was appalled when, at 11.30, he rang me up from a call box. He sounded very bad and feeble. I have worried all day lest he has had a relapse. I was so thankful to hear from him – all in pencil, almost illegible, but I made it out. Nice letters.

Sunday 6 February

There is a lot to put down since Wed but I must only make a quick note. On Friday B came to see me and afterwards I had tea with him. It was rather a bad time. He looked ill tho' he was very nice to me. I felt awful about him. He was so hurt and vulnerable. He put his case on grounds of reason, whose force I admitted, but I was not in the slightest degree moved by them. What did affect me was the childish, naïve efforts he made to please me. He would go to lectures with me even if he couldn't hear! He would read the books I liked even if he disliked them. Dismal.

Yesterday was a queer day. First a letter from E. He rang up to fix a meeting at Clapham Junction at 3.0 – sounded ill. When I went to meet him I was so moved that I couldn't read as I waited for him. He looked ill and was very feeble. It was so sweet to see and hear him. He put his hand on my heart as we stood in the sunshine on the bridge over the lines. Just half an hour.

Tuesday 8 February

A lovely, lovely day to begin this new book. First, a letter from E, a very nice letter with such lovely things in it. On the back page a half suggestion that I should meet him at Petersham this afternoon. I had an appointment at 11.0 with Porter about Lady Langford. In the middle he rang up and we arranged to meet. Porter was maddening, talking on and on about nothing. Finally he went at 12.0. I did 15 claims, signed letters, dashed in to DJ 3 times and found him with a caller. Finally wrote him a note and dashed off to lunch and to go to the 1.20 lecture by Dr Gray on *Ends and Means*. Got to Waterloo and caught 2.21 to Richmond. Had to wait for the bus but got to the Disart Arms about 3.0.

We walked I suppose quite a long way through the Park which was all big trees and ponies and green slopes. I did not look at it much but spent the hour and a half we had in seeing and hearing and feeling E. It was bliss, just utter bliss, a dream of delight. The joy of feeling his arms around me, his hands on me, his cheek on mine. We were libidinous, to repeat his word. It was gorgeous but too short and incomplete. I felt giddy with happiness and he liked it too.

Friday 11 February

A lovely week this is, on the whole. We have lunched together and wanted to love so much on Wed, Thursday and today. We are both so longing to love completely again. It is lovelier than in 1934 because I know how I shall love it now. He is better but still not quite well. He really needs feeding up and 9 weeks away. I can think of little else. When I am not with him I write to him.

Dinner with B last night. He is reasonable.

Sunday 13 February

It is bitterly cold and I am sleepy. Nevertheless I must note this lovely weekend. A north easterly gale has been blowing all the time and today we have had heavy snow showers with sunshine in between.

When I lunched with E on Friday we arranged to meet for just an hour this morning. I wrote him a letter on Friday. Yesterday he rang up (he was having the day off) and said he could meet me at Clapham Junction on the way home. I caught the 12.11 and he came at 12.55. We just walked and talked for three quarters of an hour. He said, 'I agree, we need an orgy, but could it be without prejudice?' He had found he could go for a walk this afternoon. It was marvellous. We walked over Wandsworth Common in the gale. An elm had lost a huge branch and it was lying in the road. The gulls were screaming and could not make headway against the wind. My little brown hat blew off twice. It seemed a different world from 3 weeks ago when we walked there on Sunday morning.

This afternoon is really beyond words, at any rate beyond this stuttering prose. Four hours we had. We met at the Disart Arms again at 2.45 and walked a little in sunshine in Petersham Park. We just talked about ourselves and I remember we saw a blackbird and a little horse with a fluffy brown coat and E took off his hat and I ruffled his hair again after so long – so long.

After tea we walked back to Richmond Park over a high windy place with few trees. There were deer, mostly does but one fine stag holding its head high. We walked far, I don't know where. The sun shone and brilliant grey and white and silver clouds piled up and swept over the sky. A stormy yellow El Greco sunset and at last it was dusk. By a plantation with a tall pine and partridges whirring he kissed me again. I was quite overcome – like a hailstorm I remembered his kisses, their roughness and tenderness and fragrance and sweetness. We found a big tree. It was nearly dark and began to snow – a queer whistly rustle as the hard flakes fell on the dead bracken. He held me; I could just see his face. His hands on my breast were comforting and warm.

What can one say except that it was perfect? One of the best times we have had – every brick wall between us dissolved inexplicably – dissolved by pain and sorrow. This is the rose at the heart of the thorn bush, the beauty in the midst of the fire, that after such unhappiness we should have climbed to greater heights. For whatever should happen – life or death, sorrow or happiness, good or evil, I feel safe in his love. The precariousness has disappeared. Our love is secure.

Shakespeare and the Bible are the only adequate words for this day.

Wednesday 16 February

We lunched together yesterday and today and talked about where to go in Dorset and how lovely an orgy we would have. It is lovely to be with him and watch and know he wants me and loves me. I would not have believed I could have experienced such happiness. I have not felt so secure before – the feverishness and precariousness and uncertainty and fear and lack of confidence which I felt before, except when they were submerged in ecstasy, have disappeared. It isn't that I don't realize that K may fail to give him any freedom – that I don't know, and it may have to finish. It is that I have regained and somehow created a stronger faith in our love, that in spite of everything it will endure and triumph. I don't know why this should be so except perhaps that he is telling me the whole of what he feels, good or bad, happy or unhappy. Perhaps it is that I have 'reasoned with the worst that may befall' and feel I could endure. Anyway, I have (now) a new security which makes our happiness all the sweeter. But –

> 'The slow days pass with heavy feet
> I count the hours until we meet
> Until my skin beneath your hand
> Quivers with ecstasy . . .'

Austria has surrendered to Hitler's demands. It seems that the alternative was war so perhaps she was wise to choose the inevitable and avoid the evil prelude. But things look pretty hopeless.

Wednesday 2 March

Well, the orgy is over and what an orgy. I must try to do an account before the details fade. For me it was the best yet. It makes me glow to think of it.

Friday 4 March

I am tired. I love him so much, but for the time I am satisfied physically. He said he thought he would be 'clamant' again in a fortnight and yesterday, 'You have no idea how seductive you are,' but just now we are happy being together and talking. It is so sweet. He had said when you are utterly satisfied the physical recedes and leaves your love the only conscious feeling. His lust and love have become more integrated than before. I think this is so for me too. I suppress less and realize the lust side more clearly, but this does not make my love less. It seems to increase it, oddly enough.

Saturday 5 March

I met E for coffee at Waterloo. He said K was getting better very slowly. Her heart is still weak and the Dr talks about a sea voyage. She told him her illness was due to worry and he thinks it is the effect of telling her about us. I think it may be suspense, I couldn't bear it. But she is too weak to discuss it now. I have a suspicion that the cause of her slow progress is psychological, if unconscious. An unconscious appeal to his pity – an alternative plan, since she knows the offer to have a child has failed. I haven't told him this. But the Dr can't understand her condition. This is just what one would expect. I should like Dr Malleson to see her (after being told the relevant facts).

Monday 7 March

A red-letter day. E got his promotion at last. MacIntyre told me at 12.0. We rang up Finsbury to congratulate him and found him not there. I kept the appointment hour ever wondering what had happened to him. While Dixon was talking to Harman he rang up – had a cold and a sore throat and had stayed in bed. Bruce had told him the news. E said he felt quite calm about it. I am so glad. It is official and public recognition of what I knew always, but it is satisfactory. And there is the material improvement for him. Has his and my luck begun to turn at last? If only K would rise to the occasion. I wonder if she really loves him for himself. I wish I hadn't to cope with B tomorrow. But this is good news.

Tuesday 8 March

Lunch with E. It was nice. He brought me his letter of promotion. So sweet. Bruce said, 'I'd like to see Goldstein's face on Sat morning when he sees it.' He was pleased but quite unexcited as I expected. He offered to give me the *Oxford Dictionary* (as he intended ages ago if he got it) but I said 'No'. If he wanted to give me something I'd like *Jude*. *Jude* has a significance for us, the first book we read together.

Interview with B at 3.30. We kept almost entirely to the case till 4.45. Dinner afterwards. He wants to be just friendly – like a brother – quite accepts my attitude and agrees that I may not 'get over' E. I feel mean about him.

Wednesday 23 March

Lunched with E and gave him my Budget Statement for 1937 and account of the 15 months to 31/3/38 which I virtually finished this morning. After lunch he went to a bookshop and bought *Jude* for me to celebrate his promotion. That is lovely. There is nothing I shall like more from him. It is good in itself and a book to want. Also, I should hate anyone else to give it to me. And last Sept or on any other occasion it would have been too heart-breaking. But now, when it is in a sense, inappropriate (because the parallel is triumphantly broken), it is just perfect. He also said he would give me 2 volumes of a marvellous book on British birds, but this is too much. When I protested he said, 'You must learn to accept as well as to give,' but he mustn't give me so much. *Jude* is complete in itself and makes me utterly happy. He wrote a note to Margot to thank her for her congratulations – a nice little note which she liked. I wanted very much to tell her about us but there was no opportunity.

Sunday 17 April

Wyndham is home with acute rheumatism in his back. It is very painful to move and he was reduced to staying in bed all the time.

Thursday 21 April

We had half arranged to walk today but this morning I had a note from E saying his throat had been bad and delayed his return from Sheffield till today. We had tea from 4.55 to 6.05. It was nice.

Nevertheless, I felt a bit depressed this evening. I do so *want* a baby. I am so tired of waiting for K to get well enough even to be talked to – it seems endless. It is more than 5 months since she was last talked to. And I shall be 32 on Monday. I try to be patient and our love makes me happy but I can't afford, and the baby can't afford, this endless delay.

Tuesday 26 April

It has hardly been like our birthdays with Wyndham hardly able to move. He is said to be better but it seems even more painful for him to move. Rosa is tired and edgy, tho' she is really marvellous.

I am worried about E's tonsils. They were bad from Friday onwards and yesterday he was too feeble to come to Chancery Lane for lunch. I went to Liverpool Street and we lunched at Hills for my birthday. Today he was a little better but he sees a surgeon tomorrow to talk about having them out. K is to see a heart specialist this week. Her own doctor can hardly detect her heartbeat. I don't know what to think about her. My own desires – appetites as Plato would say – lure my mind into daydreams which conflict with the way I try to look at her. I can feel this ambivalence – conflict almost – an element in E's malaise. It is even probably a strand in her own weak health. Meanwhile I must try to be patient and to keep my mind and body whole and worthy for the child I want to give him.

B sent me some red roses and a box of strawberries for my birthday, no note. They were delivered at the office by the boy from the florist's.

Wednesday 27 April

Lunched near the Bank with E. He had seen the surgeon who sounded nice, but he said the tonsils must come out. It will take 3 weeks, one week in hospital and 2 to convalesce. It is horrid but if he will be better afterwards perhaps it is worth it. I hope he will go soon if he decides to go.

Wyndham about the same.

Friday 29 April

E took K to the heart specialist who said there was nothing wrong organically – suggested a fortnight in hospital. There is no reason why he shouldn't have his operation on Sat week. I doubt myself whether any orthodox treatment will do her any good. I think this weakness is her reaction (probably unconscious) to the triangle. I had tea with him at Waterloo and we hope to go for a walk tomorrow. If only it would get warmer – a day like those in Dorset. I want so much to comfort him and fortify him.

Wyndham is probably better – the rheumatism is shifting about, legs and arms. He moves more easily but is weary and worn out. Rosa is tired and strained and depressed today.

1938

Sunday 8 May

It seems a long time since I saw E. I thought of him on and off all yesterday morning. I couldn't concentrate on work, hadn't much to do. I left the office at 12.0, looked at the shops and had lunch. At 1.20 I rang up the hospital. I was pleased with myself for continuing so unconcerned. The girl said, 'He has had his operation and is quite all right.' After ringing off I found that I had begun to cry and was feeling very weak about the knees. I couldn't go and look at pictures as I had intended.

Tuesday 17 May

E phoned this morning. He and K are going to Eastbourne on Thursday and the doctor is coming tomorrow so he had to see me today or not at all. I met him at Richmond Station. I am getting very familiar with the route. We had from 3.0–5.0 and spent most of it in Fullers having tea. He told me about the operation. He was looking fairly fit. He is coming back on Whit Monday but K is staying a month. This means I shan't see him for 3 weeks. I envy her – so much – her opportunity. I ought not to disturb them even by writing. I must try.

Wyndham in great pain.

Thursday 19 May

I have wasted a whole evening doing a jigsaw puzzle.

Wyndham's appointment with the Specialist is for Monday (£5/5/-). He has been edgy and groaned. Rosa has marvellous patience.

Sunday 22 May

The foreign news today suggests that things are very serious – Halifax in London for the weekend, UK ambassador in Berlin called on von Ribbentrop twice yesterday. In such a situation it seems idle to be much concerned with the possibility of having a baby, or what the specialist will say about Wyndham tomorrow, or the beauty of new green beeches. All the time there is the hum or roar of aeroplanes.

Wednesday 25 May

Perhaps now I can put down something of what has happened this week. Wyndham saw the specialist (Douthwaite) on Monday and is to go to Guy's Hospital as soon as there is room. The specialist told Rosa (but not Wyndham) that Wyndham has a tumour on the spine and is seriously ill. Electrical treatment can be used to reduce the pain but there is not any hope of a cure. He may live a few months. Rosa has been marvellous and is determined to keep him cheerful. Margot and I saw Dr Warde yesterday. I wanted in particular to ask how it would develop. Apparently, if the diagnosis is correct (Dr W was not entirely convinced of this) he will lose power over his legs and become bed-ridden. Ultimately bronchial difficulty will occur. The pain should not increase considerably. The nursing will be heavy and impossible at home without two nurses. He strongly advised hospital in any case, especially for further observation and treatment. There is just the possibility of something happening or being done to improve matters.

It is strange, tho' of the 3 of us I think I find it less incredible than either of the others. Perhaps it is my habit of expecting the worst, my faculty for coping with disaster more easily than with suspense and uncertainty. To me it was almost like the last piece of a jigsaw fitting in. It is of course hardest for Rosa. My job is the business side. This evening I have been talking business with him. I find it less difficult than Margot to keep up the pretence of cheerfulness and to assume that he will be in hospital only for a short time.

An interminable time since last week.

Monday 30 May

Just the facts: on Thursday Wyndham went to Guy's, on Friday he was X-rayed and we saw him 6.0–7.0. Yesterday we saw him 2.0–4.0. He was worse, depressed, mainly as he had a disturbed night. Today a more

cheerful letter but Sister told Margot and me that he would have deep
X-rays today and it might try him. I slept only intermittently last night. I
feel obsessed by the thought of him in pain. When there is nothing urgent
to think about my thought flows back to it.

This evening I weeded bindweed for three quarters of an hour.
Gardening and music are the two things that never fail to give satisfaction
however black the news.

Wednesday 1 June

A year ago today I said goodbye to E at Waterloo Junction. But I have
hardly thought of that sad occasion, tho' I have thought continually of
him today.

We went to Wyndham this afternoon (I had my lunchtime from 2.45–
4.10). He was much more cheerful, tho' rather hot. He looked better. He
had had a lumbar puncture, which is a hole on the back of his neck
through which they inject something that shows up in an X-ray
photograph. He is to have deep heat therapy now.

Wednesday 8 June

Warmer but close and thundery. I got the breakfast for Rosa and Margot
when they came home from church and caught the 8.10. I worked from 9.0
to 2.40 stopping only for a glass of water and a bun and to talk to E on the
phone. Then I went to Guy's to see Wyndham. He seemed cheerful and I
suspect they are giving him morphia at night.

Lunched with E yesterday. K is very little improved. But I spent most of
the time telling him about Wyndham. I am having dinner with him
tomorrow.

Dr Warde called on Friday and said the diagnosis had been confirmed by
the new X-rays which showed that the disease had developed considerably
since the first X-ray had been taken. They can't do anything at all. He
wanted to know if we wished to leave him at Guy's. We have decided it is
the best thing to do – in fact, the only thing.

Sunday 19 June

A full, tiring week. First, Wyndham: on Monday we had a scare – we almost expected him to die quickly but on Wed he seemed slightly better, tho' tired, and on Friday a better report. On Sat a letter from Uncle Percy* who had seen the Sister. She said they hoped to arrest the growth. We were immensely cheered by this because it is the first glimmer of possibility from the medical side that we would not just go steadily downhill. Today he seemed better. He has no appetite, tho', and he is still having morphia.

E and I have had a good week, tho' I didn't see him on Wed or Thurs. We had a short, rather disturbed dinner on Monday before I hurried home. Yesterday we had a lovely time. It was a fine morning and I wore my Tyrolese frock which opens down the front. We caught the 12.27 to Bayford (which is where we returned from our last walk in May of last year). We soon found a footpath which led into a field of buttercups with trees heavy with leaf standing around. We lounged by its gate (through which was a bean field) for an hour playing and loving and bickering. Finally we walked on to look for a hidden place to fuck. We found a wood but it had mosquitoes and we went on. He left his penknife and I insisted on going back for it. We continued on the path to a field in which was a splendid piebald stallion. It was a beautiful thing, its brown and fawn markings on pure white were like a contour map. But it was very frisky and came dashing after us so that I was afraid.

We got nearly to Hoddesdon and went to the Green Man for tea. Finally we didn't have it at the inn but at a cottage by chance, but it was an excellent tea provided by a very fat woman with a red face who wore a hat. We walked two miles along a green road, once part of Ermine Street. It was bordered with hedges with tall buttercups and honeysuckle and wild roses. We tried to finish our fuck in a crevice under an oak but we were interrupted so we didn't finish properly. Still, it didn't matter – we had a sweet afternoon. There was as much gaiety, fire and spontaneity in our loving as I have ever felt. I am so proud that my body can give him pleasure in addition to the sparks our minds can strike together. I suppose Hip is right when she says we have a glamour in our stolen

* Paternal uncle.

meetings which would fade if we lived together. Anyway, to me it is as sweet as four years ago.

The old Roman road, Hoddesdon

Sunday 3 July

It is a fortnight since I noted anything and much has happened since.

Wyndham seems better than he was a month ago, more awake mentally (last night he was restless because they gave him no morphia at all). He comes out of Guy's this week till the end of August when he is to have another course of ray therapy. We have to find somewhere to take him for the interval.

K came home from Eastbourne last Sunday better, but still feeble. Since then she has gone back. We are rather concerned about her. If after all the care she has had in the last 6 months she is no better it seems hopeless. She weighs only 7 stone 9lbs (as against 8/11) and has lost weight since she came back. We have only lunched together this week. It is so wearisome. I ache to start a child. It must be this month or not for 12 months. I suppose another year won't make any difference but I don't see how the desire can continue unfulfilled for so long without either abating or doing harm.

Sunday 10 July

On Wed Wyndham left Guy's and went to Hillside Nursing Home in Purley. He seems definitely better. He is sleeping well and eating more with better appetite. The pain in his back is gone and the chest restriction much less. He had more, tho' still very slight, feeling in his legs. He likes to be in Purley and it is very convenient for us to see him.

I have been rather dismal about E and me. This weekend I ought to have started a baby if at all, and what is he doing? He had a day's leave yesterday to make a lily pond in his garden and has probably continued gardening today. Meanwhile K is no better, in fact she is worse. Her mother gets more and more trying and K can stand the strain less and less. She is much worse than when she returned from Eastbourne.

Monday 1 August

On Sat afternoon after lunching with E I went to Croydon library and then to see Wyndham. I was much more cheerful having argued with myself that my gloom was simply due to expecting too much. I told me firmly: If you don't expect anything you can't be disappointed. Hope unfounded leads to despair. So I was quite resigned to a weekend with nothing interesting. After breakfast yesterday morning the phone rang. I almost didn't answer it. I didn't in the least expect E. He said, 'I've been thinking we might do a midnight walk tonight' – just the appointment – Charing Cross 11.15. I had some difficulty with Rosa and Aunty Paul* who thought me mad and were nervous. I tried to have a restful day. It was very hot – a humid, heavy heat. Spent most of the day in the garden doing little and tried to sleep for an hour after supper but I was too excited.

At Charing Cross E was waiting. I was relieved to see him. We tube-ed to Euston and walked to St Pancras from there. It was oppressively hot at

---

* Rosa's sister.

midnight. We caught the 12.05 Manchester train to St Albans. It was fairly full of people going north, trying to sleep and keep cool. We were glad to get out and find the air at St Albans fresher. We walked a long way through the town. The yellow sodium lights made it brilliant and I was entertained by their effect on colours. My red jersey looked mustard – also by the contrast with the green and red traffic lights, the white police lights and the bluish lights in the market place. E scolded me into being quiet and we took the road to Dunstable and Watling Street.

Once past a huge lit-up garage there were no lights except the headlights of passing cars. There was little wind and it was warm. The only birds were owls. The road descended to cross a small river. The hollow was filled with cool white mist which looked like cotton wool. We leaned over the bridge and looked at the stars reflected in the water. We turned left off the main road to a winding side road leading to Hemel Hempstead. A little way along it was a dry ploughed field. Here, under a larch we rested for perhaps an hour. Perhaps I slept a little. E was warm and I lay close to him with his arm around me. I turned towards him and he kissed me. I felt dissolved to nothing, melted into one by our love and the beauty of the night. I cried and we had a sandwich and walked on. At 3.0 E said he could see the first streaks of dawn. At 3.20 I was able to see the time by my watch. Soon after I looked back and said, 'It is the day.' The phrase stirred a memory of Shakespeare which we chased for 10 mins till he tracked it down in the wedding night dialogue of Romeo and Juliet – in great triumph. The grass suddenly grew wet with dew so we rested next on a heap of fine stones by the road. I slept and awoke to find clear daylight and the NE pink. E said with nice outspokenness, 'Are you ready for a fuck?' We loved a little and decided the road was not private enough even at 5.15am. So we went further and passed a gypsy caravan. We climbed a gate and began to fuck with resolution. A minute's exquisite agony and then exquisite pleasure. Two men out shooting and we had to stop and move out of sight of the road. The second attempt we did in the orthodox way and quickly. Sweet and fierce. We walked to Hemel Hempstead from 5.45–7.20, past the old canal. I slept in the train. Breakfast at Tottenham Court Rd Corner House – grapefruit, fish, toast, coffee. Excellent.

Wednesday 3 August

Last night dinner with B at the Strand Palace. He was very sweet to me and as generous as usual. 'Our last social meeting' according to him. He will dramatize himself but there is no harm in it perhaps. He is like a little boy. I wish I could give him what he wants – anything short of complete love won't do. I feel so mean about him. I have never failed more utterly in a relationship with anyone. Yet it is beyond my power to love him. At lunch with E today it was quite clear to me. Quite a dull lunch – we were both hot and stuffy – and yet I was never more sure I loved him and would love him exclusively. It is in the minor moods – dull, weary, indifferent, boring – that I am most certain. There is no intoxication, no ecstasy, yet always that harmony, at-one-ment.

Thursday 18 August

This new book will not start off with a flourish, rather with a misgiving, a heavy, ominous wonder about what the next six months will show.

I did not see E today. K had an appointment at 12.0 to see the heart specialist at Guy's. I felt dismal on Monday night but better on Tuesday and yesterday mainly, I think, because E talked about her. Her weight is down to 7 stone 3lbs and she says she feels no better than when she went into the hospital. Margot thinks it is psychological in origin.

Sunday 28 August

When I had coffee with E I was cheerful, even unusually so, partly because I still hoped I might have a baby from the midnight walk (I haven't), partly because I did like him so. But he said K won't go away without him, which reduces the possibility of our going away to nil. When I tell him how much I want a baby he doesn't say a word – but just looks as if he wishes I were at the bottom of the sea – well, perhaps not me, but the baby anyway.

1938

Monday 29 August

E was heavy at lunch. I wondered what was filling his mind and was not surprised to find it was the thought of war. Gardening yesterday he kept thinking it wouldn't be finished. Still, he made me a little cross by looking at personal matters (*my* personal matters) from a height, pointing out how small and unimportant they were at such a time. It is appalling to consider. I dreamed of war last night.

Called to see Wyndham (who was in good form), who thought it wouldn't come to anything.

Sunday 4 September

K went to Eastbourne for a week by herself on Friday morning so we have had 2 lovely evenings.

On Friday we decided to go to the Lyric at once to see Charles Morgan's play, *The Flashing Stream*, which had begun the night before. We easily got into the gallery. It was very good, one of the best modern plays we have seen together. It is a good subject – single-mindedness (in this case a passion for mathematics). The love story is good and so satisfactory. Nothing is better than collaborating at work as well as being in love. It is a good play because its concrete plot (the experiments on the torpedo) is adequate and yet (like the Wells film *Things to Come*) it transcends its framework. E was just the person to see it with.

Yesterday afternoon we fed at the Corner House before going to see Clifford Odets' *Golden Boy*. E had had too much wine but the play was easy. The theme is good, a study of values, mainly on their conflict in the mind of a boy who took up boxing for money and rejected music. Here again the play goes further than the plot.

Marjorie Rogers* has missed promotion. I am sorry. I wish the women were a better lot. Now and then I feel rather bad about it. Ought I to have tried hard just on principle because not bothering is letting other women down? If I were a man it wouldn't matter at all.

---

* A fellow woman tax inspector.

Sunday 18 September

A gap filled with a week's holiday at Herne Bay in the middle – Wed 7/9–
Wed 14/9. But the main thing has been the international situation over
Czecho-Slovakia which has made us listen in to the news and read the
papers anxiously every morning to see whether war appears to be nearer or
further. I have dreamed over and over again of air aids. Everyone is talking
about Hitler. Whitehall and Downing St have been packed each time we
have bus-ed from Victoria to Charing Cross. Aunty Paul and Rosa have
been to an intercession service in Westminster Abbey. Chamberlain flew to
see Hitler on Thursday but no one knows what happened. All this made us
rather pre-occupied at Herne Bay.

Sunday 25 September

We have till next Saturday in peace anyway. On Friday it looked hopeless as
Chamberlain came home. It remains to see whether the Czechs accept Hitler's
ultimatum. I cannot imagine why he didn't accept Chamberlain's plan which
appears to give him the essentials. My feeling, which is the same as that of
many people, is that if we are ever to stand up to him now is the time and not
in 2 years when he wants Tanganyika. The responsibility of deciding is
appalling but is equally serious whichever way we decide. It looks as if force is
the only language a madman can understand but it is so insane of the Germans
to allow themselves to be dragged into a war they don't want.

E was coming home today. The war scare has upset him according to his
letters.

Wednesday 28 September

E telephoned and I went at 11.35 not having seen DJ. Caught the 12.09
from Clapham Junction to Sunbury. He got in at Teddington. It was
lovely to see him, very freckly. We talked and talked and talked about the
international position. We walked from Sunbury to Weybridge and back
seeing something of the river and ferried across once.

We had a scanty
picnic lunch and tea by
the ferry. Coming back
we got lost and walked
ever so far so that we
only just caught the 6.35
from Sunbury. I was
very tired but it was
good. He has too much
imagination. I love him
so much.

There is a glimmer
of hope. Chamberlain
made a good speech in
the Commons and in
the middle of it got a
message that Hitler had
invited him to Munich
to a conference with
Daladier and Mussolini.
What makes me a little
hopeful is that it is
Hitler's invitation. He
has postponed
mobilization for 24

The Weybridge ferry

hours. After seeming hopeless this morning there is just a
possibility that he will see reason.

Monday 3 October

The immediate possibility of war has passed; peace has been precariously
preserved by giving Hitler what he wanted. The relief was immense. You
could feel London breathing again. Whatever one may think of the rights
and wrongs of the dispute and of the methods of dealing with it, it is
something to live for a few more weeks or months. I lunched with E and

felt depressed after it. He was no better than last week. He is just sunk in a torpor of pessimism. It is not that I don't sympathize with him. What I can't understand is that he should be so inactive. I just felt hopeless. He is content to go on for ever as he is. Nothing is more repulsive to him than the necessity to make a decision and to act on it. His attitude to politics is just as his attitude to our own affairs. He is completely paralysed except when everything combines to produce the right conditions for him; this is as likely to happen as that I should have a baby without his help. I considered the alternative of having someone else's, but I love him so. I don't know what to do. His inertia, whether you look on it as a virtue or a vice, drives me almost crazy at times. My feelings are natural and right but at times they make me appear even to myself as a monster. They clearly are a nuisance to him, but what can I do? How can I, week after week, year after year, be patient without emotional death? I try and try for his sake to curb my feelings, or at any rate their outward expression, but I can't do it for ever.

Thursday 20 October

I have been better. We have talked about pacifism hard at lunch every day and it is worthwhile. He is making quite an effort to reach an opinion on it. Whether it will come to anything practical is doubtful. But he is not complacent.

I have agreed with Margot that she would look after the child if I die. This should make it easier for K. Margot thinks it would be impossible if K took it. It is still, of course, the last subject E wants to talk about.

Wednesday 26 October

Last Friday E said he thought it wouldn't be long before we could tackle K about a baby. I have decided to write to her first, an account of the facts from my point of view. I have got some satisfaction out of writing it (it isn't finished), but now she has neuritis in the neck!

Had an interview this morning with Madeleine Herring (beauty business). She used to be with Elizabeth Arden. She is smart and pretty and about my age. The business doesn't flourish but so far she has had an allowance of £500 pa from a man. They are still fond of each other and he is the only man for her but as she hasn't seen him for a year, things look pretty serious. I sympathized with her. A safe job is something. It must be appalling to be dependent.

Tuesday 8 November

I am investigating life assurance policies. It is a nasty job as I hate their little books but Margot and E and Elsie have been to some extent helpful and it is all in the right direction.

Sunday 20 November

I took Rosa up to town this afternoon to a concert (LSO) at the Queen's Hall. We were in the front row, just by the first violin. It was not the highest brow but we both enjoyed it – first, Overture to *Prince Igor*, short and loud but cheerful – Mendelssohn's *Midsummer Night's Dream* Introduction to Act II – Rachmaninov's Piano Concerto played by Helmann, a young willowy creature who struck me at first as affected, but he could play. He appeared, however, to be too feeble to produce such a colossal performance. Schubert's *Unfinished* (I think it was the first time I heard it properly played and not on a barrel organ or in the street or in a Lyons Corner House). Finally Tchaikovsky's Waltz from *The Sleeping Beauty* which made one want to waltz. I wanted for the first time to waltz with E. I could feel how nice it would be. It is the rhythm shared with another person, but with anyone else unthinkable – heavenly with him. There are times when I feel just as much desire to dance as I did at 15, but only with him or alone.

Sunday 27 November

Coffee with E yesterday and I gave him the draft of K's letter for observations. I have felt a shoot of dismay every time I have thought of it since. But it has to be done if we are to get on, and the sooner the better. But I shall need some determination for he just wants peace at any price and all the action will have to come from me. I wish he wanted it too and that I didn't feel as if I were badgering him into doing something hateful.

Tuesday 29 November

E has not mentioned my letter to K. He might have forgotten all about it. I do wish I could feel the same placid contentment with things as they are. I wonder whether he would be much different if there were no impediments. Of course he would give more what I want but I am not sure he would want more. It would be easier for me if I were older and less vigorous. At times I just long for him, not merely physically, but to do things with him. I try to overcome the craving. I tell myself that most people have not enjoyed the happiness I have had already, but this is no good. The more I count my blessings the more I want to repeat them. The most effective method is to remember that unless he wants it too there would in any case be no pleasure for me and he certainly can't want it much or he wouldn't go on so undisturbed day after day, week after week, month after month. There is an inertia in his nature which defeats me. I feel about as unable to break it down as the Atlantic is to wash away the granite cliffs of Cornwall. I wish so utterly at times that I shared it. My vitality is like an engine spinning its wheels in mud. I might just as well switch it off for all the progress I make, and sink resigned into the bog. But I can't. It is against my nature. I have to go on struggling so far. I imagine from this angle he and K are completely suited. At bottom it is perhaps a question of physical energy.

Sunday 4 December

8 years ago yesterday I went to Paddington 1 and saw E for the first time in the room on the 5th floor now occupied by Wild. 3/12/30 – perhaps the most promising day I have experienced, tho' I didn't know then what it would begin.

We went to the Old Vic to see *Man and Superman*. It was the last day. He

only knew that on Friday when he mentioned it casually. He didn't think
he could manage to go but before I rang for the typist yesterday morning
he rang up and said he could get there at 2.25 – he must go home first. The
play was good, most entertaining. It has plenty of life in it yet. He liked it.
I love to see him like a thing. He likes sufficiently little for me not to grow
blasé in this enjoyment. Some rather flippant discussion on Shaw's
seriousness or lack of it.

Thursday 8 December

A nice discussion about schools and teaching with E at lunch. It is such a
pity he has no outlet for his ability in this direction. Children would be
better than nothing . . . well, but wait.

Monday 26 December

I have been waiting for an opportunity to bring this up to date. Now,
while W is asleep and Margot and Rosa are out walking in the snow
I am sitting by the fire trying to fend off a cold and making the most of
the quiet.

Most important not to let slip is Friday afternoon. It was a horrid day,
cold, the snow frozen in some places, in others a dirty mess, half frozen,
half thawed. We had the afternoon (and Sat) as privilege leave and arranged
to meet at Green Park station at 1.30. We had an ABC lunch but more
leisurely and he told me about ice expanding, and light. So we went at
perhaps 2.45–3.0 to the Spanish Art Gallery to see the Greco to Goya
exhibition in aid of the Spanish Red Cross. We paid 5/- each and had an
illustrated catalogue. It was very warm and in 2 big, lofty rooms of what
was once a private house in Chesterfield Gardens. The bigger had a
gorgeous plain crimson carpet.

There were a lot of pictures, perhaps 40, and 70 of Goya's drawings of
Spain in the Peninsular War. We looked at 3 of the El Grecos – the Virgin
and St Anne, Christ with His Cross, Magdalen and the Angel – all good
but the first nicest. Then went to the Goya drawings. I was glad to come
back to the crimson-carpeted room and look again at the El Grecos.

Another view of humanity – the spiritual and mystical. Impossible to account for the fascination El Greco has for me. His universe is completely alien and, in a way, nonhuman. But he imposes belief, he takes you into the world of his creation and compels you to see and feel that it is authentic. It lives, it is not a cardboard drawing in 2 dimensions. It has depth, reality, vitality. Possibly it is as an escape from the rational hopeless world of science that El Greco's world of miracles and visions and fantastic colours and lights appeals.

Tea at the ABC and E gave me back my letter with criticisms and said I mustn't do anything until he had broken the ice. He said I must make it more objective. I was really incapable of discussing it seriously. Every time I thought of him or of the baby or of the El Grecos I wanted to cry. It was a lovely afternoon, lovely. 'Nice,' I said at Victoria. 'Very nice,' he said.

1939

Saturday 14 January

E has been having his General Inspection Thursday, Friday and today so our lunches have been a bit cut. Tuesday's was nearly all on a technical point. I took him Mrs Bond's annuity deed for comment. It was nice to see him go for it like a dog with a bone, screwing up his nose and one eye when he got a really good idea. Although he finally agreed with me, it was quite entertaining.

Tuesday 31 January

It is perhaps fortunate that it is too cold to write much tonight as what I write will be a moan. E makes me so hopeless. Since I gave him my letter to K to read about 16th Nov he has voluntarily referred to the matter once only and then when I was too tired and full of El Greco to discuss with any sense at all. I shouldn't mind so much if he gave any indication that he was in the slightest degree interested – if he said, 'I can't do anything now, or for 6 weeks,' or, 'I just don't want to do anything,' or, 'It isn't worth the unpleasantness for me,' or, 'I think we shall have a war and I'm not going to start a baby.' But he doesn't make the smallest concession; he is just hard, as hard as granite. You would think he might show a tiny bit of consideration for my weakness – he must know after reading my diary how this uncertainty gets me down. I even find myself thinking of Buckmaster – how he would despise me! 'He flatters you with chocolates' – perhaps, but it was an honest kind of flattery based on a genuine wish to give me pleasure. It is the wish and not the chocolates that would comfort me now.

Hitler made another speech last night, more moderate than might have been expected. Apparently the economic position in Germany is getting desperate.

Wednesday 15 February

I must just answer some of the questions I have asked during the last few weeks. E does realize that it matters to me. He does intend to tell K as soon as he thinks she can stand it. He opened the subject yesterday and wrote me a note last night. He feels too pulled in half to go away next week but suggests using up our leave in days. Of course, I am disappointed but if he wouldn't be happy I wouldn't, and I am comforted by his resolution to tackle the general position soon, and also by his admission that the present stage is hard on me. He is nice. When I am dismal I tend to blame him unfairly.

Sunday 19 February

I took R to the Westminster yesterday afternoon to see *The Doctor's Dilemma*. I hadn't read it or seen it before and we both enjoyed it. There is a tremendous vitality and liveliness about these early Shaws which just sweep one along and it was well done on the whole. Moreover, he does raise and discuss interesting subjects and themes at least in this play – the satire on medicine (which I expected) and the moral questions of whether to save a good artist who is a scoundrel or a good man who is not particularly gifted, a hopelessly difficult problem.

DJ is going to Holborn and we are having LI Wyn-Griffiths (who is apparently literary). I am sorry I didn't go to hear his paper on Wed to see what he is like.

I haven't seen E since Thursday. I am hoping to have tomorrow, Wed, Friday, Monday and Tuesday with him but only in single days. I wish we could go away at any rate for the weekend. It isn't just fucking that I like. It is the peace and freedom, not having to catch trains and go home and be someone quite different. Still, I see his point and it will strengthen our position with K more than if we had just deceived her to enjoy ourselves.

Sunday 26 February

On Friday we had a lovely day. There was a cold wind high up but the sun burned my face. We started very early and went to Whipsnade. We got there before 11.0 and stayed till 2.30. It is a lovely place, roomy and unspoilt with fields and woods and hills, all the top of Dunstable Downs with a fine view towards Ashridge. We both liked it and I wondered why we had not been there before.

Ashridge Woods, near the monument to the Duke of Bridgewater

We walked from Whipsnade to Tring station. It is wooded and beautiful, mostly beeches. We found a path (or rather E did – he was very clever at finding the way) through the woods which ran straight to Albury, about a mile from Tring station. We reached an obelisk to the Duke of Bridgewater and found we had 20 minutes to spare. E sat on a tree trunk and we loved a little. It was nice after so long. I was surprised as I did not think he would want to, although I had been wanting to rumple his hair for weeks.

Sunday 5 March

E said yesterday at coffee (in reply to my question) that he had about a month in his mind when he said in his note that he did not think I should have to wait long to settle the baby question, so that means, roughly, some time this month unless something more happens.

Sunday 19 March

It is 10 days since I wrote and there is so much to note. It has been an interminable and nightmarish week since last Sunday.

First, on Thursday E and I went to see Capek's last play, *The Mother*. We had dinner at Slater's and also a bottle of Barsac. The Capek was good: a fairly stated conflict between a woman (whose value is life, and life before everything) and the men, her husband and sons, who have other values – honour (the husband), knowledge and science (the doctor), communism (one twin), fascism (the other) and altitude record (the airman son).

It was a lovely evening with him, completely harmonious, lovely at the time but even lovelier in retrospect compared with what has happened since.

On Monday afternoon R phoned me and said W was worse. It was his neck which had somehow jerked and hurt excruciatingly. The spasm passed and was succeeded by a permanent burning ache. M and I had to sit up with him Monday and Tuesday nights. Monday night was awful. He didn't get more than 2 minutes sleep on end and that in spite of having a morphia injection, a full dose of nepenthe, 2 aspirins, 2 cachets, a huge dose, bromide and some pink things. On Tuesday morning he was half crazy with pain. Then happened one of the gleams of light which just now and then make one feel the possibilities of humanity. R came in and spoke to him. He collected himself and smiled at her. I was tired after a broken night and it just finished me. It was the perfection of married love – infinite and miraculous. From that moment he was a little better. Without any more drugs he slept for 2 hours on Tuesday morning. He had nepenthe at 1.0 in the night and slept fairly peacefully and was quite lucid. On Wednesday I stayed home in the morning and R and I took him to Guy's.

He had X-rays on Thursday and a quarter of an hour's deep ray treatment on Friday. Today when we saw him he seemed a little better and said the intervals between the pain were getting longer. It is another growth, apparently, on his neck. One can't look ahead but the treatment was marvellously successful on his back so we are all hoping. But it was awful to see him in such pain and he can't move his head without agony even now.

That has been one side of the nightmare. The other is more far-reaching. Since last Sunday Hitler has invaded and annexed Czecho-Slovakia and sent an economic ultimatum to Rumania. Chamberlain made a strong (but slow) speech on Friday night condemning the German action. Everyone seems to realize the value of German promises now. Daladier has been given dictatorial power in France. It seems to be merely a question of where an attempt is to be made to stop Hitler. Unless he comes to his senses war seems to be inevitable. Things move so rapidly – Bohemia and Moravia one day, Slovakia the next. It is impossible to look more than an hour or two ahead. It seems incredible that he should precipitate the whole of Europe into a war, which must be appalling for everyone.

Saturday 25 March

An eventful week. W is slightly better. The treatment appears to be producing results. The pain is less intense and lasts for a shorter time and is less frequent. He is sleeping better and beginning to take an interest in things – reads the paper and writes short notes to R.

On Wed E and I went to see Priestley's *Johnson Over Jordan*. The play was good. I liked it best of all the Priestleys. It was skilful and well constructed as usual. But it had conviction and a sense of personal urgency in it. I thought the first two acts completely successful. The unsuccessful side of life – office and appetites – was exactly shown. The last act – the values, what ultimately lasted – was for some reason much more difficult to express. His choice was good – books, cricket, a good marriage, children, friends – but although now and then he succeeded, on the whole, for me, the tension snapped. What made the play more enjoyable for me was the feeling that E was enjoying it too. Indeed, he liked the last act best. Ralph Richardson was magnificent in spite of having almost no voice.

Tuesday 4 April

I have been dismal about E. He told me on Friday that K has volunteered to do her original job at the Government Lab if war breaks out. She 'wouldn't leave him to face the music alone' – naturally. I was edgy and strung up anyway but this was the last straw. She can face a war but not me! My self-control snapped and I said more than I intended, or meant, in a way. He was cross and I cried off and on all the afternoon and evening. I am still dismal but quieter about it. On Sat it was all right between us but the most appalling thing would be for her to spoil our love and that depends on us.

Easter Monday 10 April

The international position seems worse. M had an urgent letter this morning from the London County Council about evacuation. There was a cabinet meeting at 11.0 and Parliament is to be recalled on Thursday. The tempo of disaster seems to be accelerating. The insanity of it is appalling.

Sunday 16 April

Roosevelt made an appeal for peace to Europe yesterday. It should do good but it may not turn Hitler and Mussolini from their objects. It may however influence public opinion, even in Germany and Italy. Ever since Good Friday, through the sunny days and fresh starry nights of this miraculous spring, when the leaves have burst so swiftly, I have felt the lines of de la Mare as a running background like a small clear stream: 'Look thy last on all things lovely every hour.' The knowledge that one may not see another spring – or even the autumn, which will bury these new leaves – makes one's eyes clearer, reveals their beauty more poignantly. It should always be so but it isn't. Unless one lives precariously one inevitably takes things for granted.

Monday 1 May

Yesterday I went through a downpour to see Ella at Richmond. Ella seemed more cheerful now that she has fixed to go to Pretoria next Christmas. She wants to sublet her flat furnished for a year. If I can have a baby it might suit me temporarily. It would be so lovely, tho' extravagant. A civilized place to live and so convenient for E and not too far from town. Well, there is nothing to do but wait for him, and I may wait for ever.

Thursday 4 May

The hope of a baby gets fainter. E does nothing still. And Whitsun is only 3 weeks. If M and I have to keep the family going it can only be here and if I stay here I don't see how I can have a baby. I try to cheer myself up by remembering that I have had already more than most women, or many women – a man to love and be loved by for 6 years, from a distance except for woefully short times, but I have known ecstasy and I must be thankful. Van Gogh's saying has kept running in my head since Tuesday when M read it to me – 'It is difficult to die but it is more difficult to live.'

Monday 8 May

Lunch with E. He said he had overworked gardening during the weekend. Later – no, he hadn't read my letter (which I gave him on 21st March). He had meant to but was too tired. Anything – even gardening – serves as a pretext for not doing anything. I cannot understand him. I think he treats only me in this way. It is a symptom of conflict, of course, but he should have made up his mind what is right to do by now, and once decided there is not any point in putting off the doing.

Thursday 11 May

I hate myself. I don't know what to do. I am so horrid to E. I was just beastly to him at lunch, and he was patient and dismal. I felt so desperate. I hoped we might go and look at the 2 cottages between Reading and Oxford on Sunday and I got a bus time table and they fitted well, and then this morning he had a letter from Elsie saying she was coming on Sunday. He couldn't help it. Moreover, Elsie has a miserable time and she didn't know and couldn't help it. But it seemed just the last straw. It wasn't merely the expedition in itself. It was partly just a symbol of what is always happening. We no sooner think of doing something, and that not often, then along comes an obstacle. Also, she may stay weeks and what chance is there that K can be talked to then? This may be the final hindrance to a baby this year. I suddenly felt as if I couldn't possibly go on. I couldn't face another single week of this suspense.

I don't know what to do. I suppose I want a holiday. It is the effect of the strain at home + suspense + the effort to keep going superficially. I feel a kind of moral and emotional giddiness, almost a mental dissociation. I can only cope with the misery of the suspense by burying it and being quite different on the surface. This involves me in conversations and discussions and superficial relationships with other people that are almost like dreams. I can talk and bicker and laugh almost automatically and hardly realize what effect, if any, I am producing. It doesn't matter so long as there isn't any effect, but I am afraid of complications when I sit down and try to think with my whole mind. I fluctuate wildly between knowing what I want to do and what is right to do but not being able to do it, and not caring what I do or not even noticing what I do. I have reached the point when I must resolve this uncertainty even if I ruin my hopes.

Tuesday 16 May

Today E and I have been to Moulsford to look at a cottage and it was a lovely day. The cottage was falling to bits but the village was lovely and we walked back to Cholsey station round the Downs. We had lunch at Mead Cottage which is a Guest House – an excellent lunch. There was a most unexpected glimmer of gaiety about the expedition which was strange. In the train he felt fuck-ish. I was surprised but it was lovely. He bruised my mouth. Just a few minutes – a spark as it were – but sweet. Coming back we got down to serious discussion about my letter to K.

The bridge at Moulsford

Wednesday 17 May

Lunch with E. We talked about Ouspensky and cottages and little else as the ABC was full and it was impossible to continue about my letter.

Thursday 18 May

We had lunch at Hills and got the position clearer. It now appears that K has been making an effort to be nice to him since Nov 1937 and he thinks it would be possible to arrive at a satisfactory, or fairly satisfactory, modus vivendi. In fact, it seems that he is and will be happy living with her. He doesn't want anything else. She has become a 'great part of his life'. Apparently lunches and an odd day or evening out is all he wants of me. He is certain she could not reconstruct her life without him. It seems just hopeless. The only satisfactory solution for him is her death or my death, it doesn't matter which. I feel nothing but a problem for him. But I still want a baby. I don't care if I die having it. I rather hope I would if it lived. Margot would look after it. I have altered the letter to leave out any suggestion that he feels about our love what I feel. It seems just a question of whether they can decide together, 'Well, we have each other. Poor thing, let her have a baby if that'll satisfy her.' Heavens – it would be easier to cope with vindictiveness than this subtle pacifism. Or would it?

Sunday 21 May

I feel a bit better now, sufficiently better to be able to write something down. I was worst on Friday evening and night. I didn't sleep till after 2.0. Just as I would become quieter I would get a hallucination, his voice saying, 'You could have my right hand if it were only me,' the feel of his hair under my fingers. Yesterday I felt it would be safe to have coffee with him as I hadn't any tears left. He agreed that what he wanted now was an honest quiet life with K. I suggested that therefore all his dilemma meant was whether my baby would disturb his quiet life enough to prevent him from giving it to me if, in any case, we stopped finally. He said he thought we ought to tell her and he wasn't sure that to get his quiet life would be the best thing for him in the long run. I said I wanted to make sure of the minimum – a baby – even if I lost him. It would give me something to live for. He told me I was panicky and that I might have more than the minimum – it depends on K. I was going to say, 'A fortnight more and then we part, with or without a baby,' for I felt I couldn't continue with this strain. But I didn't, since he seems definitely to want a 3-cornered discussion.

Monday 22 May

I liked E today. He had written me a little note to say he might not be able to break the ice with K yesterday and quoting from *The Flashing Stream* which I lent him on Saturday – some relevant quotations on both sides of the argument, impartially. It is so like him and I could just see into his mind so clearly. It was sweet, so oblique and illuminating, like a shaft of light through a blind. Of course, he didn't break the ice, but this time it was perhaps not procrastination.

Wednesday 24 May

E has said nothing to her yet – says he will speak at the weekend. I feel now that it will be useless, a mere emotional tangle from which none of us will be better off, but he thinks it is best.

Friday 26 May

A lovely light day, a day of gaiety and sweetness and sunshine and exhilaration. And yet it may have been our last expedition together if K makes things impossible. I would not have believed it could have been so shadowless, and yet it was. We went to Merstham, walked along the road to Gatton and through the Park. A perfect afternoon. I wore my new sandals and he jeered at them, but he said, 'There can't be many people with nicer legs than yours.'

A crowded, odd morning. Coffee with Griff and Coleridge (SKC). We talked literature. SKC has a marvellous memory and quoted stanzas of Browning and Swinburne and Omar Khayyam. WG suggested a good psychological and literary research would be Fear in Wordsworth, through his life. SKC said he had never got over Swinburne. He is related to the poet via a brother. When we got back WG gave me a review to read from the *Times* of Freud's book on Mores and promised to let me see it if he gets hold of it. From that to Egyptian history, archaeology, Maiden Castle. Then SKC took me, on the way to catch the train, to a sherry bar in

Shepherd's Market, a thrilling place through an arch, oak beams and so on. It was a pleasant interlude and he was most careful to let me catch my train. On the whole I like him.

Tuesday 30 May

He is as far off as ever, but so unhappy, wretched, trying to make himself talk to K. I felt awful, had dreadful misgivings, felt brutal. I am certain of what is best for me – for me, and to do. But ought I to try to bend others to make it possible? The only thing I can do to relieve him is to close our relationship and forgo the baby. I cannot believe that this is right, either for him or for me. But this is unbearable for both of us. I have been able to smother my thoughts in 2 ways – (1) by ironing, washing up, playing etc, (2) by remembering the line in one of the Psalms – 'Be still then and know that I am God.' It can have an hypnotic effect. I loved him more than ever today.

Wednesday 31 May

So no further. He will not agree to my having a child without telling K even if I do not see him again. He seems certain that discussion and truth between all 3 is the only right thing but he cannot make himself take the first step. I believe he will, but when? I don't know how long he would have been content to go on as we were in 1936 or 1938. There is no more I can do but wait passively with as little worrying as I can manage. 'Be still then . . .'

Maybe if he fails I will adopt a child but this would be second best, far behind my own.

Friday 2 June

Still no further in our way. But I feel comforted by the fact that E will not accept my suggestion to give me a child and 'wash his hands of me'. He thinks it possible to do more than this in time. He has had to bend himself up. I have had a poem running in my mind since lunchtime, in and out. I have written down something. It is not good but it is true. If I could but express it. It is for him but it is about me. It began when he said that he agreed that our meeting is as Ouspensky's best type but also that it usually led to tragedy. This he was trying to avoid. Later what moved him most strongly to give me a child was that I should not be wasted. I must try to be patient and let him go on as he can at his own pace. It is resolved, I believe; he says he waits only for courage. I shall give him my poem in spite of its inadequacy.

Sunday 4 June

Yesterday I gave E my poem; not good, but it gave me some satisfaction to have got anything down. He was nice. He said, 'Just for a minute the wall was melted,' (the emotional barrier which the thought of K produces in his mind – it blocks his spontaneous feeling for me). Perhaps he has spoken to her by now. But what can I do when things are so hopeless at home? The way is dark and long.

Tuesday 13 June

Still E has done nothing towards discussion with K – 'no opportunity' during the weekend. Nevertheless I still think he has made up his mind to do so and, having resolved, makes him easier to get in touch with. He has even recovered some of his old bickering and gaiety. We may have a day off on Friday.

Friday 16 June

Today has been lovely, in spite of almost continuous rain till 4.0. We had our day and went to Reigate, walked up the hill and through the beech trees. We met four girls on horseback but no one else all the way to Box Hill Road.

My stockings got soaked from the wet grass – the path was so narrow that the grasses and sorrel just nodded water on my legs and E jeered. Along the road it continued to rain and at 1.35 we reached the Hand in Hand nearly at Box Hill. It was a most efficient re-built pub and we stayed till 3.25, first having a large and good lunch of tomato soup, roast pork and new potatoes, hot rolls, butter and cheese, cider and coffee, and then warming and drying ourselves before the fire. It looked as bad when we set out to walk to Box Hill station, with a thick Scotch mist, but before descending we loved by a green licheny beech. It was sweet to feel his hands and his lips and to ruffle his hair. I cried at the sweetness and at the pity of it – how unhappy I made him and yet I would die for him. When I had combed my hair and buttoned my mackintosh he called that the rain had ceased and the sun was coming out. There was a streak of blue sky and the land looked more beautiful than ever after the rain. We caught a train at 2 minutes to 5 and between Box Hill and Leatherhead we loved – such a waste of his precious little sperms – but still, it was sweet and I loved him utterly.

A good day in spite of the rain and E said, 'Of course,' too.

Tuesday 20 June

E kept on harping on Higher Grade (deliberately) and that is an edgy subject for me. I know I don't deserve it and shan't get it and I feel half as tho' I ought to have tried, and more if we need the money in the family. It is uncomfortable to think of. In these circumstances instead of saying nothing I gloomed to E.

Sunday 25 June

On Friday I felt desperately gloomy. I told E that if he insisted that K must know before I try to have a baby I should write to her today. Alternatively, I would try to have a baby next week and not tell her. He said he hadn't had a chance to speak to her but agreed that he had been ages. Would I not write but wait till Monday? In the end I did. Has he told her? I don't know; I doubt it. But I find the strain of these weekends of wondering impossible. Come what may I shall take a decisive step this week. It isn't as tho' we get any pleasure or satisfaction while he keeps putting it off. We don't. He is generally dismal and inhibited and doesn't want to do anything at all. If he is willing I must seize the opportunity, but I don't know what will happen at home. Well, I can just cope with one thing at a time. She is the first hurdle. If I surmount that it will be time to consider the next.

Monday 26 June

He has said nothing to K – he said he must comply with my 'hard bargain' alternative. First I felt content to snatch the chance of a baby however it came, but he looked so dismal I shan't be able to hold him to it. He says he can only talk to K on a holiday. Always something in the future.

Wednesday 28 June

I have almost made up my mind not to hold E to his promise to try to begin a baby now. We had a long discussion, the best part of 2 lunchtimes and he has promised that whatever happens, whether K is reasonable or not, whether she just crumples up even, he will give me a chance to have a baby even if he has to cut me off. It is certain that whatever she or I do or say he won't leave her – doesn't want to – but I believe he is resolved to let me have a baby somehow. So altho' the strain of waiting is intolerable there is less uncertainty and I suppose I shall do as he wishes. He was unobtrusively sweet to me today and I felt a little comforted.

WG was doing our reports today. He was nice to me – asked me if I would like a district. I would get a Special soon. He didn't see why I shouldn't get an HG if Miss Rogers could – if I didn't I must appeal etc. I hate it. I have an ambivalent attitude to the question. In a way I should be personally gratified if I could get it, and gratified as a woman. I should feel I had not let the few women down. But I hate the window dressing and discreet trumpet blowing side of most of the people who have succeeded. I am not ambitious to be like most PIs. I don't want to appeal and I think there are only two things that would make me: (a) if I need the money, (b) if I feel a sense of responsibility to the women. I can really only want one thing at a time and it is not promotion.

Thursday 6 July

E liked me on Tuesday I think, but not a word about a baby. He did not intend to speak to K at the weekend. There is nothing to do but wait with what patience I can produce. He has been quite lively.

When I got home tonight R was dismal. W was bad this morning, sick and a heart attack. Dr Warde came up this afternoon, said his heart was weakened. It is worrying as I feel R should not be alone all day. It is awful for her after the strain of these long months and the rising and falling of hopes of his recovery. M is sleeping with her tonight.

I must stop with this meagre note as I have to catch an early train. We have an appeal meeting at 10.15 and WG is taking me. I can't get up to date with the work – too many interviews.

Sunday 16 July

I have been recovering from the gloom of last week. I may perhaps be able to have a baby next time. Discussed ways and means with M this morning while we had a stroll in Marden Park and sheltered from the rain. Anyway, I still hope.

E was nice at coffee yesterday – told me about the Hoopoe swans we saw at Whipsnade. The hen wouldn't sit on 5 eggs so they removed the 2 fertile eggs to an incubator. Then the cock sat on the 3 others so they put back the 2. He hatched them and then the hen couldn't resist the babies. As he went he said, 'You're very sweet' – a little thing, but it has echoed through the weekend.

Sunday 23 July

E hopes to talk to K quietly after next weekend!!! Anyway, I have agreed not to have a baby this time but he says I may be able to next time i.e. end of August. It is surprising that he still thinks he will convert the future – 'soon', 'in about a month', 'in a day or two', 'next weekend', 'after next weekend' into 'now' – this moment.

Tuesday 8 August

Back to the office and I am so tired, partly work, partly just seeing people. First SKC. WG was on leave till Thursday. We had coffee, talked about Suffolk; he gave me my cheque (which I needed to prevent my season ticket £6/5- from overdrawing me); he kissed me carelessly; this afternoon he brought me a cup of tea and suggested a taxi as it was raining; in the taxi I said he must not be flirtatious; I don't know whether he is really hard-boiled or sensitive and this makes me hesitate how to treat him. It is obviously nothing but the most casual of past times with which he embroiders our technical chatter, casual for him and casual for me except that even so little stimulates me to want E and this makes me begin to feel unsettled and discontented and dissatisfied again, without the remotest chance of E wanting anything, even a day's leave.

Thursday 10 August

WG did me good probably without knowing it. He is the most impersonally stimulating person I have met. He can infect one with interest and make one cut through the hedge of egotism and look abroad at other things and other people as can no one else I know. Today he lent me a book about Tibet – physical and spiritual. He was interested in Suffolk and looked at my cards. He liked the devil I sent him from Mildenhall and showed it to a friend interested in music as it was playing a queer kind of organ. He must have talked for 2 hours altogether and it did me good.

Thursday 17 August

I am better than I was. Tuesday lunch was the turning point. E and I went to Lewis bookshop to get intelligence tests for David.* I felt just blocked, like an experiment that went wrong. In the evening I went to see Elsie and let off some steam. I felt a bit better and E said he knew it. He was nice. Today we talked shop and about David and I could take an interest in him without just wanting my own.

SKC has taken to calling me 'Gertrude' because he had an aunt called Gertrude 'who used to nag me when I was young'. Awful! But he 'has kept off the grass'. He betted me 4 half crowns to one that I would get HG before 31/8/41.

* E's nephew.

Monday 21 August

A bad weekend although the weather was perfect. On Saturday I cried and cried and yesterday I paid for it with a headache, but was less acutely depressed – numb. I suppose these outbursts are a kind of safety valve but they are physically bad and are getting too frequent, averaging once a week. Today I felt less bad, but for how long? I feel quite helpless to control the fluctuations, no more controllable than a cold in the head. I can feel my depression growing and have learnt how it will develop but I haven't yet managed with my effort alone to avert an attack. Only a complete diversion or a word or two from E can affect it.

The political situation is appalling. Everyone seems to think that this will be the critical week. The Germans seem to be reaching a position from which they can't retreat. The thunderstorms which burst this afternoon seemed a foretaste – the crash following the foreboding steamy calm.

Tuesday 22 August

A fine day after a terrific thunderstorm yesterday afternoon (seven people killed in a park at Ilford). Lighter and cooler and drier.

The main preoccupation has been the international situation, the announcement of a mutual non-aggression pact between Germany and Russia which came as a bombshell this morning. Everyone talking about it – we had morning coffee on the strength of it. Well, the only thing to do is to wait. It looks black on the face of it but who knows what will happen. I wish the parents were out of Purley but it is difficult to cope with W.

E was full of the situation. I don't know what to do. I am inclined to go ahead and insist but he is quite out of tune.

Wednesday 23 August

I have bought two new books for diaries for 1 shilling – an act of faith for it seems improbable to the reason that I shall fill them.

Everyone is still bewildered and there is no definite news except that war preparations proceed. Tonight a broadcast about covering lights and blackouts. But the only thing certain seems to be that no one knows what will happen. London is like an ant-heap when one occasionally disturbs it with a fork.

E was quite obsessed at lunch. He said he was full of apprehension and no good in a crisis. I, on the other hand, if not absolutely better, am, at least relatively to other people, less gloomy. I feel that war removes my personal responsibility, tho' I still feel the importance of my job of having a baby. I suggested, anyway, trying on Sunday, but he said he didn't feel he could possibly. I said that this was a final refusal and of course I could not gainsay such an excuse. He said it was not often that he could plead it. I phoned this afternoon to ask him if he would go for a walk tomorrow. He said perhaps on Friday so I hastily stopped a letter making an appointment for Friday afternoon.

Friday 25 August

I have been happy today. We have had today, perhaps the last day we shall ever have, and yet in spite of this it was lovely. Warm and close and thundery, tho' the sun almost shone at times and no rain till 4.30. We went to Shepperton. He got into my carriage somewhere beyond Norbiton, when I was getting doubtful whether he would come, looking tired and worn and worried. He said he felt awful, hadn't slept since 4.0. Upset inside and still suffering from wind. We walked gloomily down to the river and along the bank to about a quarter mile from Chertsey Bridge. We sat on the bank for over an hour and rested and I rubbed him so that the wind got better till at 1.0 he said he would have something to eat. We went to Chertsey and I made him have a whisky while I had a sherry and we went to the only possible place to eat, a little shop with homemade cake where we had Welsh rarebit and China tea. We walked back to the river and loitered along the bank and sat watching the moorhens and ducks and swans flying and little fish making rings on the water. In midstream the circles looked like straight lines coming and going. He enjoyed them and watched till it began to rain. We caught a bus back to Shepperton. He said it was a good idea and that he did feel better for it.

He rang up from Shepperton to Finsbury and heard that we had instructions to duplicate records this morning. Things still look bad, tho' I feel that it is not inevitable. Anyway, it seems that nothing will happen till Sunday. Reen phoned and has offered to have R and W at Maidenhead. Mrs Parsons has just wired (11.25pm) that she can have them too, so we are getting some plans going. M had to report this morning but came home at 9.0 tonight.

Monday 28 August

I must note a little of what is happening, altho' it is midnight. I had half a day's leave to get the parents off to Maidenhead this afternoon. R was in hectic despair – kept envying Mrs Rideout who is unconscious in Purley Hospital. She has 'worked till she dropped', R says. M went down this evening and phoned me at 7.20 to say they were settling down well and had arrived at 4.55. I am sure it is a sensible thing to do, although I wondered and wondered. It is still impossible to follow what is happening but it looks far from hopeful. Still, it does seem clear that Hitler has failed to shake the UK and France and Poland at all, and that the German-Russian pact is not without its disadvantages. Spain and Japan have definitely changed direction. Italy is doubtful and perhaps holds the key to the future.

E has moved K a little. Anyway, she is thinking about taking her mother away, possibly to Bexington, if I ask Mrs Parsons not to mention my name! He is standing up to the situation well, altho' he doesn't expect to. He has been better since Friday, partly because he has been busy getting Finsbury 2 to duplicate the records. E phoned me yesterday morning and today we lunched at Waterloo. He asked me to arrange for M to let him know if anything happened to me and he promised that I should be told if he were hurt. I do hope if war comes it won't begin till Osborne is back, then E won't have to be there. I can feel that he likes to see me and that I somehow give him confidence, probably just because he can tell me how dithery he feels. Even this little comforts me. Before he went back today he suddenly kissed my fingers, a small gesture but so much from him. I never remember him doing such a thing before. I love him too much, too much for my peace.

Saturday 16 September

It is nearly a fortnight since I wrote anything so I shall stop for ever if I don't start now. The inevitable happened. On 1st September Hitler invaded Poland and on 3rd September England and France declared war on Germany. Since then the Germans have got nearly half way across Poland, tho' Warsaw has not yet fallen. England has begun the blockade of Germany, raided Kiel, dropped leaflets over Germany and sent a force to France. France has got 12 miles inside Germany and is attacking the Siegfried Line. Up to now we have had no serious air raids but we carry gas masks everywhere. We have evacuated the big cities of children, mothers, cripples etc and there is complete blackout and nearly all buildings are sandbagged. The evacuees are trickling back, but when Poland has been coped with it will be our turn. Hitler is not at the moment concentrating on the west. We have had warnings – on the morning of the 6th from 6.50 am – 9.0. It was a perfect morning, dew and sunshine and blue sky. We had a leisurely breakfast and then watched the RAF planes coming and going and counted the balloons (I counted 175 without turning my head from the kitchen door).

We have been very unsettled. I slept at home on the 28th August alone but since then I haven't been here alone at night. This meant that M or Elsie stayed here or I had to go somewhere else. Twice I have stayed in Kilburn with the Robertsons (in M's office). Very Scots, but pleasant and intelligent. Twice in the week and for each weekend we have been to Burchetts Green to see the parents. It is rather a squash especially when King comes too as he did last weekend. R was in poor spirits and found it difficult to see ahead. She gets on well with Reen but it is an uprooting and W has not been too well. It is a difficult task for her but as there are said to be eight guns at Kenley it is better for them to be away. I feel a little guilty at enjoying the freedom, such as it is, but we do our best to see them.

E was quite knocked over emotionally by the situation and could think of nothing but the war. This week we have lunched together every day and he has improved. I think he will let me have a baby and he may go away with K and her mother for a fortnight next week, and he hopes to tackle K (again, but perhaps he will – anyway, I can't start for a month or so). He thinks the war will make it easier for me to have it.

SKC and I get on well on a clear understanding. He is determined not to like me more.

Monday 18 September

A good weekend at Burchetts Green – marvellous weather. R was a little better in spirits and I had the good notion of buying her 6 bottles of stout. M and I went to the Crown for them on Saturday evening and took Susan.* Rather a nice little pub – there was a prize Alsatian in it. Yesterday was an oasis of peace – blue sky, hot sun, fresh breeze from the north. I took R for a walk to Hurley in the morning.

The riverside at Hurley

* Their dog, sometimes referred to as 'S'.

S had a wild scamper. In the afternoon M and I basked in the sun and I read Edward Thompson or watched white clouds floating rapidly across the blue. At 4.0 Mrs Wrigley came and said Russia had invaded Poland, and shattered the tiny, perfect, bubble of peace which the beauty of the day and the remoteness of the place had created in my mind.

After tea W sat in a chair in the garden and was very pleased to have achieved it. R was jubilant. M and I realized how much difference a little thing can make.

Wednesday 20 September

Lunched with E yesterday, and wasn't too bad considering whether I would ever see him again. He gave me his address and told me to write to the PO if I intended to write, which he said was just as I liked. It was a perfect day, sunny and fresh.

Lunched with SKC at the Lincoln on ham roll and shandy and he kissed me again this afternoon. One of the things I like about him is that there is no pretence. In many ways his 'mask' is quite transparent and I feel his mind is like a child's. He says he would like to write and does write verse but is too lazy to do much as his living doesn't depend on it.

Friday 29 September

A little less cold. Bad news, tho' one might have expected it. Russia made a military alliance with Hitler and they are jointly demanding peace and immunity from interference. If not . . .

I have been neglecting the lovely things of life which are the more poignantly moving now when one lives each day as tho' one's last. Every night this week the moon has been brilliant and the light has revealed the hills utterly peaceful. No human rival light to spoil its beauty. Close to it no star could shine except Jupiter, which rivals it. I sat by the dining room window watching its tranquil loveliness – serene above a junkety sky, while the gram played 'Jesu Joy of Man's Desiring', Mozart's 'Batti, Batti' and the *Figaro* Overture. A tiny oasis of beauty which by its contrast with the rest of the day's turmoil – talk, worry, fear, regret – seemed miraculous.

Monday 2 October

The weekend was not too bad psychologically. W was weak. R was difficult to start with and she was disappointed we had not come down on Friday night, but thawed as time went on. Yesterday morning I took her for a walk towards Marlow via Pinkneys Green. It was blowing hard but was fine and sunny and warm out of the wind. We basked for 10 minutes.

Listened to Churchill last night and was quite impressed, tho' not so much as I expected. He has a quiet confidence and can joke enough but not too much. Very well delivered.

Sunday 8 October

On Friday E returned to the office. It was lovely to have a meagre lunch with him at Lyons. I was so happy to see him – I didn't know how I wanted it. He hadn't told K, but I expected that. It didn't spoil the happiness of seeing each other. He said, 'Thank you for being nice to me.'

Tuesday 10 October

A lovely sunny day today. At coffee WG told me to take some leave, so I have applied for Wednesday, Thursday, Friday and Monday to Friday next week with the agreement that I may not take all of next week. At lunch I told E and said perhaps he could take an odd day or two. He said in reply that he had heard from his uncle (Chichester) who regretted that in his short holiday he had not been able to go to Chichester, so that is that! I wish he would say 'no' point blank rather than leave me to infer. Perhaps I can discuss with K next week.

Friday 13 October

The flavour of today was unobtrusively happy, derived of course from lunching with E and 2 things that he said – first, that he may after all have a day next week to walk (either Tuesday or Thursday), secondly,

'Thank you for coming up to lunch' – which made the way from
Bank to Charing Cross glow warmly as I walked by myself along
the grey streets.

It was a sunny morning, tho' now the rain is drumming on the window.
I have been lucky to have 3 golden warm mornings for my leave. An hour
and a quarter for lunch with E, then I walked slowly to Charing Cross
looking at shops and buildings, stopping at St Paul's to walk round it. I
cannot love it but it never seemed more fitting to the city. It has some fine
wrought iron gates. It was strange to walk through the centre of London
wondering how long it would be standing and I with eyes to see.

Tuesday 31 October

It has been bitterly cold ever since last week. M went to Lychside but I
stayed with S, and Elsie came for the weekend. I had coffee with E on
Saturday. M came home last night much concerned about the parents and
certain that whatever they did they could not stop at Lychside. R phoned
this evening and said W was a bit stronger and she seemed livelier.

At lunch yesterday and today E was full of Clive Bell's *Civilization*
which he had just read and disagreed with. Quite like our discussions of 7
and 8 years ago. I like him when he is moved about an abstract. He is so
sober normally. He hasn't let me post K's letter of 25.10 yet. A conversation
with WG yesterday about a Schedule E woman who had a child because
she wanted it and wanted to claim housekeeping. I gathered that he would
be quite sympathetic.

Wednesday 1 November

At lunch E said, a definite conclusion by the weekend – the same tale, as
I'm afraid I pointed out. I couldn't prevent myself from asking him, 'Do
you not want a baby too?' and his immediate and serious 'Yes' comforted
me. Even more in a way than his 'You are very sweet' in the cold rain on
Saturday before I ran off to Cannon Street. I want so much to begin in
December. Perhaps we will be able to.

We are to have a quarter of a pound of butter and bacon per week when rationing begins next month. This in a BBC speech by Morrison. Not so bad as rumours which have been as small as 2oz of butter. We can manage.

Tuesday 7 November

W is much worse. At the weekend we decided he must have a nurse as R could not manage him. He is heavy to lift and too weak to help himself. He disturbed us all on Sunday night. He is not in active pain but it is difficult to make him comfortable. I feel that it is hopeless and that to live is a burden to him so the sooner he dies the better for him and R. They are arranging to come home on Thursday. I do so pray I may die quickly.

Sunday 26 November

I have postponed writing anything so long, in the hope of catching up, that I shall never resume if I don't try to.

Briefly, the parents returned home on the 9th and W died just before 9 am on Monday 13th November. M and I stayed home five days and arranged the funeral, the flowers, the registration and the relations. R was very good but stunned and empty and blank. Aunty Paul came up to stay on Thursday 16th and helped to fill the empty days. R threw herself into getting the house in order and completing the blackout. M and I were terribly tired at the end of the week.

Wednesday 6 December

Only 4 weeks tomorrow since the parents came home. It seems another world.

Kathleen's mother had a stroke a week ago. At lunch yesterday E said she was going downhill and he thought he had better confirm lunch today if he could come. He didn't phone so I gather she has died or is just going to. On the whole it is as well – her death has been ahead for years and it will at any rate be behind, tho' I can't at present see that K's loneliness

without her mother is going to improve the immediate future. For the
mother and for K and for E it is the best thing.

Monday 18 December

I haven't seen E today, tho' I talked to him on the phone. WG gave me
lunch and we went to look at pictures. I like WG – he has a youthful mind,
and yet serious. He and Warmsley (who is on relief) told me I'd soon have
a Special* – E told me last week. He estimated it would be in March. This
is appalling. Without any scruples I have just kept going without putting
anything into my work beyond the necessary minimum. Nevertheless, I
dislike the prospect of having it observed and underlined and made
manifest by a Special and by being passed over. I also hate the necessity of
window dressing. It is infinitely worse than an exam, which has an element
of sport about it. On the whole, an unpleasant prospect.

* Special examination of her work, in preparation for being considered for promotion to
the Higher Grade.

1940

Wednesday 3 January

A belated entry for the New Year – but it is only a hot bath that enables me to brave the cold tonight. It has been bitter for a week – the ground hard as iron and the roads like glass with frozen snow.

Christmas passed mercifully quickly, with its associations and memories.

Back to the office on Monday. It was lovely to see E. Today we talked about genetics with special reference to my baby (which I want to start the weekend after next).

Sunday 7 January

Elsie E came up to Kingston and is still there so there was no possibility of a baby. I feel perhaps less unhappy on the whole when I see E's evident contentment with things as they are. A baby will be some compensation, and I do not consciously desire physical contact with him as I did. Perhaps I am just getting older and more inert; I don't know – I may be just as bad this spring as last year. We have hardly spoken of anything but impersonal things – politics, shop, books, music – this week.

Friday 12 January

At lunch today E guessed that there had been a preliminary raid warning because all but one of the tube gates at the Bank and Chancery Lane were closed and at 2.00 we heard faint gun firing, but still the mass air attack has not come.

E has not spoken to K but intends to during the next few days and he has said next month I may have the hard bargain if he has gone no further so I must wait again.

Yesterday McCreath asked me what I thought of the marriage bar – as Acting President. The AIT is deciding on its attitude next week as Miss Le Huquet, Miss Ellis and Miss Preston want to marry and be retained permanently, and the BIR won't exercise its discretion. I made some remarks; he dropped some interesting bits of information – e.g. the Department is not concerned with what a woman does privately so long as she does not discredit the department, but it would be inadvisable to have a baby, although she would not get sacked for that – even if the facts came out. Odd to have this without any soliciting.

Sunday 14 January

E gave me back Huxley's *After Many a Summer* at coffee yesterday and we talked about it and about politics and about Reen's reply to my message from McCreath. She sent me a long typed letter by return, expressing the militant feminist view vigorously. McCreath was grateful. I must admire her for her energy and promptitude. As I told E, I just haven't a political mind. Her letter was full of tactics and bargains and fighting. I can't get concerned over an abstract point, or not that type of abstraction.

Sunday 28 January

It has been too cold even to scribble a line in bed so I am trying to make a quick summary on Sunday afternoon in front of a fire, not very hot yet but beautiful, full of thin curling flames around a black lump of coal, all gold and orange. Outside the garden is weighted beneath the heaviest snowfall yet – perhaps 6 or 7 inches. It is the coldest weather for 46 years. All our water except the cold water in the kitchen has been frozen though we have been able, with some patience, to melt the WC, the cold water in the bathroom and the geyser. It has been a bitter winter all over Europe – almost a judgement, one might say, for the lunatic behaviour of people.

E has said nothing so far to my knowledge. I was getting almost philosophical about him, almost succeeding in giving him up as a bad job emotionally as well as intellectually – a much more difficult task – but two small things prevented me. On Thursday there was a London Centre meeting on EPT* which we thought we had better go to. He went with Osborne and I went alone. Afterwards we met in the blackout and had a long coffee and went to Waterloo. Associations perhaps! but I could not help comparing E with other people and liking him so much. The other thing was that he met his uncle (Chichester) at 3.00 yesterday so we had nearly three hours first. This was lovely – the first expedition for weeks and weeks. We went to the United Artists Exhibition at Burlington House.

WG told me on Thursday he had lunched with Pullin who said that I should get a move next batch. WG had suggested a City D district or a Somerset House specialist job, very confidential. He also said, 'Your stock stands high.' I don't attach much importance to this. He is of a sanguine temperament and needs discounting in that direction perhaps as much as DJ needed correction in the other direction. Still, it was sweet of him to say so. But in spite of myself I cannot help wondering about promotion and sometimes wishing I had taken the work more seriously. I am in a neurotic state of mind about it and SKC and E both take advantage of it to torment me. I can't help thinking now how useful the additional money would be, that I have let down the women by not trying more, that I don't earn what I get now, that I cannot make myself window-dress, that I will not appeal if I get passed over, so I suppose I shall go on for at least 6 months. Whatever happens I shall not be satisfied. The best thing I can do is to start a baby which will take my mind off it.

Saturday 3 February

At last the cold has softened and now it is raining for the first time since before Christmas. And I am better too. We had coffee today and E was better. He has had a flu cold – aching in his bones – but he seems to have thrown it off. We said little; but it was sweet to be with him and with complete understanding. He had spent some spare time yesterday making

* Excess purchase tax.

an EPT computation which he gave me to look at. I must get to the bottom of it and make him give me lessons on it.

This afternoon I went to Croydon with M. We talked about how to manage my baby and what to do with R and whether M would do the Mental Health diploma at Cambridge. All very tentative but pleasant.

Friday 9 February

Alas, my doom is upon me – a Special on Tuesday next 13th. I hate the idea of being under the microscope, like a cripple naked before the world. I feel I haven't a thing worth looking at or an account that a child couldn't do as well as I. WG is very nice – is doing his best for me and bullying me to do my best. But I fear his efforts are vain. If I could but borrow Reen's temperament for the 3 days. E has been sweet to me for 3 lunchtimes (since I knew). On Monday he announced that he intended to take K to Sussex (Horsted Keynes) for 3 or 4 days next week. I was dismal. He said he would get things settled and he didn't want to start a baby this month. Then when I heard about my Special he said he would postpone the trip till the week after in order to give me moral support. He did not know how this touched me – the only time (I think) he has ever put K off, even at all, for my sake. He said it had been such a relief to talk during *his* Special and he did as he would have wanted me to do – probably mistakenly!! Today he said he would have to 'desert me' after all as his father had had a stroke and he was going to Tamworth tomorrow morning. He was nice and did his best to cheer me up but I felt completely abandoned after lunch. It was lucky I had heaps of work to do. I haven't so far done anything about the Special – nothing WG and E have advised me to do – collect statistics, pick out 'pretty' cases etc. I suppose I must tomorrow. I hate it all. I would rather (at the moment) be passed over as too bad to make it worthwhile to give me a Special. The only good in the evil is that the sooner it is over the better, and better now than when I am having a baby. It will save the effect of my worrying. Whatever the result, I am determined not to appeal. This is hideous – hideous.

Life is like an infernal wheel which turns and turns in my mind.

Sometimes the Special is at the top and most prominent, sometimes E and my vain wants. I was right when I wanted to die at 30.

Saturday 10 February

And so – my universe has rocked again. This morning I received notice of Transfer to City 10. I would prefer to have stayed at St George's for another 12 months, secure in the sympathy of WG and SKC and knowing my work so well. But there may be compensations – an easy journey – the office is in Seething Lane just by the Tower. It will be nearer to lunch (unless E should move to the west end or the suburbs). The men there may be quite nice. WG thinks it is a compliment – the first woman inspector to squeeze into the superior City Districts! I stayed till 1.05 collecting statistics and noting cases and felt a little more resigned to Wardrop on Tuesday.

Saturday 24 February

A fortnight full of ups and downs – mainly occupied for the first week by my Special and for the second with having flu. It remained bitterly cold till last Monday but since then it has been mild with some sunshine. One felt that Spring might appear.

My Special was hideous – not perhaps quite so bad as my nightmare, but the strain of having Wardrop sitting in my room and asking me questions about any case he was looking at or on any general point from 9.30 to 5.30 was terrific. I fell asleep in the train from sheer exhaustion and then couldn't sleep at night. It was so awful to keep oneself screwed up to top pitch all the time. In himself he was quite considerate. He didn't say a thing except that he thought he'd seen a fair sample of my work. There were plenty of omissions and errors but I think not having insisted on doing the 3 months supervision damned me most. He took till Friday lunch and then took me to Bertorelli's and gave me a good lunch with wine. I had two teas, one with E who made me dismal by saying he had to go to Worcester to see his uncle, and happy by being obviously sorry about it to me. He had come back on the Tuesday night and we had lunched in

Baker St all through the Special, which was a comfort.

Reen has not been promoted. I really feel that if she is not good enough I shan't be, but I was so glad to see the end of my Special that I just want to fade into graceful obscurity as soon as I can. Anyway, the suspense will soon be over.

Yesterday on M's advice I went to Hammersmith to see the American film *The Birth of a Baby*. It is good and rubbed in by diagrams and photographs what I knew before. There was a marvellous sequence showing the actual birth. It made me want still more to have one.

Sunday 25 February

I said to R yesterday if I could afford it I should adopt a baby. She said she must leave it to me. I shall let this idea simmer for a while.

Sunday 3 March

Feeling ill and coughing I went to City 10 on Thursday afternoon in a bitter east wind and sleet. I saw John* who struck me as very earnest but not unpleasant. Nicholas went through his cases – they seemed incomprehensible, but not too many. I expect it won't be too bad after a few weeks. The office is just by Fenchurch St Station, with the Tower round the corner. The district specializes in East Indies rubber companies and Ceylon tea companies with a sprinkling of shipping and produce importers and brokers. A poky little room but quiet and not too dark.

I haven't any flicker of hope for promotion. Nicholas thought Wardrop no good when he had him. WG told me they are going far down the list. I have an idea he knows I haven't got it though he hasn't said anything.

* Her boss at her new office.

Monday 4 March

I am so tired – all day at St George's packing, saying goodbye, talking to Couzens who seems mild and agreeable. SKC helped me with packing and moved into my room at the same time. I gave JWC *Texts and Pretexts* and *Poems of Today*, the D room cigarettes, and everyone cake. I am leaving a lot but it couldn't be helped.

At lunch E said his father was being moved to Kingston on Wednesday. I told him about the baby film. He said, 'I want you to have one' – in reply to a question.

Couzens had Wardrop for a Special without result too. Ominous!

Tuesday 5 March

Today to fresh woods and pastures new, meaning City 10 and an ABC in Bishopsgate for lunch. I have done little work – something on a quicksilver company who moved its control to Switzerland; a company with farms and a brickyard near Hastings; Colonial Wharves Ltd which are at Wapping etc. John still strikes me as earnest but quite agreeable; I have seen Beament who is like an old stork, very short-sighted and deaf but pleasant; the SCO Perkin who lives at Coulsdon and has a harelip; Miss Inkpen (CA) 61, and round but cordial; Billingham (formerly Paddington). I can get to St Botolph, Bishopsgate to meet E in just over 6 minutes and so can he.

A letter waiting for me from McCreath giving me a copy of minutes of meeting on retention of women on marriage. He also said that further promotions would not be made for some time.

Wednesday 6 March

I walked from London Bridge this morning. I saw some Billingsgate porters with white overalls and queer iron hats like round double saucepans. They were almost finished but a few were carrying boxes of fish on their heads and the smell of fish hung around Eastcheap.

I dictated a few letters, one of which contained an arithmetical slip of £10 which John found. I must be careful. It is easy to make slips over easy things when you can't understand most things. He came in and talked this afternoon and Salmon introduced himself this morning. It all strikes me as very cloistered and calm. All my letters typed in less than an hour! My boxes came and I feel more at home.

Thursday 7 March

E rang me up from home this morning to cancel lunch. He could say only that his father had died. He rang me again this afternoon

A Billingsgate porter

from a box and said more. He seems to have had a stroke in the ambulance and was unconscious from then. They reached Kingston at 5.00 and he died at 9.00. The local doctor won't give a certificate without a post mortem and they will want him buried at Sheffield, so the funeral will be next Wednesday. It is the best thing for the old man but it is unfortunate that they tried to move him so late in the day.

Saturday 9 March

E can't start a baby this month. I can see at least two good reasons for waiting another month: 1) I shall have recovered more from flu; 2) I shall have settled down more at City 10. Both should improve the environment. I got the impression that he will let me next month. But, of course, one never knows what may happen in a month.

I went to St George's yesterday. It took over 30 minutes from Seething Lane. I met SKC who was very cordial but on his way to the city. It seemed familiar and homely to run up to the 5th floor for my parcel. JWC showed me some shantung blouses at Dorothy Perkins and I bought a flame-coloured one for 6/11d. Then we had tea and walked through the Park to Lancaster Gate where JWC lives. Her room is very convenient and we talked. She gave me an Eversharp propelling pencil which made me feel quite moved. This was very sweet as St George's doesn't do this kind of thing.

I felt a bit better at City 10. Miss Inkpen is rather a sweet old thing. Also I got through an EPT to the extent of deciding there wasn't any!

Good Friday, 22 March

I don't know about E. He has been quite animated this week at lunch about books and work. He says he is still nervy. He doesn't say or do anything, I am getting almost apathetic. I feel I shan't say any more about a baby and I don't suppose he will. I am inclined to wait till the beginning of June and then if the position is the same as now I just finish with him. I had too great a faith in the strength of our love.

The news is still full of our air-raid on Sylt. Everyone has boosted it to counteract the bad blow of Finland's surrender to Russia.

Sunday 31 March

On Wednesday I told E that I must try next week, if at all, this time and said no more – resolving not to mention it if he did not – trying to walk 'humbly'. On Friday he did – merely to say, 'Next week did you say? You are rigid' – Yesterday I asked him if he intended to do anything and he said he would arrange to have a day's leave. So perhaps – but even this has coloured my dreaming. On Friday night a golden dream – I put our son into his arms and we were both filled with joy.

Thursday 4 April

Today we have been walking. We did not say anything till after lunch, although it was lovely all day – somehow *en rapport*. Much more than last time we went walking – (due, I think, to my knowing with certainty that he was not interested in me physically). He is in a state of conflict – said he would want what I want but for K, but he still thinks she must be told and if possible be brought to agreement before I try to have a child; but he wants me to have one. Although we are no nearer I was happier and I enjoyed the day.

Saturday 6 April

At coffee today E said, 'I feel considerably impressed by your view – but you must wait till next time' – as if with an effort, but he meant it. He was moved; I was wrong in saying we were no nearer on Thursday – we are now, anyway. I feel (and M agrees) it is useless to talk to K now, since he has decided not to suggest a separation. That being so she is not really concerned in my child, and it is merely shifting the responsibility to consult her beforehand – putting her into an impossible position of having to judge – asking her for a blank cheque. M thinks she should be told afterwards so as to avoid the necessity of deception. What makes me rejoice is that E wants a child – I can feel the strength of the fulfilment for *him*. He said Richard was the only thing or person his father took an interest in while he was at Tamworth and this was clearly owing to the feeling that he was leaving something behind. This is what I want him to feel to some extent. But he has practically promised – if nothing happens to prevent it.

Wednesday 10 April

At lunchtime yesterday the posters flared with the German invasion of
Norway and Denmark. E had bought an *Evening News* and we read such
details as there were while we were waiting for our lunch. Denmark made
no resistance. Norway was fighting but the Germans had occupied
Trondheim, Narvik, Bergen, Stavanger, Christiansand and Oslo. Today we
have heard the naval and air force help we have given – eight German ships
sunk; two of ours and another damaged; three German ships on fire. It is
appalling – hell let loose.

Last night I called at St George's and saw SKC for half an hour – he was
very cordial. I was on the way to Queens Rd to an informal party at Miss
Le Huquet's flat – she, Preston, K Bennett, Read, Rochford, Ellis, Kelly.
To debate on the alleged prejudice against the promotion of women and
what to do about the marriage ban. There was of course a lot of scandal. I
created some interest with the move to City 10 and my Special Inspection.
They all exhorted me to appeal if, as they think, I don't get promotion. It
is thought that they have decided not to promote a woman without
looking at her. I don't know, but I don't think I can bring myself to appeal.
I quite liked them, especially Bennett and Preston and Le Huquet. But
how can they feel so strongly on these feminist topics with the world
falling about their ears?

R and I talked this evening. She disapproved of M going to a lecture
after being away for a long weekend. She is really very good but there are
difficulties; she said we weren't frank with her – I said, No – for two
reasons (a) not to make her share in my worries and unhappiness (b) not to
be dominated by her personality. I think she understood and I did not do
too badly.

Thursday 11 April

I am reading *You and Heredity* and this led to a discussion at lunch. E said
when you consider inheritance it seems impossible that it 'just happened'.
Life is like a child with a Meccano set whose father helps at a crucial point
of difficulty.

I met JWC at Marble Arch and we had tea – she said nearly everyone at St George's knew we were meeting and sent their love – which is very nice. Harris (the new SCO) said he was very sorry I had had a move. I just basked in approbation. I like JWC.

Tuesday 30 April

Yesterday we intended to try to start a baby. We went to Ashtead. It was colder and dull all day though it improved in the evening. It was a lovely, lovely walk but we did nothing, though we got nearer, and were in good understanding. We may have Thursday off to try. We couldn't have yesterday as it was our General Inspection and Cox (the IO) came in to see me.

Ashtead Common

Sunday 5 May

On Thursday we had a day's leave and went to Three Bridges – walked the old route past Worth Church, through the forest to the Cowdray Arms. It was dullish but did not rain and was not too chilly. The primroses, sorrel, anemones, birches, violets were overwhelmingly beautiful and we lunched on soup and sandwiches at the inn. After this the day went wrong. We took the Handcross road past great fantastic beeches and we couldn't get back to the forest. We had to walk all the way to Handcross up the main road 2 miles to Pease Pottage. I was so tired and dispirited that I had to have tea there which took a quarter of an hour and was very bad. We went a good route along a lane and path back to Three Bridges but we had to rush it and just caught the train. E said he had intended to try to make a baby in the afternoon. It was as much my fault as his as I had not taken my map. But it was so maddening when we have so little opportunity and the best time is short. I was dismal on Friday and yesterday – so dismal that I made it worse for him, till at coffee yesterday he suddenly adopted a new tactic and said, 'You might spare a few pitying thoughts for me. I feel completely hemmed in. You flutter like a bird in a cage – don't see anything outside it' – completely successful, since the worst element in my despair was the thought that he was more or less contented. Which shows how hopelessly selfish my love is still.

WDN confirmed my expectation that I had been passed over for HG. Ten promotions and not one woman. Though I may need the money and I suppose I should have got a kick out of it I can't feel it is of much importance. E is much more concerned than I. It is so odd – he is much more moved (apparently) about this than about our failure to get on with a baby, which seems to me supremely important. I suppose I must go and see Down to find out, if possible, what is the matter with me, but the whole subject is distasteful.

Margot was 30 yesterday. I wish she could be lucky. She is lucky in her work and in her health and looks, and heaps of things, but I wish she could be lucky in love.

1940

Sunday 19 May

A fortnight, and the most eventful fortnight of the war. Last Sunday was Whit Sunday and on the Friday before the Germans invaded Holland and Belgium. Holland resisted for a few days but the Fifth Column was appallingly successful again. Belgium, supported by Britain, was more successful, but on Friday last Antwerp and Brussels were abandoned. A German attack in the Sedan region has made a big bulge and the French have had to retire. A colossal battle, and if the Germans are successful an attack on England is likely – air – parachute – navy. One again lives a moment at a time.

E went to Seaton with K and Elsie the day before the Netherlands invasion. I saw him again last Friday and found him hopeless – quite gone to pieces. He can see no way of averting the downfall of European civilization except a miracle. I talked to him, and finally asked him whether anything I said made a difference to him. He said, 'I don't know that what you say does – but you do.'

I sent in notice of appeal against being passed over. I saw Down, who said that it was due to 'lack of firmness in management'; work average till 2 years ago since when it has been better! I have also discussed it with Le Huquet (phone), KC (phone), WG at lunch on the Friday before Whitsun, Mahon (who phoned me and told me to wear a fetching hat!), McCreath at an AIT meeting, Brennan (on the stair), John, Salmon – as well as E.

Wednesday 22 May

There is almost nothing but the war. Things were worse yesterday – the Germans have almost reached the coast – claimed to be in Abbeville at the mouth of the Somme. The Government has taken dictatorial powers; Weygand has succeeded Gamelin; the French have been incredibly unprepared! It must be unbelievable negligence or Fifth Column. Moment to moment one is amazed to be alive. E can think of nothing else and is confident of disaster. I do my best with him but it makes no difference. And if we are alive I want to try to start a baby on Friday or Saturday. He said, 'Your courage is sublime but it is just sheer obstinacy and dogged faith in life.'

I went to St George's yesterday and saw SKC. He was pessimistic but there I did produce some effect. Today I have a blister on my lip. Also saw JWC. On the whole women stand up to the strain better than men. Are we blinder or braver than the men?

Monday 27 May

Still alive, and the night is peaceful. Hawthorn clotted with white, its scent and honeysuckle filling the air. But the view in London is that the position is 'increasingly grave'.

We went to Merstham and walked by Colley Hill to Redhill on Saturday afternoon. It was heavy and thundery with a hot gusty wind. E had a bad throat. There were heaps of people there. I felt utterly hopeless and just cried and cried. E was nice. All through the weekend I felt the same plus a headache induced by crying. This morning the Secretary of the Promotions Board rang me up to ask me to complete the appeal form. Oddly enough, this seemed the last straw. E said at lunchtime he would do his best to give me a baby one day this week – but I don't feel any confidence (not about him but about the future).

Tuesday 28 May

So Hitler has scored again. King Leopold has ordered his army to cease fighting and the English and French in Belgium are almost surrounded. It has been a gloomy day, but Reynaud, Churchill and Duff Cooper have spoken with resolution. I worked hard on EPT and on a shipping concern this afternoon. We were both hopeless at lunch but E said, 'Thursday.' He had also tried to do something on my appeal.

Thursday 30 May

So – an achievement and a promise to end this book. We went to Ashtead this afternoon – a lovely sunny day with a fresh breeze – a field of sainfoin and the trees in full leaf. There in a copse of young beeches with two horses and a cow in a field a few yards away, guns sounding faintly, E did his part. Now I hope – I hope so much that it will 'take' to use his expression. So short in time and so apparently effortless; he said, 'It shows what power you have over me.' May his gift not be wasted. I feel so proud that he should think me worth the effort.

I sent off my appeal form too.

Leave is to be abolished, hours to be lengthened. So we have been just in time – I hope.

May I have wisdom and strength to succeed in this enterprise and the good fortune to live again in a free and peaceful England. To have a child will make me more anxious. If I could have only a year or two to launch our gift to mankind – the pledge of our love, our tribute to life. He was gratified. He said, 'If I am hurt and lie dying in some corner it will be a consolation to know I have done this.'

Sunday 2 June

WG rang me up yesterday and I see him tomorrow morning about my appeal. He said McCreath had seen Loach about me. WG wants to tell me what to say.

Had coffee with E yesterday. I feel no sign whatever yet – I hope I shall.

Monday 3 June

A good day to begin a new book. Perfect summer weather, sunny with a cool breeze. I wore my new cerise spotted frock which fits me well and is an attractive shape. On the way to the city I called at St George's to see WG who gave me advice in my appeal. He told me to call on McCreath but before I did I saw SKC who liked my frock and kissed me. McC told me he had mentioned me to Loach who was interested. I should get a personal hearing. I must be careful not to be feminist as the Promotions Board was sure it wasn't prejudiced, even subconsciously! WG said the AIT was disturbed about the failure to promote any women and there were three 'runners' – me, Reen and Le Huquet, but McC backed me. I wondered why, since he couldn't know anything of my work but I inferred it was because I more or less agreed with him on the marriage bar question! He told me he had been impressed 'by my common sense'. So there it is. It seems that I shall have to screw myself up to the ordeal. I met R at the library and bought a new hat for the hearing at 27/11d – appallingly extravagant, but cheap if it gives me confidence.

WG said he had never seen me looking better. Is this a hopeful sign? I don't feel anything, though I am tired. Bombs on Paris today – and on Ashdown Forest near Forest Row, and Italy is almost in against us.

Thursday 13 June

E was still dismal – 'not a ray of hope anywhere', he said. He is so determined not to be optimistic, so resolutely hopeless, that I asked him why he did not drown himself, and he smiled and admitted a 1,000 to 1 chance!

Sunday 16 June

Paris has fallen to the Germans. The French did not defend it at the last but withdrew south. It seems unbelievable – Paris to be not French – the Arc de Triomphe – Champs Elysées –Louvre – Place de la Concorde – above all, Notre Dame. The army has apparently been marvellous but it is outnumbered in men and guns and aeroplanes and tanks. With Havre gone and the railway from Cherbourg cut it is difficult to keep in touch. It looks as if Hitler will very soon be free to turn against England. At coffee yesterday I think I pumped some heart into E but last night I felt very emptied of courage myself.

Yesterday morning I went to St George's to see WG. He told me what to say on Tuesday and gave oceans of good advice. He was really very sweet.

Tuesday 18 June

France has asked Hitler for terms – what they will be Heaven knows. Britain is to continue alone. Well, there seems little to do but prepare to die or suffer. E went to church on Sunday with K. It is surprising. Her suggestion, of course.

To Mannheim's last lecture this evening in a golden blaze of sunshine. It was on the forces making for social change – detached, scientific, to a point almost of frigidity in a German-Jewish refugee. At the end he was moving – 'we are living in a dynamic time – I have not told you a single positive way to cope with things. I have merely given a method. Look at the facts and use your reason and judgement. If things move too quickly there will be upheaval and uncontrolled change, but even so ultimately reason will emerge in men's minds and they will learn and use their judgement again.' From a man with his experience such faith is exhilarating now.

The threat of invasion – death, pain – sharpens one's senses. Every blackbird running across the road, the call even of a cuckoo, the moonlight, the sunset – golden, then ruddy, then purple – the thick leaved trees, the scent of roses and honeysuckle and pinks, all have the poignancy of a farewell for ever. I cannot enjoy this marvellous summer but I have never felt and realized the beauty of the earth so much. E hates it because it accords so ill with his mood of hopelessness but I cannot help loving it. It is a pledge that life goes on – beauty, flowers whatever men do.

Wednesday 19 June

No definite news of the terms for France, but ominous rumours. There was a statement that the French fleet has left French ports.

My appeal is fixed for Friday at 4.00. I wore my new hat today – I have worn it once anyway. Worked hard, mostly on EPT. Getting straighter.

Friday 21 June

No good this time.* E will have to try again – and only yesterday I said I was still hopeful. I think it was spoiled by the screwing up for this appeal.

WG rang me up this morning and gave me a final blessing. I had a lunch at Hills with E – grilled halibut and meringue. He said he had enjoyed it more than any meal for weeks – had eaten it with appetite. John wished me luck, so did Brennan. I timed it for 4.00 exactly but took some time negotiating tangles of barbed wire to find Room 33 so that the messenger was waiting for me and just put me in a waiting room and it was perhaps 4.05 when I took a deep breath and walked in.

As I expected I faced the window, Diggines immediately opposite and nearer me, obscure, hefty and brutish. On his right Cater, who helped me as much as possible. He made faces and twinkled – I was prejudiced in his favour by John and other people. On his right I guess Bradford, rather bluff looking with bushy moustache. I didn't object to him. On Diggines' left Ritson, colourless, who said little – and on his left Loach, who I guessed was anti. I took off one glove in dead silence and D muttered something which I took to be an instruction to make my 'speech'. So I began, still taking off the other. Several murmurs of denial at my wonder whether I had sounded feminist. I didn't get stuck and I didn't forget or leave anything out. I don't think I went too fast or fidgeted or was not clear. But my hands trembled a little and my voice sounded queer to me; my mouth got very dry, so did my lips. At the end I began to pick up and I lost my nervousness completely. When they came to questions D first: 'Mr J didn't agree with you on staff questions.' I said, 'Often not, though we did not argue – we knew our attitudes were fundamentally different.' He referred to a suggestion that City 10 wasn't good experience for staff management – 'perhaps a move?' I agreed but said I had started the 3 months' supervision and was not discontented in City 10. 'What kind of accounts?' I told him, 'Rubber, tea, shipping, merchants and importers of agricultural produce, metals, gum, shellac, seed, all sorts – a few property companies, some EPT.' 'Did I work the EPT on my accounts? Any trouble?' I said, 'No, I found they took a long time but were interesting.'

* She is referring to her attempt to become pregnant.

Cater's turn next: 'Are you one of our examination entrants?' 'Year?' 'I wonder if I was on the viva board your year?' I remembered Miss Fry – so did he; 'Where are you from?' I guessed he meant what university, but I made him ask plainly. I told him, adding – 'It is a long time ago.' He said, 'You are standing up to it well.' I said, 'If I took off my hat you would see my grey hairs.' Everyone laughed. Bradford on the difference between authoritarian and democratic: – 'If you gave a clerk an order would you expect him to obey?' 'Yes.' 'Would that be authoritarian?' I said it depended how it was done. I should ask his views – adapt or adopt them and explain why not. 'Wouldn't this take a long time?' I said, 'It would depend on the clerk and on me but normally I thought it was not wasted.' Cater again – 'It would have educative value?' Loach asked whether I had taken any disciplinary action at St George's. I said I had had small difficulties. Finally D: 'Would you feel confident and have no fear in taking over a District?'

There was something pleasantly English about it. Fairly informal – they were drinking tea, lounging in chairs; a lovely room and a dignified building with double doors and big staircases and portraits on the walls; and outside the river. These were 5 highly-paid men spending their time now, when England is assailed more fiercely than ever before, listening to me, an unimportant nobody, but with the rights which every individual has to be heard. The irony, the absurdity and yet the nobility struck me at the time and even more in retrospect. I can't estimate my chances at all – D and L were definitely anti; Cater was sympathetic; B and R doubtful. I think I shall get a move soon and I am possibly not regarded as hopeless for ever.

Sunday 23 June

France has agreed to Hitler's terms, which include occupation of the western coast and north of a line from Tours to Geneva, surrender of all stores, munitions, tanks, planes, ships. Perhaps there will be civil war – the overseas have declared for Britain – De Gaulle has broadcast from London calling on all who love freedom to join him. If the French government

preserves its control (Laval as vice-premier, naturally) France in effect joins
Germany against us.

Wednesday 26 June

This morning a letter from the Board of Inland Revenue – 'have been
pleased to appoint you to act as Inspector (Higher Grade) – at £590 – £25
– £700 from 1st July 1940'. I have been rather light-headed in consequence
and have eaten and drunk too much. I rang up E and R and M and WG –
saw many of my colleagues. Had lunch at Hills, cake for tea in the office,
tea with Elsie afterwards; home at 7.30, strawberries and cream and sherry
after the news. What a day! It seems incredible – like a good joke. John says
he expected it and saw Cox last week on that assumption.

If only the war would end soon in our favour. E heard yesterday that
the French fleet was in English waters – Elsie had also heard this. We had
an air raid alarm on Monday night – 1.00 am till 3.50. Everyone seems to
expect Blitzkrieg soon but everyone seems in better spirits. It is probably
partly the confidence inspired by Churchill, partly a sense that with the
defection of the French government we have touched bottom.

Thursday 27 June

We had half a day's leave today rather against E's conscience, and went to
Ashtead. It was sunny with a strong breeze. After a cup of tea we walked
up the old path and had a picnic lunch of rolls and cheese, strawberry tarts
and cherries at the same spot as we picnicked four weeks ago today. Then
we went up a path till we saw a dingle of beeches. It was strange that E was
more quickly ready than last time, but he had harder work to come to the
point. I hope it has worked but feel doubtful. Perhaps he may try again at
the end of next week. I feel less hopeful about today, but one can't tell.

Friday 28 June

Brennan and Miss Rochford rang up today. I went to St George's to pay for the cake they had. WG hadn't gone so I talked to him for 10 minutes. He said, 'I'm going to do a thing I've never done before – kiss an Inspector (Higher Grade)' – then we went to see SKC and met him going home and he told him what he'd done – so SKC did likewise – on the stairs! WG said McCreath had insisted on my promotion! I have been lucky about this, both in the time and in the people who have helped.

Wednesday 3 July

I had a letter from Hunter this morning. It was nice of him. He referred to me as a fledgling at Croydon 2. E liked this and said it just described me – even at Paddington.

Sunday 7 July

We keep expecting air raids but it is still another Sunday and I am sitting peacefully in the garden. The main news of the week was the Navy's success in preventing the Germans and Italians from taking the French fleet. M and I went to a lecture on Thursday on how to cope with incendiary bombs. It was quite effective and after dark we went out to get a bucket of sand, which we keep with a spade in the cupboard under the stairs.

Yesterday was a strange day. R went up to town in the morning and bought a fur cape, met M for lunch and went with her to the Academy in the afternoon. E couldn't arrange to be free in the afternoon so we had to take the morning off. I met him at Purley at 9.45. We intended to go for a walk over Riddlesdown till R had gone. It rained so heavily however that we got no further than the near wood. It was queer to see him walking there, where we so often walk. We listened to the rain sitting under a beech till nearly 11.00 when I went home for an umbrella and to be sure the house was empty. It was – so we came home. I made him coffee and then we went up to our room to fuck. It is right to use the word this time for it was sweet again. He liked it and I liked it. It was lovely to feel him again, and the only drawback was that it was too short – too swiftly he said – 'It's coming already' – I do so hope and hope that it will be a baby this time – conceived with pleasure and joy in my own bed, at home. It was strange to see him in the house. We just pottered until 1.00. We both caught the 1.14 – he to Clapham, I to Victoria. I had lunch and went to the Old Vic to the last day of *The Tempest*. I was 5 minutes late and the man at the Gallery door said, 'You've just missed the storm.'

It was an interesting production. Gielgud emphasized the development of Prospero; his gradually growing tolerance and generosity till the final forgiveness of the bad people and the forswearing of magic. Peggy Ashcroft was an ideal Miranda, Lewis Casson's Gonzalez was the best I remember – a slighter Polonius. The theatre was full. Somehow the beauty of the play just suited my mood: storm and calm, disturbance and peace, height and depth. May the harvest be rich and as sweet to our hearts as the sowing.

Sunday 14 July

Another summer Sunday afternoon in the garden, another week in which we have been undisturbed. E told me that material will soon not be available to make private AR shelters so we have asked an engineer architect to come tomorrow evening to advise. So the first property I own looks like being a shelter.

Friday 19 July

No good – no good! I feared it – perhaps that was why the seed was wasted – ran away – dried up – died. E said, 'I could see from your expression as you crossed the road.' And later, 'I shouldn't mind if my son was an admiral of the fleet!'

I have made an appointment to see Dr Malleson on Tuesday to ask her if there is anything I can do about it. Douches or mechanical help such as resting or not smoking or diet.

Wednesday 24 July

We had half a day's leave and came home for 2 hours together. Just a half hour of uninterrupted fuck which was sweet – may it be fruitful this time – and tea. He looked at the garage and gave his views on converting it to an air raid shelter, looked at the garden and the *Picture Posts* and books and drank tea. M was on holiday and had gone to town with R. I told her what we planned and she managed to keep R in town in the rain till the 5.20 and then phoned to say what train they were catching. We were lucky as it would have been too wet to love out of doors.

Yesterday I went to see Dr Malleson and ask whether there was anything I could do to help. She said it was simply a question of timing and patience; there is only one egg each month and it lives only two days, which may be 6, 8 or 10 days before the beginning of the period. Very sympathetic. She examined me and said I was quite good – no need to worry about my age. I hope it will come off and that I shall be able to go to her to have it.

Monday 29 July

A lovely sunny fresh day. We both came at the same moment at 12.30 and E said we had better go to Hills and have a big lunch, so we did – grilled halibut and chips, golden roll and coffee. Nothing else he said, except as we parted – 'I shall catch the 5.37 to Ashtead.' He emerged at the station from my train which he had changed into at Epsom. We had just under two hours. He said we would go the other way, across Ashtead Common. At last we found a comparatively clear place and he cut away the brambles. I was afraid he had not completely penetrated but he tried again and it was all right. He said it was not hard work – it made a difference if I were worked up – muscular reaction – reflexes probably! We both got bitten by mosquitoes but waited 20 minutes smoking a cigarette which kept them off. I lay down and turned over as Dr Malleson had told me – and lay flat in the train except between Waddon and West Croydon when some workmen going home shared my carriage. I got home at 8.30. We have done our best and perhaps it will happen this time.

Tuesday 6 August

The man (or rather a man and a boy) came to make the air raid shelter
yesterday, they have built the east and north wall and the partition to about
5 feet and taken the window out already. R is beginning to feel a sense of
security which is ample compensation for the cost.

Sunday 1 September

A marvellous sunny Sunday again and once more I resume this in the
garden, though hardly in peace; merely in a comparatively quiet interval
between air raids.

Just a quick note of the gap between 6th August and 1st September.
From 10th–17th August M and R and I were at Porlock Weir on holiday.
On the 17th we returned to Purley and on the Sunday morning following I
went to Ivinghoe to spend a week there with Ella. On that Sunday about
1.00 Purley had its worst raid yet. I came home a week yesterday. All last
week we had air raids near or distant, long or short – usually long at night,
short in the day. We spent some hours each night in the shelter on Sunday,
Monday, Tuesday, Wednesday and Thursday nights.

On Friday night I stayed in town with Elsie and went to a concert by
the LPO conducted by Boult given by invitation of the LCC. In the
interval there was a speech by the Chairman of the LCC and by
Priestley boosting the LPO. Just as Priestley began at 9.10 the siren
went; he just carried on – I saw no one go to the shelter. The concert
was lovely. I have rarely been more moved; it was the novelty – I
haven't been to a full length concert this year. It was also the sureness
and certainty of the music, like a message of confidence in the clash of
noise and fear and nerves and confusion; the upsetting of habit and
routine and ordinary business which made up most of last week – a
message that it would pass, that evil and fear and pain were transitory
while beauty and goodness and truth were eternal and would survive all
the folly of men; that beauty was above nationalism, the beauty
expressed by Bach and Brahms and Mozart and recreated by the
instruments of men in mortal combat with their countrymen. An oasis

of beauty in a hideous week. I could almost feel my jangled nerves relaxing beneath the music.

E is having a week off – perhaps 10 days, probably not going away. He seems to be surviving the raids though with some strain. He slept little at night because he invited their neighbours to share their shelter and there wasn't room to lie down. Last Monday's efforts produced no result and last time we should have tried I was at Ivinghoe, so this month is no good; next time I hope we can try, if necessary using Elsie's new room.

Sunday 8 September

Raids every day at night but little damage that I saw or heard till yesterday. We had peace till 5.00. Then, in an hour and a half, the heaviest raid of the war on England. In the shelter with R and S I could hear machine guns as our fighters tackled the raiders. When we emerged afterwards there was a huge cloud of smoke north east along the Thames estuary and as dusk fell a crimson redder than the sunset lit the sky. It was focused in three huge fires which we later heard were the Surrey docks, and other property in the crowded East End. The blaze was impressive and frightening – the biggest I have seen since the Crystal Palace fire. The knowledge that the raids would be renewed with the fire as a guide in the night made it worse. At 8.30 the sirens went again and the All Clear did not go until 4.20. Then we could tell by the duller glare of the reflection and the absence of leaping flames that the biggest fire had been controlled. The first half hour was the worst – bombs and explosions and machine gun fire, but I did not think they were very near. Then a whistle which I thought might be a screaming bomb some distance away; no explosion, but a clanky rattle very near at hand. It sounded like a cup or plate or a tray falling to the ground and I looked all round the shelter and front part of the garage for it. Then I thought it might be a piece of shrapnel on the Gregorys' roof knocking a slate off and the two falling to the ground; in a lull I opened the door to make sure it wasn't an incendiary bomb fallen on the house. It was only in the morning that I found an incendiary bomb with its tip buried in the cement of the step just beneath my nose.

I diagnosed an incendiary from 1) the splashes of white all round it

Bomb damage in Portman Street, central London

where the magnesium had spluttered out; 2) the fact that there was no explosion; 3) the size. It had not fully burned and had done no damage at all, even to 3 brooms about a foot and a half away. It had evidently hit the garage roof and glanced off into the cement which stifled the burning and prevented it from going off completely. We were not certain, however, so M told Mr Oxborrow (a warden). He came and was not sure – in fact, we had Dick O, Mr and Mrs Endacott, Mr Gurney, Geoffrey O, Alec Gurney, about 5 people I didn't know, a policeman who took away the cap, and none of them knew for certain. A man called Smith who works for the *Times* and takes official photographs of damage and unidentified dead bodies was certain and told us a lot about bombs. Mrs Vivian also was certain – 'just like 8 we picked up on the farm'. So we became quite notorious. It is at present unmoved under a bucket labelled 'Don't touch'. R was good on the whole but rather upset this morning. The official estimate of casualties yesterday was 400 killed, 1,100 injured. There was a warning this morning which we spent in the Os' shelter which is reputed exceedingly good but is in fact no bigger than ours.

It has been difficult to get on with work although I had one interview with Mr Thompson of White, Tomkins and Courage Ltd in the office air raid shelter; it was awkward without a table but not too bad and I had to chat to him politely for 30 minutes before the All Clear went.

Tuesday 10 September

On Sunday evening the siren went at 8.30 before we had finished supper. We slept in the shelter, not waking till 7.45 am. We didn't hear the siren giving the All Clear at 6.20. M and I set off at 8.35 for Purley. No trains to London Bridge, or to Victoria beyond Clapham Junction (though this was remedied by midday). I had to go on a slow electric to Balham. I reached the Bank at 10.35 and walked along King William St, where there was hardly a pane of glass intact, towards the Monument which was badly knocked about. There was a cordon of wardens to keep people out. I could see two blocks almost demolished, another gutted with just walls and skeleton standing; piles of glass and masonry all over the road, shop windows blown out. Windows were broken in Fenchurch St but improved further east. Walsingham House and its immediate neighbourhood were intact. I went up in the lift at 10.50, worked hard and went to lunch at 12.40. Nothing hot and cooked except coffee.

E phoned me yesterday afternoon. He was all right – he was duly impressed with our incendiary. He laughed when I said I wanted to try again on Friday. He is still gardening.

Wednesday 11 September

R listened in at 6.00 and heard Churchill broadcast. He said invasion was likely in the next few days. So we must hope for a gale. Anyway we shall go down fighting or we shall hit back and win. A lunatic world – but what can one do with a people who understand no argument but force?

Thursday 12 September

Lunched with E, though he said it was 'very foolish'. He seemed not
too bad though they have had bombs near them, but he couldn't possibly
try for a baby now. Though I almost expected it, it made me feel worse
than any air raid yet. It is such a short time to try and there is always
something. He can't help it, but it seems so strange to be more concerned
about raids which one can't help. He seemed to feel it unreasonable of
me not to feel the same. I don't know what to do about him. I can see
I must take his weakness with his strength as one is the shadow of the
other – but . . .

Friday 13 September

We had a very bad day. Last night was fairly quiet though the All Clear did
not go till 5.50. Another warning woke me in bed at 7.40 but I went in to
hear the news and cook the breakfast which we had in the shelter. The raid
finished at 8.40 and M and I caught the 9.11. At Riddlesdown we heard
there was a yellow warning and at Norbury the siren went. The train did
not go beyond Clapham Junction but at last we got a Brighton train to
Victoria. There we were told to take cover. As we left the train at 11.05 I
wanted a coffee but there was nowhere serving so we went into a gloomy
shelter at Grosvenor Gardens. Suddenly we heard bombs and AA guns and
machine guns and an aeroplane below the balloons. Later we heard there
had been six bombs on Buckingham Palace and one on Hyde Park. After
an interval and another burst of gunfire it quieted down and at 1.20 we
went to the big ABC and had lunch – bread and cheese and butter and I
had two coffees. Just as we finished the All Clear went at 1.58. I then tried
to get to the City. I walked from London Bridge to Walsingham House
just in time to see Salmon going home at 3.00. Everyone else had gone. I
went with him to the Bank and found McAdam and John waiting for a
tube going south. John told me not to try to get up tomorrow.
  I don't know what E has been doing – just no opportunity of phoning.
But I felt dismal about him, though more philosophical after playing Bach
and Mozart.

The AA barrage is banging away. It is amazing how satisfactory it is in spite of the noise; R is dozing undisturbed.

Tuesday 17 September

This morning it was pouring with rain and we intended to catch an early train. At 8.00 the warning went and within 5 minutes there were bangs. Perkin told me he was on Coulsdon platform and saw a bomber crash over Purley. After the All Clear went we were not too unlucky – train to Balham and lorry (6d) to London Bridge; about 30 people crowded into the lorry – a ramshackle affair which rattled along well. There was only one hold-up, at the Elephant. I got to the office at 10.50. Managed to dictate my letters, do a little assessing and some post. Lunched with E. At 3.00 the siren went and after 4.30 the All Clear and I went with Salmon to Moorgate. The usual crush but at Balham I caught a fast train to Purley – and even went to the library at 6.30.

In the lorry I heard two rumours – one that the tale that Hitler had tried an invasion a week ago, and it failed, is true, though the 'very good authority' would not give the number of German dead and doubted whether the 50,000 mentioned was right; the other that the Germans have used poison gas at Coulsdon and there have been casualties, though slight.

Salmon is getting more cordial. I rather like his brand of scepticism and his kind of mind – exact and intellectual in one way, but slack and mad in another; not too serious but not flippant.

Wednesday 18 September

Another day of raid warnings. The siren went at 12.45 just as I was going to meet E. We gave it up and he phoned at 3.0 and talked for a minute or two and arranged, if possible, to lunch at 12.15 tomorrow.

In the lunchtime raid I looked out of my window and saw the trails of white smoke which show the paths of the planes high up over the Thames estuary.

Friday 20 September

M and R are asleep and the night is again disturbed by bombs and guns and planes though not such a pandemonium yet as usual.

M never got home at all on Wednesday and though we guessed she had worked late and stayed in town the 8.00 am news announcement that casualties had been heavy – 90 dead reported – was not encouraging. I felt very dismal and worried when I got to the office with no news. My phone was dead but I managed to get to Holland Road from Fenchurch Street PO. She was all right and had not been able to phone. It seems impossible to get Purley (a toll call) from Town now. She had been detained by an urgent case – a woman on the point of having a baby who wanted to be evacuated as her house had been bombed and she was billeted in a school with no facilities for a confinement. M stayed in Chiswick and a bomb dropped in the next street. We couldn't ring R up so M went home early.

At 3.00 yesterday UCH phoned and asked me to give blood. I arranged to get there at 5.00. UCH had had a bomb through the roof and was a bit disorganized. Nevertheless they didn't keep me waiting and the boy was more efficient than the last one. There was the same difficulty in making the blood flow, but finally it did – in fact, it flowed too much after he had put a bandage on it, and dripped down my sleeve, on to the floor and he had to begin again. I kept the bandage on till this evening and suffered an inconveniently stiff arm all day, but now after a bath the stiffness and soreness is very local and slight. I was glad to give it – a tithe of my blood – since it was one pint out of the approximate ten pints available.

Lunched with E yesterday and today. We have very short lunches and talk of little but air raids and work, but it is nice to see him. It seems odd to be seeing more of Salmon than of him; I like S, he lends me loads of books which I must read. A letter (without an address but postmarked Manchester) from B reached me today – quite friendly – hoping we were all right in the raids.

Travelling was better today. There was a train marked London Bridge in East Croydon this morning. More in faith than belief I got in and though it moved with the air of an explorer forging through primeval forests it did at length get there. I noticed that Forest Hill goods yard was in a mess, due, I heard, to a landmine. I looked out south over Bermondsey from New Cross Gate to London Bridge and saw many broken chimneys and windows, roofs gone or damaged, a few gaps in the houses with heaps of bricks; on the whole I was surprised at the small amount of damage superficially visible – whole streets seemed untouched – the Bermondsey Council flats look quite whole. It made me feel that if this area – one of the worst – was not more stricken it would take a long time to reduce London to ruins.

Monday 23 September

A lovely golden day, fresh and sunny; I wore my red frock.

Lunched with E but felt dismal. He seemed so remote. He said he was just a walking machine. He felt all the time that a bomb might drop on his head and he can think of little else. It is even less stimulating than his sheer pessimism of April and May.

Monday 30 September

Still cold; and no heating in the office yet. My hands were frozen. Last night there were more bombs on Purley. An oil bomb fell on a garden in Brancaster Lane, made a filthy smother but was put out in five minutes. I was awakened about 5.00 this morning by the whistle and explosion of at least 2 bombs but R and M slept through them.

I listened to the news and to Priestley's Postscript last night – which was about meat and potato pies. He is excellent. I told M and R and E about it and even at second hand it was very successful.

Thursday 3 October

I didn't do much work today – talked a lot to Salmon who calls me Bianca (derived from Casabianca, because I dislike going to the shelter). He brought me two books by the man he lives with, and said I must come to lunch to tell him what I thought of them.

An interview for an hour this morning with an accountant who was somewhat of an expert on EPT. He began by being sniffy about my methods but I did manage to score a bit and he went away less sniffy.

Friday 4 October

Very little fresh work coming in. I am struggling with two shipping companies, EPT. It is most laborious; each ship has to be done separately. One has about 150 barges and tugs and the other about 50 large ships. Salmon came in and sympathized two or three times and we talked about the prospect of re-educating Germany to be civilized.

Saturday 5 October

Sunny, and the wind has gone south-west. A lovely day except that we have had alarms off and on all day – a nasty dive bomb over Kenley while M and I were shopping in Purley. We were driven out of Woolworths and went to a public shelter under a shop opposite. It was full-ish, and we smuggled S in under M's arm. She turned out to be an asset as she entertained babies who were getting tired of the shelter.

Monday 7 October

Worked hard today, clearing up the assessing. Three books finished, one more tomorrow. Raids off and on all day, but E was not nervous at lunch. We had rather a nice talk – just as I was getting fed up.

Salmon asked me to go to lunch at Golders Green on Thursday – a whole day's leave! He will play some records when his friend isn't talking about Art. I like his subtlety and his refusal to impose.

A letter from Elsie and one from Reen who is resigning on Saturday and marrying next week.

Tuesday 8 October

A day of raid after raid. The night raid finished at 7.15. This morning the alarm went as soon as we had started for Riddlesdown Station and 5 minutes later the air was vibrating with the sound of planes. My train did go to London Bridge via Streatham, but it took 70 minutes. We passed a Victoria train and though the side blinds were down the windows were all open and people's faces filled them gazing up at the fighting which I reckon must have been high over the Thames estuary. I saw one man in a first class carriage leaning back comfortably smiling and watching through glasses. Two women in my carriage were watching all the time. At various times in the morning we heard bombs, planes and AA. I was told that bombs had hit Bush House, a bus in Holborn, Staple Inn, Horse Guards Parade, Charing Cross Station, Billingsgate and Tooley St.

I was dismal at lunch because E was hopeless about starting a baby. He said he was doing nothing but sleeping and working and was still terrified. But at last he said when, and how – 'You are asking a great deal – I shall have to see.' Elsie had asked me to lunch at her room on Saturday, so it may be possible.

Thursday 10 October

Today I have spent a day's leave with Salmon at Golders Green. So tired now, but a lovely stimulating day. Brilliant sunshine and deep blue sky all the way from Victoria on the 2 bus and the fifteen minutes' walk with Salmon to his house.

The house is fuller of pictures than any I have seen, mostly watercolours – but three reproductions (one of Van Gogh's *Sunflowers*, one of the Canal bridges, one of Bruegel's *Winter*), several drawings and watercolours of O'Neill, several watercolours of linocuts of Claude – *Flight into Egypt* – and Edith Shackleton. I just couldn't take them in as Salmon made me look at one after another. It was too much. O'Neill is nice – looks fierce at first. I felt terribly shy. He had piercing blue eyes and a bushy moustache. Tall, almost towering. Not so fierce to talk to as to read. I felt quite inadequate except in interest. We had a large but attractive Viennese lunch cooked by

Elizabeth, the Austrian housekeeper, who has a most humorous face though she might be very trying.

After lunch Mr O'Neill has to rest and S played records – Schnabel in a Beethoven Sonata; *Eine Kleine Nachtmusik*, Lotte Lehmann in a Schubert song; even Beethoven's violin concerto with Kreisler. In the middle of it – so fateful; it is odd how associations repeat and complicate themselves – he said, 'Don't get too fond of me.' We had a queer, bitty conversation, most of which was not said at all, interrupted by turning Beethoven on the gram. There wasn't time or opportunity to say much, but I am afraid we may be hopelessly at cross purposes. I want to be honest with him. It was so queer just to be told by someone not to fall for him, and be left to infer all the rest. He said, 'It is so nice to talk to someone. You will think me a swine – your voice gives you away.' He kissed me – I liked it – I don't mind if it doesn't hurt him or E. How queerly one is made. I could enjoy his kisses (as well as his talk, for the stimulus of another person with similar but slightly different interests is always enjoyable) – but that he should want to kiss me. Why can't one be just platonic? It is quite possible to be in love with one man and yet to enjoy physical stimulation from another – partly the music and the opportunity, and the fact that E is completely cold and machine-like, reduced to an automaton by the air raids while I am not. It is difficult – I foresee another mess – at least a complication. I suppose I am hopelessly imprudent. Anyway, there it is!

I was surprised not to see any evidence of bombing on the route from Victoria to Golders Green. Today I have hardly remembered the war, except when a time bomb went off in Marylebone Road with a big crack as my bus was at Baker Street Station. It was nearer than I have been to an explosion – the dust and smoke were in the air but no one seemed perturbed – 'Time bomb gone off, I suppose?' the woman behind me remarked.

Friday 11 October

E forgot I was not going to lunch with him yesterday, and said he had 'an alarming time' – phoned me – in vain. It was only when he thought of ringing up Salmon that he remembered. He is not coming up to town

tomorrow so we cannot try to start a baby then, but he did not suggest
that we cannot try this time at all – perhaps we can have a half day next
week or two. I do so want it to come off. It seemed ages since I had seen
him on Wednesday – after the gulf of yesterday. I looked at him and knew
I still loved him. But a child would anchor me and make me more
contented. When Salmon looked at me today – touched my hand or my
hair – I could not help liking him. I am nearer loving him than anyone else
but E. If I believed it would hurt E I should be quite ruthless to myself and
to Salmon, but he doesn't want me physically. He has said so many times
that I am asking a lot when I want to try to start a child. I don't know
what to do. I hate to feel that either of them will suffer through me. 'Not
worth thinking about,' Salmon says of himself. What should I do? If I do
as usual I shall just drift into a mess from which I shan't be able to emerge
without suffering to all of us.

Saturday 12 October

A bright sunny winter's day with a white frost this morning.

ES* has written me a letter, bothering over my 'long story'. I told him a
little but there was no opportunity for a proper account. He said, 'Don't
bother about me – conflicting loyalties are the greatest cause of
unhappiness.' I don't know. What I cannot decide is how much it would
matter now to E whether I stayed in his life or went out – whether he
would at bottom prefer to be left in peace. That is what I must find out. I
am quite certain that there is more possibility of loving ES than anyone
else since I loved E but I must be honest and I must not try to have it both
ways.

At midday Ostime and ES went home and gave me a sherry on the way.
I then went on an 11 bus to Victoria. I went to lunch with Elsie and stayed
till 4.30 talking. It was good for me to talk things over with her.

* Edward Salmon.

Monday 14 October

A horrid chilly day – and I am irritable and bad-tempered. At 12.05 the
warning went and did not finish till 2.10 – so I didn't go out to lunch and
didn't see E. ES gave me some coffee and chocolate and I ate a piece of
Ryvita with my tea. E did ring up before he went home and I must have
sounded grumpy and dismal. I had by then written him a letter. After that
I wrote ES a note, as it is very difficult to talk without interruption. He
spent the afternoon sticking scrim over his windows. I found it
exceedingly difficult to work, mainly sheer distaste for such cases as the
Swedish Chamber of Commerce. ES said (with a paint brush in one hand),
'Don't go without saying good night.' He kissed me before I went. I gave
him his note and he put it away. I don't know what will happen. We must
not take ourselves too seriously, but I upset him by saying, 'I shouldn't
worry so much if you just wanted a little amusement.'

Tuesday 15 October

We had alarms all day off and on. E and I lunched – perhaps we had 20
minutes – when the alarm went. I gave him my note. I felt desperately
sorry for him. He said he hadn't slept much for three nights, he was feeling
the strain.
    My room is now swathed in scrim – every bit of glass, window
ventilator, door panel is covered with it. The effect is of living in a Scotch
mist. ES came in with a reply to my note, telling me more or less about
himself and his family and his wife. She is in the last stages of creeping
paralysis; it was diagnosed in 1926; I was horrified to think how they must
both have suffered. What can I do but try to snatch some happiness for him
and with him after such a life? He kissed me and we have snatched at least
an hour altogether to talk etc. I left the office at 4.40. There was a raid on. I
walked with ES to the Monument – underground to Mansion House – a
long queue there for a special bus. I caught a Brighton train which got me
home at 6.50. Now, once more to the sound of guns and planes, I am
waiting to go in from the air raid shelter for the news.

Wednesday 16 October

I tried to lunch with E and got nearly to Camomile St and was turned back by the police. A policeman told me there was a landmine in the neighbourhood and they were going to explode it. Everyone was being cleared out, it was horrid; hordes of people with parcels and cases and babies; fire engines and AFS men with hoses, sand, ambulances, two lorries of soldiers labelled 'Bomb Disposal', but with 'Suicide Squad' chalked on the sides.

I gave up looking for E after 35 minutes walking and had brown bread and butter and cheese and coffee in an ABC and went back to the office and talked to ES for 45 minutes. We talked about books and schools and people. We were both quite foolishly affectionate. He is sweet and it is nice to be wanted again. He is considerate and said he hoped we would not get killed. It is extremely difficult to arrange to do anything. He went early to the nursing home, as usual. There was only one half hour warning and I phoned E at 3.45. He was all right though he had had a difficult journey – got to Putney and by lorry from there. He seemed a bit less flattened out.

Thursday 17 October

A fine moonlit evening, so I fear London will have a bad night. Another day dominated by travelling. Lunched at the Bank with E – white roll, cheese, margarine and a cup of tea after a long wait. He had slept better last night but was upset inside. Men are like children. We talked of nothing but the blitz and travelling. He said he hadn't felt up to answering my note. I told him not to bother, I would not badger him again.

Friday 18 October

I went to Bishopsgate to lunch today, but lunched alone. E did not come and I don't know what happened to him. I hope it is just a chill. ES gave me a photograph this morning. We have tentatively decided to lunch tomorrow. I like him – he is sweet to me. He was better today. We are both very foolish but it is rather nerve-racking, avoiding disturbance.

Sunday 20 October

A perfect day – warm, sunny with blue sky and autumn trees. Yesterday ES had to go to Barnet at 2.00 but we had the whole morning (more or less) in the office and then 12.00–2.00. I like him, though at times I felt it difficult to get into communication with him as it were – he seemed somehow remote. I don't know why this should be. It might be easier if we had slept together as I am not sure that wanting to is a distraction which makes one aware of the other person almost through a fog; it makes everything seem slightly unreal. Yet I should hate to sleep with a person I didn't know. It is very difficult, not least to make opportunities to get to know each other better.

Tuesday 22 October

Lunched with E but spent more time with ES, making love. He kisses me and talks nonsense and then shop. And I – I should like to spend a night in his arms.

Wednesday 23 October

I had an interview with a rabid woman who represents a Geneva scent company. She called instead of the manager because 'he can't argue'. Barnes, for the Revenue, in 1935, insisted on going from a percentage basis to a profit and loss basis and now we want to go back. Poor thing! She was very fierce but she went away slightly calmed and even thought it was a pity she hadn't seen me in 1935! A case where pacifism paid!

1940

Saturday 26 October

I was rather late starting but reached the office by 10.00; did almost
nothing except dictate. ES left at 11.30 and I went 5 minutes later and we
went by bus to the Leicester Galleries to see the Epstein exhibition – 3
sculptures, 2 lovely things of his granddaughter as a baby at 4 months and 7
months and a negro girl. A roomful of watercolours of flowers; I have
never seen such vivid watercolours – more like oils, Van Gogh oils at that.
Marvellous – barbaric – sunflowers and delphiniums I liked best, they were
lovely. ES liked them.

Monday 28 October

Cold but sunny and misty; good journey to the office, worse coming home,
but seats both ways and London Bridge was open. E's journey was bad –
Waterloo closed and he had an altercation with a ticket collector who
pointed out that his season said it was available only two ways (both of
which were closed). E refused to pay and gave his name and address. In these
days – ! He has a cold but managed to eat a pear I took from the garden.

ES lunched at Somerset House and got back at about 3.00. I didn't see
much of him in the day and did quite a lot of work. He brought me some
coffee in his thermos, just for me. We made love for 45 minutes before
going home. It is amazing how easy it is to form a habit.

Friday 1 November

This morning I went to the Bank and as I emerged looked up and saw
eight planes quite clearly flying almost directly over Fenchurch Street.
They looked white, to the south but still high in the sky. I watched six
flying almost straight with others, presumably Spitfires, making figures of
eight and heading them off. Once I saw a flash in the sky as a Spitfire's trail
almost intersected the 'main line'. These planes were too high to see
anything but the vapour trails. When I went into the office I was quite
blind from looking into the bright sky.

Monday 4 November

Last night was the first night without an alarm since the blitz started. We slept in the shelter mainly because the beds weren't aired, but the joy of an evening by the fire listening to Edith Evans in *The Way of the World*. A peaceful day too with no alarms. ES was very sweet to me; he has a habit of dashing in and kissing me and dashing out to do some work, which is very appealing. He is nice; but we are effectually prevented from talking consecutively, not to say making love, by the other inhabitants of the corridor. This morning Thompson called again about EPT and left me a bottle of lavender water made by the company. I protested but he went off with an air of beneficence. I told John and he said, 'Very nice of him.'

Tuesday 5 November

Early this morning 3.00 am–7.00 am we had a continuous stream of planes with bursts of gunfire, enough to disturb us several times. It seems to have been general in London.

We received the professional newsletter today. It says that a Committee has been appointed to consider how to cope with the blackout and blitz and keep the work going, especially in London, but initiative, imagination, sympathy and broadmindedness are required! So delightfully English – it sounds like 'muddle through'.

I should miss being kissed by ES now if he were not there.

Saturday 9 November

I took the morning off and went to Golders Green to lunch with ES. It was bleak and cold and this afternoon it poured with rain but we enjoyed ourselves sitting by the fire and listening to records – Mendelssohn's *Italian Symphony*, Mozart's *Serenata Notturna*, Beethoven's *Pathétique*, Purcell's *Golden Sonata*. Lovely; we listened and made love for what must have been one and a half to two hours though it seemed very short. Then lunch and Mr O'Neill talked about Kenneth Ingram's book and scolded me for my pessimism. Then, too quickly, ES came with me to Golders Green station, I to Victoria, he to Barnet. I would not have believed I would love anyone so much and get to know him so well with so little talk and in so short a time. Bombs fell; one while we were going to look at South Square with its housing and Lutyens' church and institute, discussed in Massingham's *London Scene*; two while we were having coffee in the lounge. A lovely day. I hope so much that we live to love more.

Monday 11 November

I have worked quite hard, in spite of dallying a certain time with ES. We both find such delight in our love. I rejoiced to see him this morning, especially after the heavy raid of last night. He wrote to me in the weekend, a sweet foolish letter which I loved. I find such joy in his pleasure.

Thursday 14 November

There were two impressive bits of naval news – a successful attack on the Italian navy in Taranto by the Fleet Air Arm and the magnificent fight of the *Jervis Bay* in defence of its convoy. She was sunk but at least 30 out of 38 ships got away. Most moving.

Mrs Salmon wants to go to Paignton. ES asked me whether I wanted to go on doing IT and EPT all my life. Wouldn't I rather live conventionally and marry and have children? We talked more than usual partly because I wouldn't let him kiss my lips, as I still had a cold, though it hasn't developed completely. It seems strange to me – I love him and I have complete trust in him, though I have known him such a short time.

Friday 15 November

ES told me all about his finances today. He can't be bothered to manage, but to pay 5 guineas a week for the Paignton nursing home and John's education will be difficult. The better I grow to love him the sorrier I am for his wife. She must have been through an awful time. So must he; I can make him a little happy.

Monday 18 November

It was nice to see ES and he was happy to see me. He had written me a note. His wife had decided to go. She wired her sister in Paignton to fix up there. We arranged a job to be done jointly.

Tuesday 19 November

Cold but dry today. Last night I slept in the shelter but I heard planes and a burst of firing once. Otherwise all quiet, no alerts today at all, but this evening the sky is clear and there is more activity – planes humming, and guns, though further off than usual. We and even R are still sitting by the fire at 8.20.

ES and I have finished our job. He has asked O'Neill to try a pencil sketch of him for me. We loved for 30 minutes before we came home.

Wednesday 20 November

Last night we slept in the shelter. There was quite a lot of activity, though different from usual. The planes seemed higher and the guns further away and different.

E at lunch told me about a demolition worker who lived near a house on which he was working. He dug out a baby covered with dust and dirt and he couldn't tell whether it was dead or alive. He told the ambulance to take it to his wife first. She washed it and tended it and in an hour it was sitting up smiling.

1940

Thursday 21 November

ES made love to me off and on all day and for 20 minutes before we went home. We shall feel better when we have slept together. I don't know whether to tell E definitely or not.

Monday 25 November

Lunched with ES on Saturday. He has arranged to take his wife to Paignton on Wednesday and come back on Sunday and come here direct if possible. He is really very sweet and seems to like me very much. He says O'Neill blesses this and thinks it will be good for both of us to love. He rang me up yesterday morning.

Tuesday 26 November

Fine, sunny and cloudy, mild. R caught the 10.30 am train to Plymouth. Everything went well. It was a quiet night, no siren at all and I slept in bed. We caught a slow train about 9.00 to Victoria, taxi-ed to Paddington, found the train just coming in and put her and Susan in a non-smoker corner near the restaurant car. M and I didn't wait for it to go but had a coffee and M went shopping and I went to the city. It was queer to say goodbye to R and S and ES on the same day. We talked and kissed off and on all day from when I got to the office. He had written me a note – a sweet note, when he should have been sleeping in the quiet of last night. I hope so much for Sunday night to see him at Purley and I hope I shall be a bit late this month so that we can sleep together nicely.

Saturday 30 November

Today E unexpectedly came to the office and we had a quick coffee before I went on to Charing Cross to lunch with Elsie. Yesterday I asked him how he felt and told him I could make our relationship platonic now if he was

satisfied. I don't know what he will say. Of course, putting it more
definitely is more than just having an existing position to continue, but I
felt I owed it to him. I have heard every morning from ES. He is doubtful
about getting back tomorrow. The nursing home wouldn't keep his wife
– too much bother. I feel so indignant for them. He will have to find
somewhere else and move her there and he doesn't know how long it will
take. Apart from the facts stated, which are just news, his letters were
lovely. Anyway, I shouldn't want to sleep with him tomorrow as I happed
yesterday, 2 days early.

Monday 2 December

E had not replied to my note, but said he couldn't guess my motives. I told
him he must disregard my feelings – I just wanted to know how he felt. I
do love him still very much. Can one love two men? I think so, in quite
different ways. I have more respect for E and this is in some queer way
connected with my love for him. He represents a much higher standard
than I can ever reach. ES does too but he is more anti-social, less patient
with life. Perhaps it is just that I don't know him so well. Two letters from
ES this morning. He returns tomorrow and will come then.

Wednesday 4 December

I can't write anything. I told E about ES and E does love and wants me. I
am torn in two. I feel despicable. What can I do? I love them both.

Monday 9 December

Too upset to write anything of what has been happening since Wednesday
about ES and E.

Tuesday 10 December

Feeling clearer, but I can't begin to externalize this appalling conflict. But I slept last night and consequently felt less worn out. For the first time since last Tuesday I didn't cry at lunch.

Thursday 12 December

Still disturbed but happier – it feels as though there can be only one end – to cleave to E, at whatever cost to him, to me, to ES and to K.

Tuesday 17 December

I can't let today go without a note. The dilemma is still appalling and insoluble but today has been glorious. E has risen from the dead. He wants me, wants me as much as he ever did. That is the one overwhelming fact – miraculous, unbelievable, mad but true. He is suddenly alive – alive altogether. We went to St Sepulchre's. There was a gramophone recital, a suite for strings by Purcell and a Mendelssohn piano concerto. It was glorious – we just listened and I held his hand – and we were completely one, even physically, though only our hands touched, I wore my red frock and he looked at it. A day of blinding glory! Even the sun shone. And here all alone in the silence at 11.00 my heart glows with the remembrance. What will come of it, I don't know. I love ES but on quite another plane.

Wednesday 18 December

Still in a dream – an urgent dream – so urgent that I have planned with E to go to Elsie's rented room early tomorrow to complete the resurrection of our love! We lunched and then sat in St Ethelburga's for 20 minutes. During the last week he has said to me such words as I longed, but did not know I longed, to hear – a sweet ecstasy – fiery splendour, marred only by the bitter sorrow of knowing how ES must suffer – or, if not he, then E himself.

Thursday 19 December

A quick note of a red-letter day. I must love E very much to get up at 6 am, catch the 7.13 pitch dark train to meet him at Victoria and go to Elsie's room to fuck before going to the office. I suppose we had 45 minutes or an hour and it was sweet, lovely! I had forgotten what it could be like with him. We went to St Sepulchre's at lunchtime to hear a record of Schnabel playing Beethoven's Emperor Sonata. Different from Tuesday but lovely. Tuesday was a fiery dawn; today a serene sunset – a calm sweet echo of the morning.

Friday 27 December

A week of changes – most important. E came last Saturday at 8.45 and for three hours we loved before I had to rush for the 12.14. It was lovely – lovely. We lit the gas fire in the hall and had the electric fire too as it was a bitterly cold day. It was one of the most successful fucks we have ever had, so sweet and wild and glorious. He said I never reacted with so much movement. He gave me at lunch today a kind of poem he wrote afterwards about it. I love him completely and utterly.

But I love ES too. He is still not well but better after kissing me. I don't know what to do about him. To have E's baby while he is working next door will be brutal. I should like to write down the lovely things that E has said to me in the last 2 weeks but I can't. I just keep them like jewels to gloat over – to remember when I am sad.

Monday 30 December

A wild, damp day. The raid last night was on the City. This was announced in the 8.00 news so I was not surprised to find at 8.45 at Purley that London Bridge was off. I finally reached Victoria at 10.15. Remarks in the train, 'All the Surrey fire engines were in the city last night' – 'You could see the fire from the hills all night and at 6.30 it was just as big.'

The District wasn't running east of St James's Park so I tried a bus. A man said you couldn't get into the city at all but buses were going to Bloomsbury. I walked from Bury Place (by the BM) to Walsingham House. Along Holborn no change till I got to Wallis where there were some new broken windows; Negretti & Zambras had been burnt and another building opposite Holborn Viaduct. The station seemed intact; St Sepulchre whole; Holborn tube had a notice: no Central Line trains further east (but I discovered they were running to Liverpool St missing Post Office). There were clouds of smoke in Farringdon St looking both ways from the viaduct; at Newgate Street I was turned off by a barrier and went down to Ludgate Hill. There, hoses and fire engines all the way and several buildings round St Paul's still burning, but the thing that moved me most in all this obscene squalor was the Christmas tree outside St Paul's still bravely burning, bearing its star and all its coloured lights.

Along Cannon St there seemed little more damage; Southwark and London Bridge were intact but clouds of smoke were rising from fire on the south bank; Eastcheap was unchanged and I was just beginning to think I had come through the worst when I turned a corner and saw more smoke than ever in clouds round Mark Lane station and All Hallows and the Tower. I turned up Mark Lane and into Hart St and quite expected to find Walsingham House hit but it wasn't damaged at all, though the buildings opposite the PLA in Seething Lane were still burning. At one place I saw a notice – Danger: Falling Walls. The whole office reeked with the acrid smell of damp smoke.

Two and a half hours (lunch and coming home) with E have made today supportable. It was lovely, and we may just possibly have Sunday together.

1941

Sunday 5 January

E phoned at 11.0 to say that K had decided to go to town so he would be free. I phoned Elsie to ask if we could come and see her first. She was in and said 'Yes' cordially so we went. She gave me some lunch to prepare – bacon and egg, Ryvita, prunes and coffee and then went out and left us. So we had a lovely peaceful time together by the fire from 1.0–4.15. First lunch, then fucked from 1.30–3.30, about; then just sat quietly and talked. We made the most of our rare opportunity to enjoy privacy in comfort. He did not use a French letter but I cannot be very hopeful that we shall start a baby this time as it is the wrong bit of the month. Still, perhaps – ! And it was a lovely fuck to commemorate with a baby. I should so love to have it (except for the sake of ES).

Sunday 12 January

At 7.45 yesterday morning E phoned and suggested meeting at the Monument at 9.0. I rushed and left home about 8.20. Got a lift halfway to the station and reached London Bridge at 8.55. We had coffee at Fullers for 30 minutes. In the afternoon I went to Golders Green with ES, and we had a couple of hours to ourselves. I made him dismal by talking about E but I felt I must be certain of not misleading him. He said he was quite clear about the position and didn't want to talk about it. I still love him in his way and I feel a pig.

1941

Saturday 18 January

A lovely, lovely day, hideous outside – cold and snowing all day and a bad
start; a cold wet half hour waiting for E at Victoria. He had not got up till
8.30 owing to a mistake in his clock. By then Elsie would have started for
her office. I tried and failed to get her on the phone at the house. So we
walked through the driving snow to her office and found she hadn't
arrived. E waited in the hall while I went to try to phone again and failed,
but when I got back to the office E said she had come, so we went up and
warmed ourselves by her fire and smoked a cigarette for 20 minutes and
talked. Then we went back to Victoria to get a bus to her room. We got
there about 10.30 and turned on the fire. We were soon warm and dry.
Then we loved. It was one of the quickest and loveliest fucks we have ever
had – so easy and light-hearted and gorgeous, just unbelievably lovely. It
was a kind of *vivace* fuck. Afterwards we dressed and were peaceful and
quiet from 11.30–1.15. We went on loving on a smaller level but still nice,
like echoes of music coming and going. I didn't want to go out into the
snow, and yet I minded less than sometimes as we had had the quiet after
our *vivace*. It was complete, a rounded cadence, I thought as we walked
towards Victoria. I shan't mind being killed by a bomb tonight after such a
perfect morning.

  I lunched with ES. I hadn't wanted to but I didn't mind at all. I was glad
in a way that he should get the benefit individually of our happiness, for he
did – a kind of reflected glow. So did Rosa; I met her in Croydon during a
warning. She was rather nervous and the flag was up at the Town Hall
signifying imminent danger. We went to Grants but their shelter was
closed, so we went to Kennards and spent 45 minutes buying a carpet for
the dining room. It is to be delivered on Wednesday and Rosa is very
pleased. It gave me a lot of pleasure to let her have it, so one way and
another this has been a lovely day.

Sunday 19 January

It has turned warmer and the ice and snow on the roads has begun to melt,
a dangerous process as it was like wet glass. But so pleasant to feel a soft

wind and see blue sky and sunshine. I caught the 1.43 to Victoria and ES met me there and we went to Golders Green. We had one and a half hours – tea and the Pathétique sonata and then he came back to Victoria with me. Rosa and Margot went to a fire watching meeting and learned a few hints on tackling incendiaries. Margot volunteered for herself and me. I have also volunteered at the office 'if enough other people do'. It seems mean to leave it to the men just because women are not yet to be compelled.

Monday 20 January

A continuously bad day, pouring rain, cold wind, the relics of frozen snow under foot – dark and dismal. Lunched with E; he was still glowing after Saturday morning and so was I. He said he thought the books were wrong in saying a man should take care to warm up a woman slowly – I was as quick as he.

Wednesday 22 January

Last night was quiet. At 9.30 a warden called Beckett came and Margot and I became Fire Spotters 28 and 29 respectively. We have to watch till midnight on Sunday, Tuesday and Thursday. He took our full names, ages and professions as the Council insure us. We have been given the post phone number about which there was a mystery. We must not divulge it to anyone. When we spot a fire we have to blow whistles and phone the post. Beckett advised not to volunteer at the office.

Monday 27 January

A quiet night and day. Rather depressed. It was lovely to see E at lunch. We arranged to go to Elsie's room on Wednesday afternoon. He had read 37 chapters of *Pillars*★ I lent him and liked it. But ES was very sweet and had written me a letter in French. I felt a pig to him. I can't love him as I

★ *Seven Pillars of Wisdom*, by T. E. Lawrence.

love E and he knows it; he says he just doesn't want to talk about it and ignores it as far as possible. I don't mind if this satisfies him, but of course it doesn't and he is jealous at times. Still, he does enjoy doing as much as we do.

Saturday 1 February

A devastating day. I had the morning off and met E. We went to Elsie's room and just saw her before she went to the office. It was lovely; we fucked for half an hour and then had coffee and sat peacefully till 1.0. It was sweet but I had a sort of 'last time' feeling in the end, probably because Elsie is having to give up the room and move to Leamington as she has a new job in the Camouflage Department of the Home Office.

I met ES for lunch and he told me I had had a move to Belfast (HO Relief), to report 3.3.41. I was simply dazed and couldn't take it in. He was desolate but said I needn't go to Belfast if I don't want to as I have a good case of domestic hardship. I should hate it in peacetime, but in wartime with travel difficulties and curtailed leave I should be completely isolated. It would be hideous. We went to Grey Close and I was just dismal. I don't want to leave E or ES or Margot.

I am just flattened out.

Monday 3 February

The whole day I have been concentrated on my move to Belfast. Saw John this morning. He was surprised and said he was sorry 'but not too hopeful about the possibility of getting the move altered or cancelled'. He was not pleased with the prospect at City 10 as Herrick has had a Special, is a year junior to me and is likely to get a move quickly if he is promoted. He offered to arrange an interview with White who is PI (Establishment) at Somerset House. I went to see him this afternoon and he advised me to take the move. I might get a worse one if I protested! Northern Ireland districts were pleasant and had good conditions of work! I might get a district there after a short time! I should probably be there at least 4 or 5 years, as the law was different and it would be wasteful to move people there for a short time. E was upset when I told him at lunchtime, but hardly realized what it meant. ES was sweet to me and refrained from expressing how it upset him but considered only how it would affect me. I don't know whether to write to Loach or not. White said definitely that he would not attach weight to the hardships in my case. It seems to me I must either resign or go. The only thing to do if I go is to have a baby there, tho' this would be difficult. It would be miserable cut off from everyone completely. Except in emergency it is impossible to get a permit to visit England more than once in 6 months, and even letters are censored. I am just devastated. It will be almost impossible ever to see E.

Tuesday 4 February

The great topic is still Belfast. I have done very little work. ES is miserable and I find I still love him quite a lot. So he was a little less miserable tonight. I went to lunch with E late as John had kept me. E had slept badly. So had I. McAdam came in and told me (being a Belfast man) that I should love it! I told John I was considering resigning. I have arranged to see McCreath tomorrow morning for advice. He was quite sweet when I phoned for an appointment. I met E at Victoria for a cup of tea. He has finished *Pillars* and liked it. He has had it only about a week.

Wednesday 5 February

Bitter cold this morning. I went to see McCreath who talked for an hour. He was looking ill, having come back on Monday after a fortnight's sick leave with his heart. He was sympathetic about Belfast; thought it was a most unimaginative move; very hard in my domestic circumstances. But the AIT could not make a case of it. When I mentioned resignation as an alternative he was shocked and told me to go and see Loach at Llandudno if I was so desperate. He thought if I was prepared to go to that length I could get the move cancelled, but he asked me to think carefully and advised me not to for my own sake and because of the effect on the position of the other women. This last reason (which had been in my mind from the first) weighed more than anything. He said he was lunching with King (President) and would talk to him. I am to ring him tomorrow.

Then I went to see Griff. He talked to me for an hour and a half and he was sweet. He advised me to accept the move with all its misery and use it to enrich life. All he said was true and really relevant since he guessed the real reason why I didn't want to go. He talked to me like a grandfather and kissed me before I went. He completed what McCreath had begun. I reached the stage of feeling it was a choice for me between wise and foolish, between positive and negative, right and wrong, so that whatever I do I shall be unhappy. I lunched with E and met him for a cup of tea. Before we parted he had told me he thought the right thing to do was to go. I just cried and cried but I agreed. It is now a question of how to do it. I shall write to Loach as a protest, otherwise in the future (when I may want consideration) there may be no evidence that the move was anything but what I wanted.

Thursday 6 February

I am getting weary of talking and badgering people about Belfast. Today I wrote a letter to Loach but phoned McCreath before posting it. He said he had discussed it with King who, like him, sympathized but hoped I would not do anything desperate! McC had heard that Loach was coming down to the House & thought it would be useful to see him. I must wire him to ask for an interview. McC and King would be pleased to go with me but we both thought I should be better on my own. McC asked me to let him know when the interview would be and what happened immediately afterwards so that he or King could then see Loach and tell him what they thought if necessary. It was good of him. Brennan came to commiserate and gave me the name of a friend of his in the Passport Office who might help over permits to England.

I met E this morning and agreed that I must go unless Loach reconsidered the move. I must not push my objection to extremes. At lunch we talked about a baby. It is a question whether we can or should try hard to start one this month or whether I should go to Ireland to see how things were first and try to get over on leave at Whitsun, say, and start one then. He is trying to decide whether to be candid with K about it. He will probably, if I do go to Ireland. She is run down again and wants to use his 3 days leave to go away.

Monday 10 February

Yesterday ES came for the day, ostensibly to meet Rosa as a possible lodger in my place. Rosa had a cold at its worst. She liked him, decided that he needed 'looking after'. He reminded her of someone she had met ages ago. He liked it; we went for a walk over Riddlesdown. It was mild and blowing a gale and just not raining. Thick mud in places, especially where all the old grass has been ploughed. We were late for dinner but listened to the concert in the afternoon. He looked at the garden and decided that there was a lot of work to do there. I think he would like it, and Rosa would too.

We listened to Churchill last night. His speech came through well; he told us little that was new but spoke magnificently – an artist in words.

Lunched with E. I wore my red frock and brown coat. But he had looked up the routes to Belfast and my heart became like a stone! I met him and went to Victoria where we had tea. A little better in spirit – but as I looked at him, so near, so often seen, I felt desolate. He said we could take 28 days leave which means at least a week more. I thrilled to think perhaps we might have a few days together and he said, 'Your face is like an April sky – suddenly the sun shines after clouds.' We talked of a baby and he said, 'I just want one thing – and that is to fuck you.'

Tuesday 11 February

I met E at Cannon St and we went to tea at Elsie's to borrow Epstein's *Art and Biography*. She went out to dinner at 5.40 and we fucked very quickly for 15 minutes. Sweet! Of course, he would not go on wanting to for long but it is hard to part from him when we are again so much in love.

Margot and Rosa are now beginning to realize how inevitable the move is. E was very sweet.

Wednesday 12 February

Lunched with E and we talked about a baby. I don't know whether to begin before I go to Belfast or whether to try in 2 or 3 months. The synchronization of time and place will be difficult. ES told me I must do something useful and engrossing when I leave London, which is true. Also, that I am useful and don't use my brains. Met E and had tea at Victoria.

Friday 14 February

Had tea with E and lunched with him at Euston where we had gone to enquire about routes to Ireland. I have to go Stranraer–Larne on 2nd March. In the morning I went to the Northern Ireland office to ask about permits. It is worse than I thought. Rosa can come once in six months, but not Margot and no one else. I am not sure about me. I think I can't come till September and then not till March. I am more anxious than ever to start a baby now.

E tells me I should accept Elsie's offer to give me ordnance maps of NI for Christmas. He says he will want them to follow my walks. I must keep my diary in loose leaf form and send it to him instead of a letter or with a letter. He must be attempting to construct in imagination how we can live together, tho' separated, putting into practice what Griff said: two who cannot grow separately cannot grow together. It comforts me just a little.

Sunday 16 February

I met E at Clapham and we went to Ashtead. Not far towards Headley on the old footpath we walked. There was a great deal of mud as army vans and lorries had been up the lane churning it up, but we could walk on the beech leaves. The lamb's tails made a shower of gold, dazzling against the blue sky, and the sun was hot on our faces. There were larks singing over the field where we picnicked on cherries last summer and saw a hare two or three years ago. But this was just the setting to the ecstasy – yes, ecstasy

again – of loving E. It was too wet on the ground to fuck completely but
for me it didn't matter. To be in his arms, to feel his hands and his kisses
while over our heads the bare branches made a pattern against the sky – I
was utterly happy. I even forgot the sorrow to come. It was a golden day,
another jewel in a necklace I thought was complete.

Today I met ES at Golders Green. Before lunch O'Neill talked to me
but during the afternoon ES made love to me. I loved him and was nice to
him, but in quite a different mood from yesterday with E. It is
extraordinary and I suppose neither would understand how it is possible
for me to love or even tolerate 2 different men. It amazes me, but to love
ES as I do does not affect my love for E at all. I feel he is a tired, unhappy
child who must be cherished and comforted. But E's love is a magnificent,
terrifying thing which leaves me humble and yet proud; like Leda or
Alcmene.

Tuesday 25 February

Today has been lovely, lovely, a day to remember with joy. I met E at
Clapham Junction. We just caught a train to Leatherhead having a carriage
to ourselves all the way. We loved between stations with some intensity so
that at Ewell he leaned back quite exhausted and in the middle of an
ejaculation! After this we were ready to concentrate on the walk and did
not spend any time love-making – anyway, it was too cold to pause. We
walked about 16 miles – through Fetcham, skirting Bookham, to Ranmore
Common, over the hill and down to Gomshall for lunch at the Compasses
and back through Shere to West Horsley. It was loveliest from Bookham to
Ranmore Common because we had no maps and the path was new to both
of us. A mile or so out of Bookham we were very politely stopped by a
soldier who wanted to see our identity cards. The road became a path
running up and down into hollows of the Downs, quite unspoilt, showing
misty in the distance, or clear between bare branches. I began to get
hungry when we turned from Ranmore Rd along the path down to
Gomshall, which we reached at 1.0. The Compasses is beautifully placed
by the Tillingbourne river and I had heard much about it but never been
there.

The Compasses Inn, Gomshall

We had a good (but expensive) lunch of bacon, egg, potatoes, cabbage, carrots, pancake, cider and coffee. The road back to Horsley was familiar and as lovely as ever. All the evening I have had an afterglow of happiness in my heart, which not even our parting and my going to Ireland has shadowed. One of the loveliest days we have ever had.

Friday 7 March

I could write nothing more till now because this diary had to be censored and had been sitting in a sealed case at Euston till yesterday. On Thursday 27th, in pouring rain I took 2 cases of my own books, snaps, papers and diaries + 2 packing cases of official books, already sealed by the man from Somerset House. I had lunch with my friend Mary who gave me the name of her cousin in Belfast and aunt in Ballymoney.

Yesterday morning I went to see Dr Malleson and she confirmed that I have started a baby. She thought it was lucky I was going to Ireland and I am glad for Rosa, Margot and K, and for ES. Both E and Margot are glad and I am thrilled, tho' the job does seem stupendous now. I lunched with Margot and told her and had a long tea with E at Euston. I was good on the whole, especially as the morning sickness period described by Dr M lasts 8 weeks and I haven't been sick in the morning yet. She said I probably would have by now if I were going to, so it is late enough to be going.

Saturday 8 March

It was awful to see E on the platform at Euston as we puffed smokily away. I looked at the *Standard* and out of the window while it was light, till beyond Tring I looked with sentimental feelings for the familiar canal. It is 7 years since E and I first walked its towpath. Soon after Bletchley I had dinner, and finished after Rugby. At Nuneaton the second occupant of my compartment got in. I must have slept quite a lot. It seemed quite a short time before I heard 'Stranraer Harbour' and I had to get up. It was still quite dark (5.0 am) but the stars were shining. I found a porter but could understand little of his dialect, but he collected the luggage. I queued up on board for permits and then censoring. A man looked at the hatbox and case, especially my camera (to see if there was any film in it) and handbag (for sealed letters). At last I got safely on board and had some breakfast – a good breakfast except that there was no marmalade. I felt better after that in spite of my cold. When we started at 8.0 I went on deck. It was a lovely morning with a pink & gold sunrise over the hills, tho' it was very cold. It was a smooth crossing but we waited an hour outside Larne, landing just after 11. It is a pleasant little run down the coast to Belfast. I taxied with my luggage to the hotel. I found it a typical private hotel with the independent elderly ladies always to be found who have nothing better to think about than food and their health. A few officers and nurses who have their meals apart. My room seems very small and full of luggage. Its saving grace is an electric fire so I retire there for solitude since I can only just put up with the other people for meals. The food is quite good and apparently unrestricted except that each person has a separate tin of sugar, distributed on Thursday.

I went to the office at Moore House in the afternoon and sought out Reville. He had expected me before. He said I should be in Belfast all the time I was on HO relief and told me my district would be Enniskillen subject to Diggines' signature – probably the easiest district in the UK but isolated. I should be quite on my own. Hardie, his assistant, told me I should probably go in June. Reville is very busy as he is CI and BIR for all NI.* He has a general permit to England but no one else can go more than twice a year.

Belfast is a hideous place. I go to the office in a rattle-y old tram (for 1d) along a street without one building worth looking at except, perhaps, the new BBC building. The shops are not bad but expensive. It seems strange to see them all with unbroken windows. There are plenty of surface shelters and a few balloons to protect Harland & Wolff's shipbuilding yards.

I could not face hunting for digs so I buried my gloom in the cinema for 3 hours – 2 American films, neither good, but it was dry and distracting. I can hardly bear to think of E or of home. To unpack Whisky, the little horse, last night made me cry. Bed is the best place.

Sunday 9 March

On the whole I have got through today better than I expected. I ordered a paper at the office and was mildly surprised to be able to get the *Telegraph* on weekdays and the *Sunday Times*, tho' the *ST* didn't arrive till noon. It made me quite at home to be reading it as usual, but more thoroughly. After lunch I wrote to Rosa and Margot and went out to post letters. I found 2 small parks, saw the University and the river Lagan and eventually got by another route to the centre of the town. I found 3 of the addresses where digs were advertised but only one was even possible. After tea I wrote to Elsie and after supper I went to the lounge. The inmates tend to talk to me. They can't quite make me out. I detect some ill feeling between the elderly lady party and the 'Services' party but the most interesting thing was the general dislike of Priestley's *Postscript* – general, but much stronger among the military and their wives. They complain that he is boring and ask how his wife can live with him. But he makes them

* Chief Inspector and head of the Board of Inland Revenue for Northern Ireland.

uncomfortable and I suspect this is because he gets under their skins. This war will have achieved some good if it manages to shake up, even a little, the people who live in this hotel.

Tuesday 11 March

Two possibilities for living have emerged: Hardie knows a young woman with 2 little girls, husband in Admiralty, who takes Paying Guests at Holywood, the suburb where he lives. He is taking me there on Thursday. The other is a furnished flat at £2.2/- per week at Sydenham, a slightly nearer suburb. The flat attracts me because of its independence but it would probably be more expensive. Anyway, it will presumably only be until June. Someone at the office said that he had heard that Marjorie had complained that the men weren't nice to her and hence possibly I was being put away by myself at Enniskillen.

Had an interview this morning with a nephew on behalf of his widowed aunt. Her husband had 9 children by his first wife and 12 by her, and 18 survive. She has £104 EPT to pay on a pub and wanted to claim HK and for a son of 21 learning motor engineering. The typist at Belfast approves of my dictation and wishes I were there permanently. She told me there was a lot of feeling against England and the war in Belfast – 'Just as soon live under Hitler' – but not so openly said as earlier.

Saturday 15 March

I have had 2 late nights – hence the silence here since Wednesday. On Thursday Mary Roney's cousin Jack phoned and suggested going to the cinema. He is a nice lad, 6 feet high and handsome. We went to the Ritz. The best thing was the MOI* film *Christmas Under Fire*. It was the first of its kind I had seen and I thought it good. Some of the photographs were lovely – country churches, hills and fields patrolled by soldiers, evacuee children picking holly, Christmas leave, finally Christmas trees down the tube but you couldn't see what station it was. The picture of London, even

* Ministry of Information.

the bombed shops and houses, made me homesick. The main film was *Saturday's Children*, an American 'social document' – not bad, tho' rather gloomy – domestic happiness threatened by insecurity and poverty. Jack Roney suggested that the immunity of Belfast from raids (up to now) is due to the Germans' hope of getting it intact!

Reville came in to see me while Williams was talking about the Recorder procedure on appeals. On any appeal the taxpayer can claim a re-hearing before the Recorder or the County Court judge. You have to be very respectful and call him 'Your Honour'. I must try and get to a hearing before I go to Enniskillen.

I have had one letter only from E. Margot said in a letter I got yesterday that he phoned last Saturday and told her he had a bad throat and would be tied to the house. I can't help worrying. Had a letter from Dr Malleson on Thursday enclosing one from her patient who gave the name and address of a woman doctor in Dublin and an account of how she had her baby there – quite useful. I shall go and see her before I go to Enniskillen. I still don't want to smoke or drink coffee – otherwise normal.

Sunday 16 March

A really lovely day again – sunny, misty and no wind. A frost in the morning but quite hot walking. After breakfast I set out for the wall of hill behind the town which you can see from anywhere. I just walked towards it from the hotel, first through squalid small houses and across a dreary big bog with an engineering factory on it. Hundreds of small children, some of them pretty, most of them dirty and stupid-looking, were playing in the street. I counted 82 in about 3 minutes. I have never seen so many children living in such a small area. I reckon I walked about 6 miles altogether. After lunch I listened to Roosevelt's speech, recorded, and wrote to E and to Mary Roney. Not too bad for a Sunday!

Tuesday 18 March

Rain this morning but it cleared this afternoon, tho' it is cold. I couldn't go to see the flat at Sydenham but I am going tomorrow. The thought of the baby is the one thing that consoles me.

Wednesday 19 March

A very satisfactory letter from ES today (one of two) saying John is very cross about my move – now, when Herrick's lack of experience is showing. I could not help some satisfaction from this. I should like to flatter myself that C10 would go to pieces without me! I bought 8oz of baby wool at lunchtime. This evening I went out to Sydenham to see the furnished flat. It costs 37/6d a week including use of cutlery, linen etc., gas and light. There is a dining room, rather gloomy, a large light bedroom, a room between hall and kitchen and a big kitchen. There is a grand piano in the bedroom. I could manage with 2 rooms, kitchen and bedsitting room, but Mrs McIlroy wants to let the whole flat. It is on the ground floor. I am thinking it over till tomorrow, but I am tempted by the quiet and independence and piano.

Friday 21 March

The night before last London had its heaviest raid since the city fire raid at the end of December, the first serious raid since I left. I did not get really worked up until the evening and then the news fixed my mind on the one subject. I could not keep my thoughts off E and the family. I felt simply desperate, so helpless in the complete silence here – infinitely worse than I have felt on any occasion in London – a nightmare feeling. I finished a letter to E but cried and cried. I tried to comfort myself with probability, with the stupidity of worrying whatever had happened. Nothing altered my feeling. If it hadn't been for the baby I should have tackled Reville this morning in desperation. At last I fell asleep, only to be awakened by the unmistakable sound of a mouse somewhere in the room. The last straw!

By being very strong minded I made myself do nothing. In the morning I found it had been in 2 of the 3 drawers of the dressing table and I heard it before I got up. Horrid! I told the office that something must be done and I think they have looked in the top drawer, but I doubt whether anyone has finally coped with it.

I am glad I am moving to the flat on Tuesday. Mrs McIlroy phoned and said she would collect me and my luggage at 5.0 and ask the milkman and the baker to leave their goods. I hope it will work, but I am sure I shall prefer it to living in a hotel. I made a budget and I don't think it will be so expensive as living here.

We have reduced the new accounts to nil and I begin to get a little post. Have got one of the books Dr Malleson recommended, but the other is still not in. The delays are awful. I heard that in normal times now (i.e. with no serious raids anywhere) it often takes 10 hours to get a phone call through to London.

Saturday 22 March

A vile day – cold, and it has not ceased raining all day. After going to the office this morning I came back to lunch and didn't go out again at all. I began a vest for the baby, did my MO diary and continued Margot's blouse. Reville came to see me this morning. I am to stay at Belfast 1 for another 3 weeks, that is, till 19 April. The more I think of it the more scandalous it seems to send me to Enniskillen, an easy district where I shall forget all the EPT I ever knew and have to learn about farms. Any oldish HG man could do it – a man who is getting decrepit and hasn't the mental energy and the will to tackle EPT. They should keep me in a heavy EPT district doing my bit hard. They don't know I am trying to do 2 jobs – taxes and a baby.

Thursday 27 March

I moved to the flat on Tuesday evening. Mrs McIlroy called for me about 5.45 in her car and took me from door to door. At first I seemed all thumbs, couldn't remember where things were kept. The blackout took me ages and I overslept on Wednesday morning till 9.0. But I am getting used to it. It is lovely to cook what I like when I like and to have my own books and pictures and the little horse and E's photograph which all make it more my own. The geyser isn't fixed yet – won't be till Monday – and the water doesn't get hot enough for a bath. The blinds in my bedroom are a nuisance and have to be folded up, but these things will right themselves and are small. Mr Bennett upstairs is in the navy & Mrs B is a hearty north country woman from Darlington. They are friendly and I went up to hear the 9.0 news last night and was shown photographs of her family.

I have had bouts of depression, usually in the office when I haven't had enough to do. This morning I wrote to E, not having heard from him since Monday morning, and felt dismal. But I went to lunch and got my ration book dealt with and then joined the *Times* book club and got out a book at once – Herbert Read's *Annals of Innocence & Experience*. I felt much better after this – almost resurrected. When I got back Miss Harrison said there was good news from Yugoslavia. After the government had given in to Hitler there was a revolution early this morning. So I felt still better, had a small snack lunch today and was quite ravenous for my dinner.

Sunday 30 March

Yesterday I shopped in the afternoon after lunch in Belfast. Just as I was leaving the office Wardrop paid a social call. He was quite cordial (for him). When he asked me how I liked it I told him. He takes the official view: when you get your HG you must have a district. I said I thought this too rigid for wartime, and much as I should like my own district, I thought I should be doing more now on EPT. He was lunching with Reville, so perhaps he passed it on! I had a chit from Establishments, asking for amendments and additions (if any) to preferences. I said my preference for London had been strengthened since I came to Belfast but I would prefer almost anywhere in the southern half of England to NI.

A lovely long letter from E on Friday morning – lovely, so lovely that I cried a little in the bus as I read it.

1941

Monday 31 March

A letter from E saying he thought from what my letters didn't say that I must be very unhappy.

Reville came to see me and I told him I wanted all my leave in September. A fortnight at most, he said. I pointed out that I could only go to England once and I wanted my leave to go there, but he couldn't do anything. I must see what PI Establishments said. I told him I would probably have an operation while I was in England and he was quite sympathetic about that. Maybe I would like to go earlier than September. On medical grounds something might be done – official business. From his standpoint it would be more convenient to take sick leave before I go to Enniskillen.

The geyser is still not fixed. I long for a bath but they have promised to come tomorrow morning without fail. The rice pudding I made was marvellous. I thought it would last 2 nights but I finished it – and after steak, cauliflower and fried potatoes, but I had a snack lunch.

Wednesday 2 April

Last night I went rather reluctantly to see Mrs Darling (with whom Mary Roney had put me in touch). She turned out very nice – a dentist, practising with her father – married last August to a man in the Colonial Office who had to leave for Trinidad the same day. Has a sister here working as nurse in a maternity hospital, another living at Blackheath, married to the MOH of Woolwich. I hope I see more of her. She may be able to help a lot about doctors etc. She lent a map of Belfast, which is a boon, and gave me a supper of egg and lettuce sandwiches, sponge sandwich, shortcake and tea.

Thursday 3 April

An accountant in this morning who said he thought I had struck a bad patch of weather; it wasn't usually as bad as this. I wondered – was this a form of local patriotism? A lovely fire tonight which makes me lazy. My own superior coal has arrived at last (ordered on Monday!), moreover I have had a pleasant, well-balanced dinner – fried sausage, boiled potatoes, lettuce, baked apple and custard, tea and bread and butter. An altogether better day.

Saturday 5 April

I got back at 4.0 and found that the geyser was working enough for a hot bath. The luxury! Since then I have been just lazy and have done nothing but cook some supper (fried whiting, brown bread and butter and one of Mrs Bennett's tarts); otherwise I have just toasted myself by the fire and read *The Voyage* – I am enjoying it very much.

Sunday 6 April

My *Sunday Times* came today. A pity we have lost Benghazi. Germany has attacked Yugoslavia and Greece. I can't get it out of my head how they are suffering. And what looks like a pro-German resolution in Irak may be the most serious of all. To bring a child into such a world.

Tuesday 8 April

Last night I heard the siren again, for the first time since the 6th March when I had to taxi to Kennington to lunch with Margot. I had just fallen asleep and gunfire awoke me and a few minutes later the siren went. I considered, and decided there was no point in getting up. There are 2 bay windows in my bedroom but the bed is in the far corner and it is on the ground floor. I heard the Bennetts above me getting up and she was excited. I hadn't heard the plane come over. She reported that there was a big fire (which I heard today was a timber yard). The AA sounded very poppety & shallow after the heavy London barrage. The earlier planes kept high but later they evidently found the AA was not much risk and came lower. There were long gaps when I must have slept, but several times planes and bombs and gunfire awoke me. They dropped 3 landmines. Two fell in the lough but one hit a factory for spare parts and killed workmen rumoured to number anything from 6 to 100. One plane was brought down by a fighter near Larne – exploded in the air. There was some excitement this morning. I could hear people running about the road and also the patter of shrapnel. Machine guns kept popping at the flares. Miss Harrison, who was with her people over their shop, just by the river, said their shop window was blown out and the front door blown in. I was not so jittery as I was after the heavy London raid last month, worrying about people, but it was worse here than at Purley because it is a smaller place. One feels more conspicuous, more part of the target.

Good Friday, 11 April

2 days' gap because I have left the diary till after the news and lingered, talking to the Bennetts, till my fire had gone out and the only thing to do was to go to bed. So tonight I am beginning at 8.10.

Just a few footnotes to Monday's raid: casualties were 8 killed and one or two not found. The rumours soared to 150. Almost all were in one factory on night shift. I hear that an unexploded shell came through the roof of a house across the road, through the ceiling and made a mess of the bedroom. The people had just gone downstairs. Also, we have a smoke screen on moonlit nights when the weather is suitable. Mrs Bennett thought it was poison gas the first night. We have had instructions about what to do if the office is damaged. I have called at the Blood Transfusion office and offered mine if necessary up to 6th June.

I begin to feel a little curiosity stir. I got *The Face of Ireland* (Batsford) from the library and made tentative plans to go to Dublin for a weekend, Saturday afternoon to Monday (taking a Monday instead of today). I could explore Dublin and see the doctor on the Monday. I might also perhaps go out this Monday if it is fine. I have thought of Newcastle if there is a bus. It is a pity not to see the places within reach of Belfast while I am here.

I get a lot of pleasure at present out of food. This may be a kind of zest due to the baby. I enjoy planning my breakfasts and dinners and get hungry for them. It may be partly the scarcity of some things, for instance,

I felt triumphant this evening when I got some cheese, and enjoyed every crumb of my dinner – fried cod and fried potatoes, brown malt bread, cheese and lettuce, stewed apple & post toasties, tea and a tiny piece of bread and butter – especially the second course. Since I got my delayed marmalade ration I have appreciated a little of it for breakfast as never before.

E's letters are lovely; I don't feel I am getting out of touch with him at all.

Saturday 12 April

I have found out about buses to Newcastle on Monday. If it is fine I shall try to go. Buses are much better than trains.

It is milder but damp and this afternoon I felt more depressed than I have been for some days – the holiday perhaps. Also, the scarcity of work makes it seem so pointless to be here at all. And I had difficulty shopping. Nothing but stewing beef, no stamps at the Sydenham shop, no firelighters, no brown bread except Veda which is 6d for a small loaf; and everywhere packed.

Easter Sunday, 13 April

It is the spring at last. I went for a 2 hour walk just after 3.0 and it was warm. I found a good walk up to 562 feet past the Parliament Building at Stormont which I could see only from the side.

Wednesday 16 April

On Monday I developed a cold due, I think, to sitting frozen in the unheated office on Good Friday morning. Not a serious one, but sufficient to make my head ache on Monday. I was not detained from my expedition to Newcastle and duly caught the bus, being lucky to be on the front seat after starting in the front corner. The weather was sunny and warm, with deep blue sky and puffy white clouds racing across it. I didn't trust it fully and was right, but till 12.15, when we got to Newcastle, it was perfect.

We went via Ballynahinch and Castlewellan – little grey country towns looking surprisingly French owing to a paved and gravelled *place*, with flat grey houses and a *mairie*. Castlewellan had chestnuts with seats and was bustling with life. All the shops open, the whole population out, old men with wonderful whiskers and hats; the ubiquitous swarms of dirty children; lads driving cows and sheep straying perilously in front of the bus; a market consisting entirely of old clothes stalls.

You would think to hear people talk that Newcastle was a veritable Brighton but in fact it is a toy seaside town. One big hotel with a station next door, a mile of shops and houses, a swimming pool, a tiny harbour with a tiny harbourmaster's office. It is all grey – grey houses, grey sand, grey rocks, grey shingle and looks charming with sun out but sombre when the sun and clouds are grey too. The country is attractive – the route was lovely – mostly cultivated except on the hill top. Water of all kinds – sea inlets, streams, lake, mere, pond, bog – all sizes. Men working in the fields, usually with horses, but once I saw a man striding across a field with a bag slung round his shoulder, sowing by hand, left and right, rhythmically.

Last night was disturbed. I went up to hear the news with the Bennetts and Mr B told me the *Formidable*, our newest aircraft carrier, was in. She was launched from Belfast just before Christmas. On Monday about lunchtime the sirens went in Belfast. I heard something that may have been guns but I thought was thunder and also machine guns but there were swarms of soldiers everywhere. Apparently they were on reconnaissance. The sirens went last night at 1.40 and the All Clear (in the middle of which I heard what I took to be a time bomb going off) at 5.0 am. From 11.0 to 4.0, with scarcely 10-minute intervals, German planes kept coming over continuously dropping heavy stuff – must have been heavy as the vibrations were remarkable. The AA kept up a continuous barrage but it couldn't even keep them high. You could hear them dive low before releasing their bombs. Our fighters were up 2 at a time, there was incessant machine gunning. It was the worst night I have had, either at Purley or here. The Bennetts came down to my dining room and I made tea. At 12.0 I went to bed in the dark thinking I was as safe there as anywhere and, tho' it was impossible to sleep, I should be resting physically. Several times the bed swayed like a cot being rocked. Doors and windows rattled and I could see against the blackout the glare of fires. The most nerve-racking thing was when the Germans glided in silently. The only thing one heard was the crump of bombs. I went over poems in my head: Keats's Nightingale, Grecian Urn, Autumn, bits of Hyperion; Shelley's West Wind and Night; Shakespeare's Sonnets, 'Let me not to the marriage of true minds' and 'To me fair friend you never will be old'; de la Mare's 'When I lie where shades of darkness' – so apposite with the last verse: 'Look thy last on all things lovely every hour' . . . They seemed even more beautiful and permanent in that inferno; and from those to hymns – 'Oh God Our help', 'Jerusalem' and the Magnificat and 'I will lift mine eyes unto the hills'.

This morning it was good to be alive and I enjoyed every crumb of my breakfast.

Friday 18 April

We have had 2 quiet nights' rest, which were welcome. But on Wednesday London had its heaviest raid yet. I felt I should go mad yesterday. Belfast first and then the anxiety of wondering about the London people. The post hadn't come, so when I got home I found a lovely collection. E's letter was posted yesterday, after the raid, so I was glad to know he was safe. His letter came in record time, while the one postmarked 28th March, which arrived 15th April, was a record the other way. None of them was opened. After this I felt a bit more cheerful. There is not enough work to distract me and I worry and freeze, sitting in my coat with no heating.

Last night Mrs Bennett said she had had the offer of a furnished house and was moving there next Thursday, tho' she was sleeping there from yesterday. It was thought to be safer, being further from the aerodrome and having a solid cupboard under the stairs. They were both concerned about me and I certainly would not like the flat so much with no company upstairs. They will have a bedroom and a sitting room to spare but had to offer them first to friends, tho' they would both prefer me to have them. The other possibility is to lodge at the house across the road. Mrs Hay – Yorkshire, very nice, more 'genteel' than Mrs B. She and her husband are wardens, but she had a fall and mustn't go out at night so she is alone when he is on duty.

When I had a bath last night I thought the baby was showing a little in increased bulkiness but perhaps it was fancy.

Saturday 19 April

Reville came to see me today & told me about his landmine. I told him there wasn't much work at Belfast 1 and he said he would move me round to another district. My cold is still bad and I froze in the office. I did my shopping and got back soon after 3.0. Tried the piano for 30 minutes, but there was nothing to play and my fingers were woefully stiff. At Mrs Hay's last night I heard that the Dublin, Dundalk and Cork fire brigades came to Belfast's help in the raid. I was impressed and quite cheered. Perhaps adversity may make the Irish more civilized. Also, firemen from Glasgow and Liverpool came to help. They were brought in destroyers and were in action at 2.30 am.

Mrs Bennett is having a job to clear up. She says I can go there to live. I am going to see it tomorrow. The points against Mrs Hay's place are gas lighting, no privacy and the fire has to be lit specially for bath. There is a piano at Mrs B's and the hot water is good. I gave them tea when they were here. They have left me their wireless set.

Thursday 1 May

It is 8 weeks since I left Euston. I was rather excited this afternoon about Raper, who is going to try to wangle a permit to go to the AGM 3 weeks on Sunday. Apparently, if the permit question is solved, I could go on the Friday night, take the Monday as Good Friday and get back on Tuesday. It would be heavenly. No one wants to go as delegate as London is thought to be too hot! He invited me to Bangor at the weekend. I may go the weekend after. More work today. I solved the lunch problem by having soup and a roll at a milk bar and then 2 salmon rolls and a bun at the Snackery. This morning I got a lb of oranges at the local shop! Lovely!

Tuesday 6 May

A full 5 days since last I wrote. On Saturday I caught the 2.45 train to Dublin. I was lucky to step into a non-smoker in the middle of an argument between a man who wanted to smoke and 3 determined women who insisted on their rights. Finally he said, 'I'm not liking your company,' and went out with his woman, leaving the corner seat vacant for me.

The journey, when we were moving, was interesting. Portadown looks a dead, dull place. Gradually we climbed until we were passing the Mourne mountains, leaving Newry to the east in a hollow of the hills. It looked big and more interesting than Portadown, perhaps because it was further away. At the next station we stopped for Immigration and examination of identity cards. Through a cutting in grey mauve rock we ran down hill, leaving the highest of the Mourne mountains between us and the sea and so to Dundalk, the first town in Eire. A long pause for customs. The country seemed to change its character and grew softer and more lush and spring was much further on, sheltered from the north. We got lovely glimpses of vivid blue sea till just north of Dublin. We were running by the shore and watching lazy, crawling waves on the sand and the red sails of boats in tiny harbours. Coming back on Sunday it was just as sunny but more misty.

I loved Dublin which seemed much more attractive than Belfast. The hotel was palatial – the Gresham in O'Connell Street. Imposing but not overwhelming on the outside, rather like Versailles, with chandeliers and urns and mouldings inside, but less expensive than I expected. It worked out at 12/6d for bed and breakfast. The shops were interesting in these days – my mouth watered at windows full of jam and marmalade, unrationed butter, bacon, meat.

I went to the Abbey Theatre to see *The Money Doesn't Matter*, a comedy, but serious with an Irish setting. Quite good, but I thought one or two of the character parts were overacted. The audience was interesting and I had the last 1 & 6 pence seat. It was strange to come out at 10.50 to find street lamps full on, lighted shop windows and buses fully lighted. But I had a feeling of depression; I couldn't live in such a precarious peace 'purchased' as it were at other people's expense while they were suffering. I feel more content in the blackout and blitz.

It was another brilliant day. After a large and leisurely breakfast I walked round Dublin along the Liffey to look at the Custom House; then the other way to see the 4 Courts, both lovely 18th century buildings. The river reminds me of the Seine and the RC element – friars, nuns, orphans in crocodiles – and the second hand bookshops made me think of Paris. I loved Stephen's Green, a lovely little park with mallard and baby ducks. There is a grace and individuality about Dublin and an intellectual life which make it more attractive than Belfast.

I went to see Dr McCormick at 12.0. She looked like a char in what appeared to be a pink flannel petticoat and had a mop of grey hair. I liked her. She said I needn't bother to see a doctor till August unless I get puffiness or severe headache (meaning kidneys are not standing up to the strain). She said I could not conceal it after June and thought Enniskillen a place which would enjoy making a scandal. She did not approve so whole heartedly as Dr Malleson. She thought a child should have both its parents. She will give me a doctor in Belfast in case of emergency and says if I go to England it must be at least 6 weeks before the baby is due.

I caught the 6.0 train and came from Belfast by tram reaching the house at 11.25. 45 minutes later the siren went and we had a real blitz. Our side of the river got it worse than on Easter Tuesday. The first half hour was the worst. We were in the dining room and the windows were blown out. I saw a piece of shutter fly across the room and a huge cloud of smoke and soot came from the fire before the gas went out. We went into my sitting room with an oil lamp as the fire was not lighted. All the windows were damaged except my sitting room and a little one upstairs. The ceiling of the larder came down and some of the moulding of my bedroom ceiling fell. The noise was terrific. It went on without a lull at all till 2.30 and gradually eased off till 4.0. We went to bed at 4.50. There is no water, no gas, no electricity. I believe the dockyard is badly damaged and there were some appalling fires. The centre of the city – offices, shops – had serious fires, and the office was saved by the fire fighters who were a good team, reinforced by Cartwright & Baillie & Co who came in to see if they could help, altho' they were not on duty. The first floor non-revenue people had no one. By great efforts they put out the fire which began to spread from other buildings and the damage was limited to windows and window frames.

Wednesday 7 May

[continued]
(forced to stop last night because it was too dark and we have only candles). We did not wake up till 9.0 but I had only about 2 and a half hours' sleep. The All Clear sirens did not go because the electricity which works them was off. People emerged from shelters or were bombed out and made a lot of noise so that it was difficult to get any rest. The sky was alight with fires. But before I slept I heard the birds' dawn chorus – a miracle of sanity and sweetness. Had to boil a kettle on the oil stove. Had an orange and some cornflakes for breakfast. I took the wise precaution of taking cheese sandwiches and an orange for lunch, thinking correctly that it would be impossible to get anything in the city. We could get no milk, bread or tea in the office. The heating and lighting were off and by the afternoon there was no water. I was lucky to get a lift in a warden's car to a point normally less than 5 minutes from the office. We had to go by a devious route and I was soon quite lost. We saw appalling destruction of small houses, street shelters, a church quite flat, but I was told the casualties were not large because so many people had fled to the woods and hills.

The baby seems more conspicuous, especially after meals, tho' apart from fatigue due to lack of sleep I am very well. I bought some calcium tablets today. On Sunday night at the height of the bombing Mrs Hay said, 'I do feel very sorry for expectant mothers.' 'Especially in the late stages,' I said. She said, 'No – more dangerous in the early stages, before the child is fully formed!' I wrote to Loach yesterday about Enniskillen giving a strong hint of the real objection. I gave Reville a copy but he made no comment on this at all. He was quite cordial and sympathetic, but, 'just bad luck your name came up in conjunction with a vacancy there'. He didn't want to come himself and it cost the Treasury over £200 to move him, not counting the heavy expense he had which was not refunded.

Friday 9 May

Today the inconveniences following the raid were more in evidence than ever. Some of our building had to be vacated because adjacent buildings were being dynamited. Water has been turned off in the city all day as well as being still off in Sydenham. Gas was turned off in the city so that I had to have a sandwich and a glass of cold milk for lunch; traffic was more congested than ever. As against this, gas at Sydenham has reappeared; it was cold all day so that I sat in my thickest coat and was still not warm. I spent most of lunchtime visiting the Food Office to ask where I get my cheese, bacon and jam rations now that Bank buildings had been destroyed. I was given 4 alternative shops and got some bacon after a long wait at Liptons. Also, for the first time since reaching Ireland, I managed to get lamb cutlets as my meat ration.

Queuing for rations

Wednesday 14 May

The landing of Hess in Scotland has provided one of the few comedies of the war, quite apart from its importance as a symptom of Nazi dissension or its practical use to us.

I have been applying for an exit permit to visit England as delegate to the AGM. Cartwright saw Headquarters and gathered it would be granted, so I had to do the formal part. The local police station is in an area roped off. They told me I could write now as I should get it, but this seemed too Irish to depend on, so I went to another police station at lunchtime and after a long tale persuaded them to give me a form which I completed and delivered to the local police station tonight.

Thursday 15 May

A letter (of 9th) from the family tonight. They hadn't had my letter punctually either so we are making the same moan. NI centre meeting at 4.15 – 12 people there and I was chosen representative to the AGM. We went through the agenda and discussed it. At the end Miles, in the Chair, made a nice little speech welcoming me as the first woman in NI. Rather sweet of them and it illustrates the difference in the large membership, with its virtual anonymity, of the London centre and a small provincial centre where everyone knows everyone else.

Friday 16 May

Letters this morning – a spate – from Rosa, Margot, ES, E and an OK card from Margot after last Saturday's raid on London, Mass Observation and my permit to go to the AGM. A lovely collection. Reville chatted for 45 minutes this afternoon. He is not going to be rigid about leave and agreed when I said I shouldn't apply for any next weekend, taking Good Friday on the Monday. He said he would wink at odd days or long weekends, tho' he couldn't put anything in writing, so long as the work didn't suffer.

Monday 19 May

Sunny and really warmer today. Swallows were darting and squeaking over the houses at Sydenham and gnats flying. A letter from Loach in England, from which it is clear that I am for Enniskillen and no avoiding it. I am inclined not to try. But he says he is not clear whether I consider my health unfits me for charge of a district and if so can he have a medical report for consideration. I shan't reply till McCreath has given his advice, also E, but the question is whether I ought to show it to Reville (who is going over this weekend and seeing Loach on Friday) and how much I should tell him. Have progressed with him quite a lot in the last week – talked to him for 45 minutes today. I have bought my ticket for London – £4.19.3d including sleeper. I seem to be bulging a lot today. I hope it won't be noticeable at the weekend.

Tuesday 20 May

Fine, but cooler today. Went for a walk round Circular Rd this evening with Mrs H. It was pleasant. The trees and gardens are lovely. Showed Loach's letter to Reville. He thanked me but made no enquiry beyond confirming that I didn't intend to suggest that my health would unfit me for charge of a district. I said I should reply to it, but not till I had seen McCreath at the weekend.

Thursday 29 May

A week's gap – and what a week. I left Belfast on Friday at 5.20 and got back Wednesday at 11.20. The journey to London was tiring and not too comfortable though I was thrilled at every mile nearer. It took two hours crossing to Stranraer and it was a damp, misty evening with a NW wind blowing strongly. Reville and I had a pleasant but odd meal before we sailed – haddock and chips, toast, biscuits and jam and coffee. We went on deck as soon as we left and he looked rather green. I felt completely comfortable, though the crew said it was rough and the *Princess Margaret* certainly rolled most exuberantly. We left Stranraer about 10.40 and reached Euston about 10.20 on Saturday. The other three sleepers were occupied – one by a young woman who smoked too much and another by one with two small children. I didn't get much sleep.

At Euston I rang up E and was so happy to hear his voice that I just stood and cried all over the phone box. I had already been worked up by the beauty of the country between Bletchley and Watford, so well known and full of associations. We arranged to meet at 11.50 as he had to be in the office since Osborne was at a committee meeting. I rang Margot up and talked a little and then went to Marble Arch to shop, but had no time to buy anything. E and I had lunch at a Mecca in Cannon Street and then went on chance to Rina's flat – he had not had my last letter so had made no arrangements with Elsie or Rina as suggested, but we were lucky – just caught her and she left us the flat to ourselves. We fucked for a lovely afternoon in her bed. I had not consciously wanted him since I left England, and I believe the physiological basis is altered, but it was lovely. He hurt me more than for ages but it was sheer ecstasy. 'Not bad, considering we are out of practice,' he said. In the middle the phone went. It was Elsie, so we were able to fix up with her.

Here the black came uppermost. Margot met me in the rain under the cliff. Rosa saw almost at once that I was bulging and I told her the truth. The shock was great and she was quite prostrate all the evening. Margot kept going from me to her and back. It was dismal for her. I felt awful as Rosa had prepared to celebrate my return and it seemed so awful. It was a relief to have Elsie there. Eventually we went to bed. I heard 2.0 strike before I slept and I was awake at 7.0 and saw Rosa for an hour. She was still upset and seemed to have developed a cold. Elsie stayed till 11.30 and talked to Rosa. Both Rosa and Margot were grateful to her. I caught the 9.13 to the AGM.

It was my first experience and I found it interesting until I got sleepy about 4.0. The meeting began at 10.0 and finished at 5.0 with an hour for lunch and was at the Strand Palace Hotel. King was very good in the chair – strong but good-humoured – witty and very skilful at guiding the arguing in the direction desired by the committee. He could say devastating things without rousing bad feeling. Quite a number of young members made interesting and good speeches. I saw Brennan and had lunch with the other women – Ellis, Le Huquet, Preston. I like them all especially the last 2. They were most sympathetic about NI. I saw Reville for a minute and he told me the transfer letters would be issued this week.

McCreath caught me at the beginning of the interval and said he had written as he was not certain whether I could get to London. He said that he had told King about me and the 2 of them had seen Bradford last week. Bradford was surprisingly broadminded and said if I could avoid any scandal inside and outside the office a broad view would be taken of medical certificates and I should get a long period of paid sick leave. If there was a scandal it would be unpaid sick leave. McCreath said if he laid down this condition he must see that I was in a district where there was every chance of carrying it out. He agreed and McCreath has written to Loach saying he has seen Bradford and I must not be given a district yet and I have good ground for being moved back to London. McCreath said, 'What about the city?' and this took a load off my mind, especially the assurance that at worst I should not be dismissed or have to resign. McCreath has done very well – 'a pretty problem you gave us this time', he said. He and King thought I had done the best thing in writing to the Association. He said that while he did not agree with my view he fully admitted my right to act on my own judgement. Bradford apparently insisted on treating it as an unfortunate accident. People find it easier to condone this than a deliberate decision.

The office newsletter had an announcement on leave which gave a little more latitude, so I stayed another day. On Monday I went to town and shopped with Margot in the morning. After coffee I went to Treasure Cot and bought a maternity belt, surprisingly light and comfortable at 20/5d; a brassière (they had only one – I have to order another) at 7/11d; a 2 piece, light frock and sleeveless coat, 5 and a half guineas, nigger brown with a squiggly cream pattern over it, quite office-y and comfortable. Then to lunch at Guy Pearce with E. The girl remembered me quite well. It was lovely to see him again and he was relieved at the official news. After lunch I went to see Dr Malleson. She was cordial and surprised to see me, gave me a urine test and one for blood pressure and said I was very good. She approved of my belt but said I shouldn't carry the baby flatly. I was bigger now than some people a month later! She was most interested to hear about the department and told me to write to Queen Charlotte's now about having the baby there. It is at Hammersmith and she did not think raids were much risk. She asked about Rosa.

After this I went and bought a ring at Woolworths (as I intend to tell Mrs Hay I am married, since I shall hope to stay here till I go to England). To Selfridges and bought *The Single Handed Mother* with no trouble. I met E at Victoria for tea and caught the 6.10. Rosa expected me before and seemed disappointed in spite of the fact that I seemed to make her worse when I was there! But she picked up a bit in the evening, tho' on Tuesday morning she seemed worse again. I was afraid I shouldn't be able to lunch with E, but I told her I wouldn't and she made me go. So we had another lunch. Saying goodbye was not so bad this time. I met Rosa and Margot at London Bridge and we went to Euston, had tea there and caught the Stranraer train at 4.50. The journey was excellent. Rosa decided to go to Largs with Margot and they came to see me on the boat. She was much better in spirit and quite enjoyed her dinner on the train and a cup of tea at Wigan. Her cold was in her throat, but otherwise she seemed better. It is excellent for her to be going away. The change should do her good physically and she will be away from Purley and prevented from doing anything on the spur of the moment which she might regret.

I dawdled on the train and so missed the queue for permits and luggage on the boat and had no trouble. I had a good breakfast and went on deck. I got chilly after a time and went down to the saloon where I went soundly to sleep and did not awake till the crowd collected to go ashore! Mrs Hay was disappointed not to see Rosa but very cordial to me. I found quite a lot of work accumulated but I was so tired. It was a hectic weekend with a shortage of sleep and full of emotional heights and depths. But on the whole it was most profitable. I was glad to have faced the inevitable task of telling Rosa. I had done some essential shopping. I had seen Dr Malleson; best of all, I had the relief of knowing the official attitude and finding it better than I had hoped.

Last night we had an alert from 1.15–3.30 but no one heard anything and I was too tired to get up until things happened. Still tired, so I shall go to bed early. I still have the task of telling ES. E thought it would be too much to tell him to his face.

I spent £12 at the weekend in addition to the fare, £5! Cheap if it brings me 3 months paid sick leave!

1941

Sunday 1 June

At last we have had some summer weather, yesterday and today. I have just
basked in the garden in a cotton frock without stockings. Have told Mrs
Hay I am married but have to keep it dark for my job, also about the babe.
She was quite thrilled but couldn't understand how I could be so well
during the first half.

No letters yet. I have written to ES.

Friday 6 June

At last a letter from E. He did not write till last Friday but it took till last
night to reach me. Letters from Rosa and Margot yesterday. Rosa still
seems very upset, tho' she seems to be making an effort to hitch this next
experience on to something she knew before. She compared it to
Guinevere in Tennyson and Hawthorne's *Scarlet Letter*. She has written to E
what Margot calls an exclamatory letter.

Tuesday 10 June

A queer 'turn' this morning – the worst I have had since the baby began.
I awoke in the night and felt slightly sick, but nothing happened and I
slept after perhaps 45 minutes till Mrs Hay called me. Then I felt very
queer – just general malaise, not very sick, not a violent headache, but
not at all good. I staggered dizzily to the bathroom to be handy in
emergency and knelt on the floor but I couldn't see. Everything seemed
in a kind of brown dusk for a few minutes – then nothing more and I
gradually felt better. I happened to see my face in the bathroom mirror
and I looked very green so I loitered a bit till I got a colour so Mrs Hay
would not notice. In 20 minutes I was actually eating bacon and drinking
tea. I don't know what it was – too big a dinner; too hot a bath; or just
liver, but it is a warning not to be silly.

It has been chilly today but the sky cleared tonight and I walked for 35
minutes in the sun. Two nice letters yesterday – one most magnanimous

from Salmon, on the lines of 'take care of yourself and good for you'. One from Elsie. This morning one from E, rather dismal, but I loved him for it. He hadn't had a letter from me for a week so one of mine, at least, must be lost. He is more affected than one would think by Rosa's letter. He thinks it is hopeless to expect reconciliation. Queen Charlotte's will let me have the baby there.

Wednesday 25 June

I believe it is exactly a year since I got my promotion and what a year! E's letter did not get to me till today and I had a letter from Rosa that made me weep. Feeling quite fit but rather melancholy. I wrote a nasty letter to E yesterday. There is more work to do in Belfast I and I get more interruptions. Raper and Miss Harrison are regulars and this afternoon Miss Mathers and Miss Ray. She is attractive and good looking and I liked her. She knows Miss Rogers. She has a boy 6 months old. She worked up to a fortnight before and began again 6 weeks after but she is taller than me and of course there was no urgent need to conceal it.

Saturday 28 June

I have been rather depressed most of the week but better today. I think the root cause is Rosa. She replied to my 'tactless' letter, making an effort and being rather sweet, but it indicated the gulf between our views. I have read it twice and it has made me cry each time. The last 2 letters I had from E did not decrease my depression and I fear I wrote him 2 rather dismal letters this week. He expects so much of me and takes everything for granted. It is partly an inability to let himself go, partly the conflict in his mind, but I feel he should make an effort now, if at all. Also, it may be partly Rosa again as her letter did upset him. Anyway, the old dismal circle was revived in my mind – K and E and Me till I could have wept. I felt worst in the office – in the evenings I listened in and sewed and knitted.

Today Mrs Hay came home elated, with 9 lemons, 2 or 3 pairs of stockings, 1lb of marmalade, some chocolate and ham from Eire! Their weather was better than ours and they managed to do quite a lot in the week.

Monday 30 June

This morning I had a letter from McCreath saying he supposed I hadn't had a transfer letter yet but he thought that satisfactory arrangements had been made. Most tantalizing! More serious – he was sorry that the question of pay on sick leave was not so clear as Bradford had told him. The Treasury was considering the question of principle and the Board would have to follow their ruling, so I may not get paid. Anyway, he finished up by saying that tho' a special visit was unnecessary he would like to see me 'when I was next in London'. Does this mean I am being moved to London? Or does he mean when I am on leave (sick or ordinary)? Cremin came to see me and said he would prefer Enniskillen to Belfast 8. He is now on HO relief. He said he thought Reville was a bit cross at his plans being upset.

Tuesday 1 July

Very busy today. I dictated for over an hour, saw 2 accountants (one this morning about a coal merchant's EPT and one this afternoon on a minor enquiry). I didn't feel so good either. Early this morning I woke up and felt rather queer. After a time I got up and lit a candle but could hardly see it – another dizzy attack. I knelt on the floor as before and sat on my heels and eventually my eyes cleared and I felt better, but what causes it in the middle of the night? I looked at the time after I recovered – 5.45! It is similar to, but lasts longer than, the dark giddiness you get after stooping to weed, say. All day my head has felt a bit heavy, otherwise quite fit.

Sunday 6 July

Have had one letter from E since Thursday week, a letter of 24/6, then one
of 28–29/6. Yesterday Margot's letter said he had forgotten to lunch with
her last week. I was quite dismal and cried most of the afternoon. I suppose
there is nothing the matter with him, but if not it is inconsiderate. He can't
do much – less than most fathers – but he doesn't do even that. And at the
moment he is having a better time than either me or Margot. I decided to
write him a short note to the office and then not write again. Felt better
after posting it and going for a short walk in the rain.

Tuesday 8 July

My move arrived this afternoon – London HO relief – to report at
Somerset House on August 14th. Reville came in 3 or 4 minutes before my
letter arrived and pulled my leg by saying 'Dumbarton 1, in charge'! It is
convenient for me as it is cheap living here and gives Margot time to look
round in London.

Wednesday 9 July

I think the flutter I have felt very faintly for 3 weeks or a month (and
thought must be tea or something squeezing past a narrow place in my
inside) is the baby. It is so uniform and is more and more frequent. I am not
sure I didn't feel the heart beat this evening. This, combined with my move
back to London, has given me a kind of quiet thrill all day. It is a
reassurance to feel the child move – a kind of assurance that it (or nature) is
doing its share, that the miracle has begun and is continuing.

Thursday 10 July

Feeling better today. Everyone was out so I played the piano this evening.
Also had letters from home and from E this morning. I wrote to and liked
him better than I have for a week. I begin to think that the emotional

cyclone of last weekend was physiological in origin. I wrote him quite a cordial letter – even though he is beginning to prepare to spend all his leave with K.

Very nice letter from Margot, which has glowed in my mind all day. I don't know what I should do without her, especially now when Rosa cannot resist digs at me in every letter.

Sunday 13 July

The post has been very poor, but yesterday I had a surprise delivery – a brassière from Treasure Cot (opened by the censor!). Letters included ones from Ella, ES, A Paul. E had just got 4 of mine, all on the 7/8 of July. The worst was mine of the 17/6, delivered the 7th July. He consoled me by saying it was a nice letter which didn't suffer from its delay!

We are having a Centre meeting next Thursday instead of only one a year, as the committee is trying to stir up interest. I shall have to go and just hope no one observes my bulge because they want me to say something about promotion machinery (having had the most recent experience of struggling for my HG).

Saturday 19 July

I have been slack at the office and consequently bored. Went to the Centre meeting on Thursday. It was intended to rouse more interest on current topics among the rank & file. Quite an interesting meeting – nine people there.

Sunday 20 July

I dreamed on Friday night for the first time that I remember about the baby. I was holding him by the hand – about two to two and a half, a lovely child with wide mouth and wide dark eyes, dressed in jade shantung knickers and blouse and a linen sun hat. I wore a wide hat and it was a sunny day with holiday-ish atmosphere. A voice (sounded like a woman's, but don't know whose) said, 'It is quite all right to take him to Egypt now.' It was connected in my mind with the flight into Egypt. A very vivid, detailed dream.

Sunday 27 July

I have been busy packing my trunk and 2 big suitcases. It is a thankless job especially on a hot day but I did it with more pleasure than when I came to Belfast. First I had to note for E the censor numbers and sort my letters.

Thursday 31 July

Raid on London on Sunday night. I was relieved to hear from Rosa and Margot today. Expected to hear from E but I suppose the post is bad. Margot wrote a long letter – she has found a woman who might come and look after the baby who sounds most promising. I have written to her. To get this settled would be a great advantage and she sounds the right type. I hope I can afford it.

Sunday 3 August

My permit arrived on Friday morning – very quick. It seems hard to believe I have only 10 more nights here. A letter from Margot came yesterday afternoon – Mary Roney offers to share a flat with me. This was an offer Margot jumped at and E jumped at. In fact, Margot said she had never seen him so pleasantly relaxed as at the lunch when she told him about it. There is a lot to be said for it and I always wonder when I have lunched with her why I don't see more of her; also, it would help with expenses.

Saturday 9 August

An exciting, mixed day. At 10.45 Margot phoned. She booked the call from Purley last night and got through quite quickly this morning. It was lovely to hear her. She is deciding this afternoon with Mary between two places: one in Earls Court Road and one in Cromwell Road. She said the censor from NI had eased off and consequently letters have been coming more quickly. They have even had my last Tuesday's. So I wrote another today.

This morning I fell over. The first time (and I hope the last time) since the baby began. Skidded on a small mat in the hall and just sat down plonk. I don't think any harm was done but Mrs Hay rushed out very concerned. I was relieved to feel the baby flutter afterwards, as if to say 'Be careful of me!'

Sunday 17 August

What a week! I can't remember much before Wednesday. The office at Belfast was very sweet to me and I don't think they can have suspected anything. I treated them to cake for tea on Tuesday, and on Wednesday morning the women took me out to coffee and gave me a magnificent buttonhole of 2 roses with asparagus fern. Then Miss Harrison and the typists gave me a very nice hankie as a memento of Belfast! I met Mrs Hay at 4.0 and we had tea at the Carlton. She had brought two of my suitcases and saved me taxi-ing all the way. I then went back to say goodbye to Reville (he had a typist there so I couldn't discover how much he knew!), Hardie, Williams, Raper, Robinson and the typists who came down to put me in the taxi. So to York Rd station and goodbye to Mrs Hay.

The train went at 5.50 with the wind howling and the rain beating, but before we reached Larne the rain had stopped and the sun came out, and there was a glorious rainbow. I was rather nervous about the crossing but decided to have high tea (tea, toast and marg, fish and chips!), anyway thinking it would be better to be sick on something than nothing. Before I had finished, the cups were skidding about. I crept cautiously up on deck holding on all the way and found a seat. It was deserted except for a few tough men tottering about. Once settled I knew I should be all right. It was easily the roughest crossing I have had, at any rate in a small ship. I heard it was blowing at 60 miles an hour, but it was magnificent. The sea was vivid jade green and navy blue, covered with white horses, and against the precipitous Scots coast we could see the waves dashing high like a deep scalloped lace border. I had a sudden overpowering feeling of exhilaration which made me want to sing with happiness – something blatant or raucous like 'Land of Hope and Glory'!

This exaltation lasted all the way to Stranraer but evaporated in the long and tiring business of getting ashore. It was still blowing hard and we had to queue on the deck for censor's examination. He didn't look at my luggage but went through every single thing in my handbag except one or 2 censored letters from England. Finally I found my sleeper and the train went at 11.0. I didn't sleep at all well and the baby didn't like the train as much as the rough crossing. I was glad when morning came. I had a cup of tea and my sandwiches. It was a lovely summer day and the country between Rugby and Watford looked beautiful.

We reached Euston at 10.40. I cloaked my luggage and phoned E and Margot; arranged to lunch with them at Kennington; had some coffee and bought a paper; phoned Rosa and so to lunch; it was lovely to see E and Margot. They both arranged to come to Kensington after tea to show me my room (Mary is away all next week, and is not joining me till Monday week).

I went to Somerset House and saw Davenport – had an entertaining hour's chat. He doesn't know the facts and pumped me hard, obviously intrigued at my return to London. I was glad to hear I was to go on relief to St Marylebone, to McCreath. He offered me a tin hat (but then found the man who keeps them was not there). He gave me heaps of instructions and a cup of tea and I set off for St Marylebone office, which is now at the Bond Street end of Grosvenor Street.

McC was very cordial and made great efforts – gave me a room to myself (in spite of protests from Notting Hill who use it to play pingpong!). Selected a very discreet typist, asked me what type of work I'd like and gave me the Met Electric Supply Co and its subordinates to browse over. It is a big job as it needs re-working back to 1934/5. He heard from Bradford on Friday that the Treasury have decided on sick leave without pay. I heard the story: a woman clerk is having a baby (unwillingly) and went to their association for advice. Houghton sent her to Miss H, the woman Establishment Officer (appointed solely to protect and watch the interests of the women in the department!). She said Sick Leave without pay. Houghton wasn't satisfied and went to Bradford who said Sick Leave with pay. Miss H got on her high horse and went to the Treasury who, after consideration, supported her. Bradford is cross, partly on general grounds (he is sympathetic), partly because he has lost face! It is clear that nothing can be done inside the department. McC was very nice and said he could probably arrange a loan from the Benevolent Fund if necessary! E is inclined to advise me to agitate outside, tho' he agrees with no pay, but disagrees with the discrimination against unmarried women. I shall go and see Dr Malleson this week and ask her advice. She has had some experience on agitation. I shall, of course, have to cut down the sick leave as much as possible. E says if I have 3 months, after deducting income tax, I shall have about £40 in the next 6 months!

This room is rather palatial and it is clearly expensive to live in London. It is on the second floor and has a private bathroom. Quiet; it looks out on trees and a church with no windows. There are a lot of gaps around and 3 of my 4 panes are gone. There is no means of cooking whatever, which is the main weakness. I may get an electric ring, tho' one can order dinner in the morning. The rent, 37/6d per week, includes plain breakfast, light service, which is no more than the McIlroys' flat. I can get to the office easily from Gloucester Rd to Green Park for 2d. Margot came for a picnic lunch yesterday and Rosa for tea after her art class. Both Rosa and I felt it to be an ordeal, I think. I found I was very tired afterwards, but it was better than we expected. She had made me a pasty. I rang them up today and Rosa asked me to go there next weekend after dark on Saturday and back on Sunday! Margot said she felt better this morning.

It is lovely to be in London again. Even Sunday in London has seemed enjoyable all on my own. I begin to unfold again and become myself – fixedly and unavoidably Cockney!

E says he would have known only my face. Margot says I do not bulge as much as she expected. Last night when I was putting cold cream on my breasts (in accordance with Dr Batten's instructions) I noticed for the first time that there was just a hint of a milky secretion. I am rather relieved as this wasn't noticeable at all till then. I hope it means I'll be able to nurse the babe.

Wednesday 20 August

Have worked quite hard this week and have now got the Met Electric
Group as far as I can at this stage. It is lovely to be lunching with E again.
We meet at Chancery Lane as in old days but have a solid lunch because I
have a toast and tea breakfast and MacVita, cheese and salad supper. I lunch
with WG tomorrow. When I phoned him he said, 'How nice to hear your
voice again.' I go to see Dr Malleson at 5.0. Margot called on Monday and
I had tea with her tonight but we don't get long enough to talk properly.
Rosa has invited me to go home on Saturday and stay till Sunday so
perhaps that will help! Margot approves of E's suggestion that besides
Margaret we call the babe Miriam after his mother (if it is a girl).

Friday 22 August

I have had a busy two days. Lunched with WG yesterday and told him of
the baby! He said he was glad but was very severe about living in
Kensington – read me a hair raising lecture about raids. He was entertained
by the thought of Establishments. He has been doing wood carving and is
in the middle of a novel about Wales after the Napoleonic wars. McC came
in to see me and told me his wife is keen on a hospital at Barnet. He thinks
I should take my two weeks ordinary leave beforehand. I went to see Dr
Malleson at 5.0 and she tested my blood pressure and gave me a certificate
to get coupons for baby clothes. This morning I went to Queen
Charlotte's. It was a lovely place (when I found it!) and is not finished. I
saw the almoner (oldish but quite nice) and gave her the letter I had had. It
was clear that the hospital had bungled. They are absolutely full up. She
couldn't find my letter of 30.5 and was rather dished when I read her a
copy which stated all the facts – 'Said I should come in August and asked
them definitely to reserve a bed.' She had two suggestions: I might try
Westminster (but I should have to go to Woking) and there was a nursing
home run by a Miss Ping, but she might not take me. She worked by rule
of thumb and talked about the Welfare Officer with whom they usually
put 'unmarried' girls in touch – but I didn't seem to require that. I felt
depressed and tired when I left her, because I liked the place. But one never

knows. Hammersmith has had a good many bombs. I have written to Dr Malleson for advice in this situation. My new coat is good, but I grow larger with some rapidity. Dr Malleson was quite satisfied with physical condition.

Monday 25 August

I went home for the weekend on the 7.48 to Purley on Saturday and back by the 9.53 last night. It seemed so natural to be going to Purley, as tho' I hadn't been away any time. I had lunch with E on Saturday as he was seeing Elsie who was in bed with flu. After lunch he came to my room for a while and Margot came straight there and stayed till we caught the train home. Rosa was quite sweet except for one short discussion on Saturday night which upset me so that I couldn't sleep. Apart from this she was better. She made great efforts with the meals and we had quite pre-war feasts including clotted cream twice! She made Mr Zimmer's favourite apple and almond tart for dinner yesterday and gave me buns to take back. She even went to church so that Margot and I could have a chance to talk (Margot had a headache and went to sleep actually!).

McCreath told me today that the place at Barnet is full.

Have worked quite hard. McC gave me Marylebone Council accounts on Saturday and today one of Chaplin's EPT cases to check.

Monday 1 September

It is difficult to keep this up at present. Mary arrived last Monday and when we have both been in we have done a lot of talking. It is odd how we make each other talk. I suppose because we are interested in the same things and she has different and interesting experience and an independent mind.

First, about the confinement, Dr Malleson gave me a strong note to the almoner and told me to try again. I did. They were rather more communicative.

Wednesday 3 September

Hot, sunnier and hotter.

To continue – I liked the Doctor at Queen Charlotte's, who examined me very thoroughly and said all was well. Later I saw him again and he said Dr Malleson was an old friend of his and he would admit me if he could, but the government limited the number of their inpatients and he couldn't do anything now. He asked me my job and whether I was having the baby adopted. When I said, no, I wanted it, he said, 'Oh, I see! Planned for, was it?' The almoner phoned St Mary's Paddington and arranged an appointment. I went next morning to see their almoner. I didn't like the place – it was the old part and semi-basement, 1897! The almoner was younger and more business-like. Yes, they could take me, till in filling up the form she came to husband's name. Then she said they were not admitting unmarried women apparently because they were officially limited to 16 maternity patients. She would put me in touch with someone who might advise.

This week I had a letter from someone at the Society for Moral Welfare. Margot said, 'Don't waste her time.' (I was inclined to see what she would be like!) 'It is a nasty job and she will be busy!' Meantime Mary had phoned Suffolk House at Stanmore (which was given me by Queen Charlotte's the first time) and found out they didn't mind whether or not one was married so I went to see the matron yesterday. I liked the place. It is still recognisable as country till recently and is open. The roads have hedges. It is just over 10 miles out and will be better undoubtedly if blitz starts again, tho' they had a lot of noise last autumn. The home is a large detached house with a lovely garden in a road of similar houses. I liked Ping the matron. She had nice eyes. She talked to me for an hour and I decided to go there and have the double room which is £5.5 per week. She told me all about costs in addition and gave me a list of things I should want. The main snag is distance but if I can go a week before and (say) stay with Ella at Pinner it is only 15 minutes in a car. So the confinement question looks like being solved. I have now only to fix on a doctor. The matron gave me the name of one at Edgware who is said to be good.

Robertson from Somerset House phoned to say that he had sent me instructions to go to City 10 for the 3 weeks and would I regard them as cancelled as they were leaving me at Marylebone. The explanation was that McCreath had been talking to White and said he intended me to work at home. White said he wouldn't take responsibility for that but if McC wanted my spell at Marylebone extended – well and good. So I am to work at Kensington from Monday and McC will send me work which Mary is to collect and pass on to me. Really, McC is being exceedingly good and if this scheme works it will reduce my unpaid sick leave considerably.

Went home for the weekend as before. Rosa was better on the whole, tho' she said some things that upset me. She is more inclined to talk a little less irrationally. M is a rock to lean on.

E came to dinner at Kensington this evening, which was lovely. So pleasant to talk to him quietly and privately. He is having a week's leave from Saturday week and going either to the farm in Essex or to Gloucester.

Thursday 11 September

This week it has been cooler. Elsie came to Kensington on Saturday afternoon, and came to Purley on Sunday morning. She brought 2 jumpers (30 shillings the two) which her friend, who used to design for Jaegers, was disposing of. One was green and pink and suits Margot beautifully. The other brown and pink not so good, which may suit me. She is very busy but hopes to get more money. It was interesting to see her and Mary together since they had not met since 1925. They each thought the other had improved enormously and they got on very well. Elsie thinks I am lucky to have Mary to keep an eye on me.

Margot called on Saturday afternoon but not for long as she had promised to pick blackberries with Rosa. I made the result into 2lbs of jelly on Sunday morning. I had a pleasant Saturday. E worked on Friday night and took the morning off. We went to the Victoria and Albert Museum. There was a children's exhibition of mixed things. This week I have been working at home, going with Mary in the morning who called on McCreath for work which she handed over to me. I have missed a bit because Margot has been on a week's leave and did not go away. On Monday we went to see the Soviet play *Squaring the Circle*. It was enjoyable and light but interesting. Interesting, too, to see a few threads connecting the old theatre with the new – the traditional dances, a certain echo of Chekhov, The Technique. We had a big tea afterwards as I had lunched with E at St Pancras at an ABC which appeared to ignore people in the hope that they would walk out unserved – two sets at our table did so; we managed to get sardines on toast and coffee! On Tuesday, apart from a more successful lunch at St Pancras station café, I worked hard. On Wednesday I caught the 12.20 to Ashtead and met Margot at Sutton. We had a picnic and watched mechanized harvesting. Afterwards we picked blackberries, sufficient with those Rosa and Margot picked the day before to make five and a half lbs of jelly. We couldn't get a cup of tea so had a fizzy mineral to quench our thirst and then regretted it. Yesterday Rosa and Margot went to *The Cherry Orchard* while I worked all day and met them for tea. Today Margot lunched with E and me and I spent the afternoon with her. We sat in Lincoln's Inn Fields admiring the dahlias for some time. We went to Pontings and bought towelling for nappies, had tea and came to the flat before Margot went to dinner with the Robertsons.

I am still well but the baby is getting very cumbrous. It is an effort to walk up the tube stairs. I bulge very obviously. Occasionally, usually in the morning, I have a very sore spot at the front of my waist. The baby is very lively at times. I rest a lot on my divan and get sleepy in the day, but Mary and I tend to talk a lot in the evening.

A Health Visitor called on Monday and handed over fifty clothing coupons for the baby, for which I had to sign a receipt. I rather like her. She chatted for twenty minutes and said possibly Kensington borough might have got me into Queen Charlotte's as they have a few beds earmarked. However, it may turn out for the best.

Tuesday 16 September

After a dull and chilly few days this afternoon the sky cleared and the sun shone golden as it does in September. E has gone to Essex all this week and I lunched with Margot at Victoria today – rather hastily. Still working at Kensington. McCreath doesn't send me enough to do a whole day's work, and I rest quite a bit. I went home for the weekend and R was very sweet and more inclined, I thought, to talk rationally. M went out to tea on Sunday and R and I had a very amiable tête-à-tête. The weekends fly very quickly when I am home only from 8.30 Saturday to 9.30 Sunday. It is lovely to play the piano when all the notes sound (contrary to Mrs Hay's), even if they are rather out of tune. The Rapers came to tea yesterday. They are pleasant children. I told them about the babe.

Mary told me last night that her stepmother (who is French) knows several Free French. Apparently there is almost a regular service from Brittany to mid-channel, of fishing boats bringing Bretons who are transferred to the British ships halfway. The German garrisons are almost reduced to middle-aged reservists. There was a small amount of gunfire on Friday night and I heard planes but no warning. On Sunday in daytime we heard some queer bangs too, but nothing much.

I bought some blue wool on Saturday and have now spent all but 20 of the babe's coupons and 3 more of mine on it.

Friday 19 September

This week I have been suffering from a mild sense of grievance or self-pity about E. It does seem strange that just now he should go off for a week's holiday with K without even giving me his address. I certainly had a short letter from him yesterday which (in my state of mind) I hardly expected. He has been lucky with the weather and is staying on a farm eating the fat of the land.

Mary's cousin has recommended a doctor in Stanmore and I am going to see him tomorrow morning. Still quite fit, but I get very tired and am generally slothful.

Yesterday I lunched with Margot at Kennington and then met Rosa and took her to see *Fantasia*, the Disney film. It consists of six visual interpretations of music – most interesting technically, tho' extraordinarily unequal! The Bach, quite abstract, was the best in my opinion. It is a new art form embracing colour, form and movement and has immense possibilities. He certainly has genius, tho' at present it shows itself more in the range of possibility of the form he has invented than in his actual achievements. R found it stimulating, as I guessed. We walked to Victoria through St James's Park and had tea with Margot. A perfect golden September day.

The last 2 evenings I have been busy sewing with Mary. We have tackled an enormous roll of Turkish towelling and begun to convert it into nappies.

A restless night – I kept dreaming about the Russians. Nothing consecutive – the clearest memory was of strings of place names, but vaguely disturbing and anxious.

Friday 26 September

All this week it has been warm, either close and misty or golden sun. I have felt the heat with increasing force till today I wondered if I had a slight temperature. Have lunched every day with E and had tea with him on Monday, Tuesday and today and with Margot on Tuesday and yesterday. I was very depressed up to Monday but since then I have felt less so, and in a kind of coma of remoteness. Very lethargic and sleepy – living in a kind of dream. I haven't done much work but HO has given me another 3 weeks at Marylebone. I went home for the weekend and Rosa seemed definitely better – more inclined to sensible discussion, tho' the more she sympathizes with me the more bitter she is to E.

On Saturday morning I went to see Dr Byworth and liked him. He said 'baby work' was his favourite branch of his job. He knew the nursing home and appeared to be on friendly terms with Ping; examined me and said my measurements and the position of the baby were satisfactory and that the heart beat was good (only one, so it isn't twins). I think I shall have confidence in him.

1941

Wednesday 1 October

Met Ella on Saturday and we had lunch at Fullers; sat in the sun by the Round Pond for two and a half hours and then came here for tea. I shall probably go to her flat on the 16th but I shall have to go to the nursing home on 25th anyway as she is going away for a week and won't leave me alone. She knows quite a lot about babies with 2 nephews and a niece.

The heatwave continued until midday on Sunday when we had a downpour of rain. I had to borrow shoes, mac and umbrella to get to the station, but I was glad it was cooler. I made another 2 lbs of blackberry jelly and Rosa made some crab apple and elderberry jam which is a success. She gambled with the sugar as it was quite an experiment. There are masses of elderberries in the garden and she was given the crab apples.

On Monday Mary invited me to use her electric kettle which is now working and E was not going home till the 7.40 so he came to tea here. He enjoyed my brown bread and butter and blackberry jelly. I met Margot tonight. We had tea at Victoria. Yesterday I had quite a lot of work, and it was probably due to the heavy case that I felt rather shaky at lunch, so that E was quite concerned and even suggested a taxi back!

Friday 24 October

The 3 weeks' gap has been so full of new experiences that it is a hopeless job to try to note them.

On Friday 3rd October E went to Worcester to attend to his uncle who was said to have had a stroke. I met him at Paddington and he seemed a bit concerned at having to go, although I didn't worry as the baby wasn't due for 3 weeks. He had a rush and we had only about 20 minutes. It was a lovely day so I stopped to buy nappies at Derrys on the way back. The day after was wet and I caught the 6.51 to Purley in the evening.

For a day or two I had had a slight colourless vaginal discharge and I vaguely wondered what it was. On Sunday morning I felt quite fit, tho' it continued and increased. I didn't want my dinner, tho' I enjoyed it when I had it, but the discharge had developed into a regular trickle and I began to wonder if it was the beginning of the waters breaking! We sent Rosa up to rest and Margot rang up the nursing home which was noncommittal, and the doctor, who said, 'Lie down and see whether it stops.' By 2.00 I had very slight pain like those one gets with a chill. I went up and lay on Margot's bed and the trickle continued while the pains got more intense and recurred about every five minutes. We decided that I had better go to the nursing home. When Rosa had gone to church Margot would get an ambulance (I insisted on this for her sake as she was coming with me and the first aid men would relieve her of some responsibility). She tried Purley UDC, but their ambulances were reserved for AR casualties; the LCC, but they couldn't do it as both Purley and Stanmore were out of their area; the Red Cross, but they hadn't one free; St John's, and they could do it. But when they arrived they had run out of petrol, tho' they had coupons. The driver on the job before had used the spare can. There was 45 minutes' delay till they interviewed a Brigadier-General and persuaded the army to let them have some to get to a garage. They carried me downstairs all dripping and still having spasms. I put a hankie over my face in the hope that the neighbours wouldn't notice me and we set off. I had been sick 2 or 3 times and was sick again in the ambulance. The pains were more acute still and always seemed to coincide with our being held up by traffic lights. At 7.30 we got to Suffolk House. Margot paid the ambulance men and Sister Ping helped me to walk upstairs. By this time I was dripping not only water but also blood and was most concerned at the mess. I sat on the bed and with an effort took off my frock and smock and put on a nightie. I was sharing a room, and as the other occupant was expecting her husband to call, I went to the theatre.

They didn't give me an enema or a hot bath as the pains were very frequent. I watched the clock above the bed and tried to relax between the pains and to push down when they began. Sister Ping said later that she expected a 5 or 6 lb baby and no difficulty at all. About 9.30 the pains decreased in intensity and frequency, tho' she said the baby should be born by 10.0. She phoned for Dr Byworth, who appeared in a huge orange rubber apron. He gave me two tablets (bromide, I think). My back was aching all the time so I could only just distinguish it from the periodical pains and I had very little energy to push. The doctor said the baby's head was only 1 and a half inches in and one or two 'good strong' pains would bring it far enough for them to give me chloroform before the actual delivery. But the whole thing slowed up and progress stopped. He put a dark cone over my face and there was a sickly sweet, overpowering smell, which was chloroform. I pushed it away with my hand, tho' I had been longing for it. Dark clouds like smoke seemed to roll up and extinguish everything. At 1.0 am Sister Ping's voice, urgent and summoning, came from an immense distance waking me up. I said, 'Is the baby all right?' and she said, 'Yes, you've got twins! A boy and a girl.' I couldn't believe it. I learned later that Andrew (3 lbs 12 oz) was born at 11.30 and Margaret (6 lbs 4 oz) at 11.50; that no one knew there were two till Andrew had been born and they had thought what a fuss about nothing. Sister Ping put her hand on my tummy and said, 'There's another,' and they gave me more chloroform. It was a forceps delivery and I was badly torn. The doctor was quite annoyed with the twins for catching him out. He hadn't suspected them at all (and nor had Dr Malleson or the doctor at Queen Charlotte's).

I wished I hadn't been awakened as I found I had a violent headache and I didn't sleep for the night. I was raging with thirst but wasn't allowed to drink even water. All night Keats's 'Ode to a Nightingale' went through my head, tho' I never got it consecutive and completed. At 6.30 am I had a cup of tea and discovered the painfulness of the stitches. Five minutes later I was sick; I had some tea and a piece of toast for breakfast and was sick; a little fish for lunch and was sick. In the evening they just gave me carbonate of soda and glucose to drink. I did sleep a little on Monday night. On Tuesday I just managed to eat one third of the small amount of meals I was given and I kept dozing all day. Each time I awoke I was very sicky. On Wednesday I felt better and let them take away the bowl I had been sick into. From then I improved and my appetite came back. I got up for four minutes last Saturday and felt very feeble. On Tuesday I had an ordinary bath and, tho' I have to stay another week (four altogether) it is only because I haven't got anywhere to go and Hobday* isn't free till November.

---

* Vera Hobday was the person Margot had found to be a nanny. Her husband was in the army and was to visit from time to time when on leave.

Saturday 25 October

The twins are quite different in looks and temperament and you could say which was the girl by looking at their faces.

I didn't see much of Andrew the first week. He seemed pathetically tiny with a little pointed face and fine fair hair. He made the most extraordinary faces, wrinkling up his forehead (which was high) and his nose and mouth. He had a strangely sophisticated expression, as if he were weighing up all the facts and knew one could expect little in this world. His forehead, eyebrows, eyes were just like E's only smaller. Margaret was darker but her skin was fair and her face was rounder with a pointed chin. She had beautifully shaped eyes and lids, and reminded me of Margot when she was a baby. She seemed less reflective than Andrew, readier to express her immediate feelings. Andrew looks now as if he will have red hair. They both appear to be developing grey or blue eyes and both have light skins. Neither is at all like me except that both have big toes with a gap between them and the other four toes. Margaret is a fierce little thing when she is hungry and reminds me of a lamb in her eagerness to suck. They both appear to smile (and this is the only expression in which they have any resemblance to each other), but nurse says it is wind! Nevertheless, when E saw Margaret's smile he said it had haunted him till he saw her again. He said Andrew was like one of the heads on a capital at Wells and was perfectly sculpted. He had a shock when he saw Andrew as he hadn't been told how tiny he was, and he was depressed after the first time thinking he wouldn't survive. But he soon saw that he had a lot of vitality and called him a go-getter. Margaret crows with pleasure when she is fed, but Andrew just grumbles and talks to himself. He doesn't sleep so much as Margaret and cries less.

I think they are sweetest when they are put on their backs at 5.0 to wake up. They take ages and stretch and yawn and blink just like grown ups. They are both having Cow & Gate to supplement my milk. It is astonishing how attached one can get to them in a week or two. I should feel deprived now if I had only one. If only I can cope with them it is lovely to have two at once, tho' how it happened I can't think. There are no twins on either side of the families so far as we know.

E is very thrilled – more doting than I should have thought possible considering that it was I that wanted them primarily. He is quite impractical, tho', and just does nothing but admire them when he comes to see me. I haven't the heart to make him talk business. He said Andrew's small squeaks and murmurs were like the dawn chorus of birds and sweeter to hear than Bach. He brought me some scabious and some bronze chrysanthemums – so queer from him. I was quite touched.

Margot has spent over half of this week looking for somewhere for me to live. All day Tuesday she looked at Clapham and Wimbledon with no success. It is clear that I shall just have to be extravagant for three months and spend what I have saved. I have heard from McCreath and sent the medical certificate to Bradford – for four weeks. McCreath is trying to arrange for me to be in London indefinitely and hopes I shall be at Marylebone.

I feel guilty about Margot. She had all the worry and bother the weekend they were born (which was the day of full moon – Hunter's moon, and a Sunday). She had the bother of packing up and coping with the flat (Mary helped her here)

Doreen and E with the twins: Andrew (left) and Margaret

and the job of looking for somewhere to live. At the same time she had to cope with Rosa, who relapsed badly. This was partly owing to the publicity of the ambulance. She hasn't been to see the twins and hasn't given them anything, tho' she bought me a green woolly bed jacket which is useful and elegant and extravagant. M says she has improved and she has made efforts, but she finds it impossible to accept the situation. Yet she would adore the twins if only she would let herself, and is just depriving herself of pleasure in them. Anyone else, almost, finds it easier. Lots of people have come to see me and admired them and quite accepted: Ella, Mary, Griff, Netta Cameron, Elsie, the doctor and the sisters here, and ES. Preston, who wants another herself, wrote to me and I told her all about them. She told Le Huquet. I think Griff must have told Williams, who told Cole, who asked Preston whether I wished to have the rumour killed – decent of him. I was cross that Williams knew and still more that he was spreading it, but it can't be helped. People will get over it and forget about it, probably, in a short time. Griff came to tea and brought a Stendhal and Enid Bagnold's *The Squire*, which he selected for its topical interest – all about a woman having a baby! I finished Trollope's *Doctor Thorne* and read Arnot Robertson's *Summer Lease* and now halfway through Chekhov's *Letters*. I have also finished a blue jersey for Andrew and knitted two vests.

It is lovely to feel well again. It gives an extra savour to everything – the taste of food, the luxury of a hot bath, the feel of sunshine, the sight of the trees against the sky, the clutch of the twins' little fingers on mine. The nursing home is excellent, two sisters who run it in particular. Sister Gordon is older and has a beautiful face, iron grey hair, dark eyes and a humorous mouth. Her father was a solicitor and she tried working in his office for a time and hated it. Has worked on a farm and now works furiously at this and finds time to be an ARP warden and to garden. Ping is energetic too and is surprisingly like Reen Hosier in looks and manner – just that brusqueness. They grow nearly all their vegetables and have had 113 lbs of tomatoes. There are two nurses – Topless, the night nurse, who comes from Lincolnshire (Louth) and looks square and solid like a Dane (but shorter), and Crow who is small and dark and marvellously efficient. She was married in May to a man who runs a garage, under great difficulties now, at Ringwood. They see each other about once a month at weekends. She is intelligent and good-natured, but uses a cynical manner which is quite superficial. I get on quite well with all of them, I think especially Crow who is very fond of the twins, especially Andrew. It is a completely different world for me and I have learned a heap of things in these 2 or 3 weeks. Nurse Crow has taught me how to top and tail a baby, to feed it and to bath it and dress it. I was horribly nervous the first time I bathed Margaret but I have done it twice now and begin to have more confidence.

I have watched the trees outside the windows turning colour. On Wednesday the sirens went and I heard a few guns in the distance and worried a bit about the babies, but the All Clear went after about an hour. If the blitz begins again I shall be much more afraid now because of the twins. I must find somewhere outside London as soon as possible.

Monday 27 October

This morning I went out for 45 minutes, just around Stanmore village and up to the hill, to a farm. I felt feebler than I expected, tho' it was glorious to be out in the sun. It was cold and the trees had completely turned especially the chestnuts. I seemed to have been indoors for much more than 3 weeks.

Yesterday E came in the morning and Margot in the afternoon. They had found a house at Addiscombe and been to see it. E said he had one of the worst hours of his life on Saturday afternoon interviewing the agent and being cross-examined. He had concocted a whole story, which the agent had accepted. The only snag was that E wasn't certain what Margot had said the day before! He showed the agent his post office savings book with £700 in it and told him his job, but the agent insisted on a reference from my former employer, so I had to write to McCreath again.

The house belongs to a widow and the furniture is in good condition. It is small and has a small garden. Shops near, including Woolworths. A box room is reserved but two bedrooms, bathroom, two living rooms, kitchen, electric water heater, power plugs, one gas or electric fire. Margot had lunch with E on Friday and transformed him after 30 minutes' talk into a very practical person. He was full of such things as adequacy of the blackout, getting gas and electricity connected, airing beds, getting coal and provisions. He will probably know today whether the widow agrees and if so we shall have an agreement to sign. It sounds good – rent £2/5 pw, which is no more and probably less than a flat would be. Ella's unfurnished flat at Richmond was £120 p.a. He was also rather drawn to a house advertised in Ashtead at £3 p.w. but it would have been awkward for Margot to get to, tho' further out in case of blitz. Margot said Rosa had been very good and went to the agents with her and had been most helpful. She had even shown concern for the twins – afraid the little one would get cold – he ought to be wrapped in an eiderdown. She sent me a note which was rather sweet. I guessed (tho' she didn't say so) that she thought I ought to close relations with E for the sake of his babies. Margot brought me a spray of roses (four on one stalk) and eight apples, as well as my clothes. E left me the *Sunday Times*.

Andrew has gained 4 oz in the last 3 days and is 4 lbs 12 oz (one pound over his birth weight) this morning and he has discarded the last of his cotton wool and his woolly hat. I bathed him and he was good and loved being in the bath – kicked his legs with great pleasure. Margaret was 6 lbs 7 oz (2 oz gain in 2 days). The milk continues better. I am making Margaret a bonnet to go home in.

Wednesday 29 October

It is cold and unsettled – a gusty north wind, sunny patches, hail, rain and snowy squalls.

Yesterday I went to Edgware, a typical suburban shopping centre with no individuality and nothing of interest. Today I went to register the twins. It took me from 10.00–12.00. I went to Redhill Hospital and waited there only to learn I had to go five minutes away to the Middlesex County office. A well made up young married woman was the sub-registrar. No comment when I said I was not married. It was queer to give Andrew Wyndham born at 11.30 and Margaret Miriam born at 11.50, as though they were being given another official birth. I remembered the last time I went to a Registrar's office almost two years ago to register Wyndham's death. I signed the book and paid 5/2d for 2 copies of the two certificates which I suppose will be wanted for the adoption order.★ Tomorrow I have

★ Doreen planned to formally adopt the babies, as she was an unmarried mother.

to go to Harrow to get their ration books and identity cards. There was some fuss at the beginning because I hadn't a present address – was so short a time at Kensington, only 4 weeks at Stanmore and not yet at Addiscombe. The Registrar had never seen such a case before.

A letter from E last night and one from Margot this morning. The negotiations for the house are going well. The agreement is to go direct to me. I can buy about a ton of coal in the shed. Have written to the gas and electric people.

Reading Stendhal's *Charterhouse of Parma*. It is very pleasant. It reminds me of Voltaire, regarded simply as a novelist, for Stendhal does not appear to be serious as no propaganda to put over. His irony and detachment are similar. McCreath sent me letters he had had from Bradford and Loach, L wanting to know my domestic arrangements and assuming I wished to be regarded as a 'fully effective unit'!

Thursday 6 November

Since I last wrote I have been settling down. On Thursday last I went to Harrow to get the twins' ration books, clothing cards and identity cards. The next day I got the milk form which Dr Byworth signed and also bought a blanket for Andrew to be wrapped in. When we got to the new house Margot was there. She and Hobday (the nanny) had done shopping and got the house warm and comfy with a good fire. Hobday came to see the twins and brought her sister with her, with her small daughter, but she was not really arriving till Sunday night. I was on my own till then but managed to cope with the twins not too badly. We had a warning about 10.00 and I heard 2 planes and a lot of gunfire. I was just feeding Margaret, with Andrew upstairs and I was very worried. After an hour the All Clear went. Margot and Rosa came to tea on Sunday and before they went Rosa went up to see the twins for the first time. She was very upset and it was clearly an ordeal for her. I had to give her brandy afterwards. But I was glad she had seen them. I had a bath at 9.45 and had just got in when I was knocked up by a warden who said light was showing from the bathroom fanlight across the landing to the box room fanlight and so through the window. Hobday arrived about 10.30.

We seem to have settled down quite well. She is good with the babies and cooks well. She flies around and gets through a lot but we shall have to get a woman to do two mornings a week for turning out. She has prepared gigantic meals in the evening but doesn't seem to have much lunch. On Monday I went up to town and did a hard day's work. First to the Bank for money; Bumpas where I got Mary *Decade 1931–1941* and for Margot Augustus John *Drawings*, as tokens of gratitude for all they had done to help; McCreath to arrange to resume on Monday. He gave me Bradford's message that if I repeated the performance I should get the sack. But he told me that he had told Bradford that tho' he would give me the message the AIT would protest against such unduly harsh treatment and he felt that Bradford himself would not go to such a length if the occasion arose. McC seemed surprised to see me so fit and remarked that maternity had not changed me at all. I left him to meet E for lunch, having arranged to call at Kennington to pick up my cheque and the voucher for my watch which had been repaired. I collected it at Walkers, Victoria. It was a relief to get it back.

I then went to Fulham to look at a second hand twin pram in a depository. It was 12–14 guineas. I wasn't sure about the condition. The tyres might have needed renewing soon so I thought about it first. I just caught the 3.51 to Croydon and went to the Food Office to get emergency coupons and to the Milk Office to see about the twins' extra milk at 2d a pint, a little shopping and so back at 5.15. A very good day's business.

On Tuesday I went to Purley to see Rosa and collect some clothes and my electric iron. She was very glad to see me, very cordial indeed, and she made me a cheese omelette. I collected my luggage and phoned Millsons, the best pram people. They had a second hand twin pram at £19/19s and said there were no new ones with springs. Yesterday I went up to town to scour London for prams. The new twin prams to government specifications have no springs and are only slightly larger than single prams. They are hideous, tho' this is not important. They are only made to order, which means a month's delay and would be £17 or £19/19s. When I got to Millsons I saw the second hand one – navy blue and in very good condition and I thought I had better buy it. It cost £20/3/6d and reduced my Current Account to £28! I went to the Food Office in Croydon to register the removals and get pink ration books for canned goods. I also went to the Public Health Department about the 50 clothing coupons for the other twin. They said I had to get another certificate, signed by the doctor or midwife, before they could issue them, in spite of the fact that I produced identity cards for 2 and they could confirm from Kensington that I had had only 50 coupons. Red tape with a vengeance! All this took over an hour.

Had lunch with E. Margot came in the evening and had tea. Today I met Rosa in Croydon, had lunch at the Express and came back for the afternoon while Hobday went out. Rosa was still cordial and enjoyed her tea. I gave the twins their bottles in the dining room so that we could talk and she began to take an interest in them. When I came to Margaret she took her in her arms quite of her own accord and nursed her while I got the tea. This was a great improvement. She also gave advice and expressed opinions such as that Margaret would walk early. She went home in a pleasant frame of mind at 4.45.

Thursday 13 November

It has poured with rain all day and been very dark, but it has been very mild since Tuesday. I left the twins with Hobday and went back to Marylebone on Monday and resumed Marks & Spencer. McCreath also gave me Selfridges and later on Coty (England) Ltd. I felt very rusty at first; it was 9 weeks since I had worked in the office and 5 since I had worked at the flat but it is astonishing how quickly one slips back. We have now worked out a routine: 5 am wake up (if not already awakened) and feed Andrew; 5.45–7.15 sleep again; 7.15–8.00 get up, breakfast, get dressed, wash up; 8.30 feed Margaret; catch 8.43, office 9.30. I catch the 5.40 from Charing Cross, get in, feed Andrew, have dinner, feed Margaret, drink Lactigol and bed. So far it works and the milk seems to be continuing. I now have a thermos and milk to drink at 11.00 in an effort to keep it up.

Margot intends to come tomorrow. I have lunched with E. He is very keen on the twins – talks about their education, their abilities, what our attitude to them should be. He intends to tell K this weekend. I am sorry for him because the conflict in his mind must be intensified. He so clearly loves the babies and I want him to have a lot to do with them. It would be so lovely if K would rise to the occasion and remake her life without him. I have written him a note to thank him for giving me the opportunity to have the twins. They make me so happy. I have complete faith that we have done a good thing and I have regained a zest that I thought had gone for good, and I feel happy in a more peaceful, less precarious, way than I have ever experienced. It is so satisfying to have done, and be doing, such a constructive job amidst the destruction of the war; to have made a channel for the realization of such a miracle of creation.

Andrew and Margaret, photographed in January 1942

Epilogue

The arrival of the twins marked the start of a new chapter in Doreen's life. Although she had been unsure whether E would remain in touch with her and her growing children when they first arrived, he did in fact do so. He eventually found the courage to tell K about them when they were 4 months old. His concern had been that K might have taken this news as badly as she had taken the news of his and Doreen's affair in 1937. On this occasion, however, she showed considerable magnanimity by recognizing that the twins needed to know their father. From time to time she sent small presents of ballet shoes of increasing size as Margaret grew. Eventually she agreed to E spending every second weekend with Doreen and the twins at the home that Doreen created after the war near Oxted in Surrey. E and K remained married until E's death in 1974, aged 80.

Doreen was able to continue to work full-time and her career flourished. Hobday, the nanny that Margot had found, was instrumental in enabling Doreen to continue working and she remained with the family until they moved to Oxted after the war. Margot and Rosa were also enormously helpful with child care at times. Unfortunately Rosa remained fiercely hostile to E and would never meet him, a situation that created many tensions and difficulties for Doreen.

The twins grew up, married, and had their own families and careers. They are now both grandparents. They saw nothing of E's side of the family during E's lifetime, but met, and were welcomed by, several members after his death.

Doreen and E remained close until E's death in 1974. Doreen's diary had become intermittent by then and she made no direct reference to the death. However, at the relevant point in the diary she wrote out a poem by Vita Sackville-West, addressed to Harold Nicolson:

I must not tell how dear you are to me.
It is unknown, a secret from myself
Who should know best. I wouldn't if I could
Expose the meaning of such mystery.

I loved you then, when love was Spring, and May.
Eternity is here and now, I thought;
The pure and perfect moment briefly caught
As in your arms, but still a child, I lay.

Loved you when summer deepened into June
And those fair, wild, ideal dreams of youth
Were true yet dangerous and half unreal
As when Endymion kissed the mateless moon.

But now when Autumn yellows all the leaves
And thirty seasons mellow our long love,
How rooted, how secure, how strong, how rich
How full the barn that holds the garnered sheaves!

Doreen herself died in 1994, aged eighty-seven.

We ['the twins'] knew that our mother Doreen had written a diary throughout most of her adult life, and she had told us we could read it after her death. On doing so, we, together with Doreen's sister Margot [M], found it so interesting that it seemed publishable. The original version for 1934–41 is about three times longer than the version published here, which is edited to be more manageable. In addition, Doreen continued to write a fairly full diary until the mid-1950s, and a sparser diary for much longer. Doreen also contributed a diary to Mass Observation intermittently from September 1940 to November 1944, which is a shortened version of her personal diary.